How Enemies are Made

Volume 1
How Enemies are Made – Towards a Theory of Ethnic and Religious Conflicts
Günther Schlee

Volume 2
Changing Identifications and Alliances in North-East Africa
Vol. I: Ethiopia and Kenya
Edited by Günther Schlee and Elizabeth E. Watson

Volume 3
Changing Identifications and Alliances in North-East Africa
Vol. II: Sudan, Uganda and the Ethiopia-Sudan Borderlands
Edited by Günther Schlee and Elizabeth E. Watson

How Enemies are Made

Towards a Theory of Ethnic and Religious Conflicts

Günther Schlee

Berghahn Books

New York • Oxford

First published in 2008 by
Berghahn Books
www.berghahnbooks.com

©2008, 2010 Günther Schlee
First paperback edition published in 2010

Library of Congress Cataloging-in-Publication Data
Schlee, Günther.
  How enemies are made : towards a theory of ethnic and religious conflicts /
Günther Schlee.
    p. cm.
  Includes bibliographical references and index.
  ISBN 978-1-84545-494-4
  1. Ethnic conflict. 2. Social conflict--Religious aspects. 3. Conflict management.
I. Title.

  HM1121.S34 2008
  305.6'970890096773--dc22

                                                    2008026232

British Library Cataloguing in Publication Data
A catalogue record for this book is available from the British Library

Printed on acid-free paper

ISBN 978-1-84545-494-4 hardback
ISBN 978-1-84545-779-2 paperback

Contents

List of Figures and Tables

Figures

Tables

List of Abbreviations

ARPCT	Alliance for the Restoration of Peace and Counter-Terrorism
AU	African Union
CAP	community action plan
DDR	demobilisation, disarmament, and reintegration
EC	European Community
EU	European Union
GPS	Global Positioning System
GRIT	graduated and reciprocated initiatives in tension reduction
GTZ	Gesellschaft für technische Zusammenarbeit (German Technical Assistance)
GTZ IS	GTZ International Services (the part of GTZ implementing projects sponsored by institutions other than the German government)
ICG	International Crisis Group
IFSP	Improvement of Farming Systems Project
IGAD	Intergovernmental Agency for Development
IMF	International Monetary Fund
JVA	Juba Valley Alliance
LTTE	Liberation Tigers of Tamil Eelam
NATO	North Atlantic Treaty Organisation
NGO	non-governmental organisation
NIF	National Islamic Front
OLF	Oromo Liberation Front
ONLF	Ogadeen National Liberation Front
OPDO	Oromo People's Democratic Organisation
PICD	Participatory Integrated Community Development
RC theory	rational choice theory
RRA	Rahanweyn Resistance Army
SDU	Somali Democratic Union
SNF	Somali National Front
SNM	Somali National Movement
SoSh	Somali shillings
SPLA	Sudan People's Liberation Army
SRRC	Somali Reconciliation and Restoration Council
TFG	Transitional Federal Government
TNG	Transitional National Government
UIC	Union of Islamic Courts
UN	United Nations
UNDP	United Nations Development Programme

UN-HABITAT   United Nations Agency for Human Settlements
UNHCR   United Nations High Commissioner for Refugees
UNOSOM   United Nations Operation in Somalia
USC   United Somali Congress
WFP   World Food Programme

Part I
Introduction

Figure 1.1 Map of north-east Africa with some of the principal ethnic groups mentioned in this book.

Chapter 1

Why We Need a New Conflict Theory

We expect science to provide insights we cannot gain from a mere everyday view on things.[1] A systematic conceptual understanding, a methodical process, and data gathered in some standardised fashion or at least intentionally and with a sense of purpose are supposed to sharpen our awareness of hidden connections. To differentiate between science and an everyday understanding does not usually pose problems for natural scientists. Simply, by concerning themselves with different scales of phenomena from the ones accessible to the human senses without technical support – for instance talking about molecules or galaxies – they mark their knowledge as clearly distinct from everyday knowledge. They do not have any difficulties in defining science as a special form of knowledge. On the contrary, their problem is rather to make their knowledge generally comprehensible: to explain to an audience not trained in their own specific discipline, to laymen in their field, what it is exactly they do – and this includes the politicians who are to provide them with the financial means for their research. Their problem therefore is translation of their scientific language into everyday language. Some social scientists seem to reverse this process. They translate an everyday experience into a special jargon, and call that professionalisation. Whoever sees through the trick will become suspicious and ask about the scientific gain: that is, the proportion of knowledge which would not be available to society without a separate functional area of science.

A major problem of the social sciences is that, contrary to the natural sciences, their objects of interest are no different from the interests of their non-scientific surroundings. Social scientists concern themselves with wealth and poverty, war and peace, love and death, and much more, all of which is of a general human interest, and about which non-scientists talk just as much. Do social scientists display any knowledge at all which is superior to everyday wisdom? Only that would justify consulting them in policy matters or as experts in court.

In this volume I will show that a systematic conflict analysis can lead to different conclusions from popular perception. I will start by demonstrating that there may be something wrong with popular perception. This is not merely my personal point of view; particularly in the area of 'ethnicity', scientific and popular opinions have differed significantly for a long time. Starting with fundamental questions, my next chapter will try to develop a sounder perspective.

---

1.   This chapter is based on my inaugural lecture *Identitätspolitik und Gruppengröße* at the Martin Luther University Halle-Wittenberg, Halle (Saale), 30 June 2004, and on parts of the 'Einleitung' to Schlee and Horstmann (2001).

The phrase 'ethnic conflicts' has come to be used rather naturally, particularly since the end of socialism and the rejection of the perspective of class struggle. Nobody asks what exactly is 'ethnic' in ethnic conflicts. It is assumed that ethnicity (and according to this model every form of difference, particularly also religion) represents the cause of conflicts. Every media consumer constantly learns that the ethnic factor is the reason for political fragmentation, be it in the former Soviet Union or Yugoslavia, where we seem to be confronted with a continuation of the processes which had once led to the dissolution of the precursor states, namely the Habsburg and Ottoman empires. Thus, ethnicity is perceived as a constant or recurrent factor which, resistant to time, generates conflict. Unfortunately, this is also the view taken by the political elites, who therefore have difficulty in negotiating ethnic or religious differences constructively.

The convictions on which this opinion about ethnicity is based can be subsumed under six points:

1. Cultural differences, i.e., ethnicities, are the cause of ethnic conflicts.
2. The clash of different cultures reflects ancient, inherited, deeply rooted oppositions.
3. Ethnicity is universal: that means every human belongs to an ethnic group.
4. Ethnicity is ascriptive: that means as a rule one cannot change one's ethnic affiliation.
5. A people is a community of shared descent.
6. Ethnic groups are territorial. They strive for a united territory and, eventually, for national sovereignty.

Regarding the first proposition of ethnicity as the cause of ethnic conflicts, such a proposition would only be supported if the extent of difference between the conflicting parties reflected the intensity of their conflicts. Observation, however, shows that the degree of such difference is not in the least connected to the existence of conflicts or their intensity.

The prime example for the ethnic factor as a cause of conflict is supposed to be former Yugoslavia. As is the general belief, oppositions originating in the Middle Ages have broken out once more, and indeed the Serbs refer to the Battle of Kosovo Polje and identify modern Muslims as their then enemies. Ancient ethnic oppositions, only temporarily suppressed by a communist regime, have been said to collide. But, if ethnicity is a form of social identity, then it is fixed by definitions of self and other. That means nobody can have an ethnic affiliation which is unknown either to themselves or to others. Ethnicity cannot exist unless people are aware of it. Some children of Yugoslavian immigrants in Germany had entirely lost this awareness by the end of the 1980s. There were cases of teenagers who had no idea to which ethnic group they belonged and what the language they spoke at home was even called. They would have to ask their parents first. Today, probably every single child from former Yugoslavia, be it in Germany or elsewhere, knows their ethnic affiliation. At least in such cases it should be obvious that the new emphasis on ethnicity is a result, not the cause of ethnic conflicts.

By subdividing their countries into constituent republics mostly named after a titular ethnic group, Yugoslavia and the Soviet Union actively contributed to preserving an awareness of ethnic affiliation as a part of identification in the minds of their citizens. If indeed ethnicity was the factor that undermined these structures, the central powers had their share in it. In national censuses the citizens were regularly asked to which ethnic group they belonged, and in cases of doubt had to make a decision. In spite of this, about 5 per cent of the persons questioned refused to identify with one or the other nationality and declared themselves to be 'Yugoslav'. Where are these 5 per cent now?

In the mid-1970s, an American anthropologist wrote a book about the Bosnian Muslims called *European Moslems* (Lockwood 1975). One of his findings was that, in an urban context, ethnic and religious identifications were fading. His prognosis was that the ethnicities of Yugoslavia would dissolve and in the end there would be a Yugoslav nation, whose previous ethnic subdivisions would be reduced to historical reminiscences or regarded as of folkloristic interest at best. In this evaluation he followed the line of prevailing modernisation theories, all of which assumed that, in the course of the advance of modernism, ethnicity would only survive for a while in rural areas, if at all.

Apparently in the 1970s, ethnicity played a minor and, compared to earlier realities, diminishing part. The political will corresponded to that. The vast majority of Bosnians – in the sense of the entire population of Bosnia, not one or the other ethnic group – were up until the 1990s determined to keep the significance of the ethnic factor to a minimum. In the face of the developments in Slovenia and Croatia, they wished to preserve the pluralistic character of their republic as a 'Yugoslavia on a small scale'.

Many thousands demonstrated in the streets of Sarajevo to support the preservation of their multicultural community. These demonstrations were terminated by a few snipers, and the spiral of violence and counter-violence resulting from this is only too well known. Only then was every person forced to choose an ethnic identification. To be a 'Yugoslav' could not protect one from being killed or exiled as a 'Croat', 'Serb', 'Muslim', or, in a later phase, as a 'Kosovo Albanian'; in order to escape this fate one had to join together with those presented as one's own kind according to the ethnic principle – a development called 'becoming hostages of the militias' (*Geiselhaft der Milizen*) by Dizdarevic (1993).

An examination of the actual or alleged cultural differences between the ethnic groups of Bosnia shows that the linguistic differences between them are not significant at all. They all speak Serbo-Croatian, with only slight variations. Slovenian, on the other hand, is a distinct Slavic language and markedly different from Serbo-Croatian. If one looks at the levels of violence accompanying the processes of separation in the different cases, it is striking that the linguistically clearly distinct Slovenians managed to secede comparatively peacefully from the federal state of Yugoslavia, whereas, among the linguistically hardly distinguishable Serbs, Croats, and Muslims of Bosnia, atrocities took place on a scale which had been believed to be no longer possible in Europe.

The dialectal differences within the Serbo-Croatian language are far smaller than the ones between the different German dialects, which obviously do not prevent their speakers from living peacefully in one and the same federal state. However, cases in which a low level of difference coincides with a high intensity of conflict are frequent. One is almost tempted to postulate a negative correlation between cultural and linguistic differences on the one hand and levels of violence on the other.

The element of differentiation between Serbs, Croats, and Muslims which also seems to play a political role is religion. For the Muslims, the denominational term has become an ethnonym, i.e., an equivalent to the ethnic terms 'Serb' and 'Croat'. This probably means that, after several decades of an agnostic or irreligious regime, the Yugoslavs had to a large extent forgotten their respective religious practices, and in today's conflicts identified with the religion of their grandparents, rather than referring to actually held beliefs and actually practised forms of worship of their own. This interpretation is supported by the fact that, though the entire Muslim world showed solidarity with the Bosnian Muslims, Bosnian refugees in Malaysia caused bewilderment due to their ignorance of religious practice.

In the case of Somalia, an extremely high level of factionalism and violence likewise coincides with little or practically no cultural differences. Somalia is a state with a culturally, linguistically, and religiously homogeneous population,[2] which was often called the only 'national' state of Africa. It is well known from the news media that the factionalism here takes place on a subclan level. In concrete terms this means that the respective opponents belong to descent lines of one and the same clan which have separated for only a few generations and whose founders are known by name. Linguistic or other cultural differences, any more than religious schisms, neither are to be suspected nor in fact exist in this case (Schlee 1996, 2002b).

Cultural homogeneity is not a guarantor of peaceful coexistence. Kenney (2002) has shown that the opposing groups in Northern Ireland cultivate symbolisms which are very similar even in their details: the marching bands, the parades, or the iconographies of violence painted on the walls. It is a conflict taking place within a single cultural system of signs. The enemies understand each other all too well (ibid.).

Now let us look at the second proposition, which claims that, in ethnic conflicts, ancient and deeply rooted oppositions erupt. Where these have not surfaced recently, they are said to have been submerged by other forces, say a communist regime or colonialism. This is countered by the fact that ethnicity is constantly redefined, not only regarding its cultural contents but also with regard to the collectivity of persons defining a respective ethnicity (Barth 1969). The border between 'us' – the 'we' – and the 'other' is constantly being renegotiated.

Concerning the age of conflict groupings we find a very high degree of empirical variation. For the Armenians and Azeri – again selecting an example that has made the headlines since the dissolution of the Soviet Union – it is claimed that they fought each other in the same groupings as long as 1,000 years ago. Indeed, such ancient conflicts do recognisably exist, though possibly with changing reasons, mutable front lines, and in different historical forms. On the other hand, we have

---

2.   This is true for the parties to the conflict. In the south, there are also rural populations, among them Bantu-speakers, who partly fall outside these parameters, and until recently did not belong to the forces actively engaged in the conflict. Rather, they were victims or part of the loot, as former nomad clans appropriated them as forced labourers along with the land.

the example of the so-called 'Kalenjin' (see Figure 1, p. 1), which van Nahl (1999: 306f.) describes. The Kalenjin are an ethnic group in Kenya. However, once the old people of today never knew they were Kalenjin. Although the history of the Kalenjin cannot be traced back further than colonial times, and although originally only the educated knew how European linguists drew dialect boundaries and defined language groups and families, today the existence of the Kalenjin as an ethnic group, even a highly politicised one, is beyond doubt. It is the group of former President Daniel arap Moi, who knew how to place numerous members of his group in important positions and in this way thoroughly excluded other ethnic groups in Kenya from effective power. The first letters on the number plates of Kenyan government vehicles always read 'GK', meaning 'Government of Kenya'. But in the jargon of the Moi era they came to mean 'Government of Kalenjin'.

Aggressively articulated ethnicities can therefore be very old or very young, and their age has nothing to do with the intensity of ethnic mobilisation. Frequently, the seeming antiquity of ethnic differences and ethno-nationalisms is, of course, a back-projection into the past. Each nationalism tends to refer to ancient oppositions and differences (see Elwert 1989: 441). It is a virtual feature of nationalisms that they assume venerability, and always assert their historical roots, which are often driven into the past only through this act of assertion, like a tree drives its roots into the soil and does not grow out of its roots.[3] The age of ethno-nationalisms may be a contested issue but it has nothing to do with the intensity of ethnic conflicts. There is not a shred of evidence to support the contention that older antagonisms are more intense than younger ones.

The third proposition under discussion concerns the universality of ethnicity, i.e., the claim that every human belongs to a people. Unlike this claim, ethnicity is on no account a natural or universal structural principle of humanity. In pre-colonial Africa it could be observed that a given group with a self-chosen name would regard the villages a little to the east or a little to the west as still affiliated to its own group: two or three villages further away, however, the inhabitants would be perceived as foreign. Changing the point of reference and switching to one of the neighbouring villages, we find that this group also considers itself the centre of distribution of similar features. In other words, in such a setting no ethnic 'group' possesses a fixed outside border and that means that we are not dealing with groups at all, but rather with a continuum in which the border between the 'we' and 'the others' shifts depending on the point of view of the observer (Elwert 1989: 445). Needless to say, without groups [4] we cannot have ethnic groups or ethnicity in its proper sense. Here, ethnicity frequently only emerged as a result of colonial administration, when districts were divided according to the tribes allegedly settled there. Furthermore, ethnicity cannot be viewed separately from modern science and education. How, if

---

3. Contrary to a misconceived metaphor, nothing 'derives from its roots'. Plants, the origin of the metaphor, start from a seed on the surface and then grow upwards and downwards. So it is with historical roots: they are driven back in time from the present; the present is not derived from them.

4. Mathematically, a group is a finite set. If we knew all the members of a group at a given time, we could enumerate them.

not ultimately from ethnographic literature, should an Inuit from Greenland know where exactly the distribution area of the Inuit as a whole ends? Where, if not in school, should they hear about Alaska or the north-eastern tip of Siberia? In this way, scientific ideas – correct ones as well as incorrect ones – about similarities and differences are occasionally reimported into local political discourses, and influence the modern boundaries of community sentiment. In particular, names of language families often undergo curious careers.

Proposition number four states that ethnicity is ascriptive, an irreversible attribute from the individual's perspective, which as a rule cannot be changed. In Kenya's arid north, however, which is used by several pastoral-nomadic groups speaking different Cushitic languages, we find many regular forms of transition between ethnic groups, which are open to at least the more competent bearers of local cultures, i.e., to those who know the relations and opportunities of transition and know how to use them manipulatively. Due to historical conditions, the discussion of which is not within the scope of this text, different clans are spread out over various ethnic groups so that different linguistic and cultural entities – i.e., ethnic entities – consist of sub-entities they share with each other. In times of drought, for instance, or when all livestock is lost as a result of violent conflicts, members of a particular clan in a particular ethnic group can appeal to their clan brothers in a neighbouring ethnic group for help, or they can go there as immigrants or refugees and make claims to pasture and water rights. Should they and their families stay there, ultimately their ethnic affiliation will adjust to the new surroundings, i.e., via the clan bridge, one's ethnicity can be changed, although this process may take a few generations.

There might be institutionalised bridges between ethnic groups like the ones described for Kenya elsewhere in the world, and the cultural features perceived as distinctive for the ethnic groups involved will not necessarily change when members move from one group to another. Only the groups' membership changes. The individuals switch from one cultural container to another. The ethnic groups themselves remain: they only exchange a proportion of the individuals they consist of (Barth 1969).

For example, in the lower reaches of the Omo in southern Ethiopia, Turton (1994) also observed that politico-territorial groups like the Mursi and Surma (see Figure 1, p. 1) consist of clans which are partly the same in both ethnic groups and seem to have existed prior to the emergence of the present ethnic configurations.

The fact that the 'tribes' – which became established during colonial times – have shared subgroups is even more remarkable among the Madi and Acholi (see Figure 1, p. 1) in northern Uganda (Allen 1994), because the languages of these two groups belong to quite different language families. In all these cases, the existence of common clans does not rule out the possibility of military conflicts between these groups.

The fifth proposition was that an ethnic group is a community of shared descent. After what has just been said, this must be considerably qualified. But even without institutional bridges of transition, the connections between ethnic boundaries and boundaries of descent groups are rather loose. In many cases the circle of people with whom one intermarries is smaller than one's ethnic group; on the other hand it can comprise elements of other ethnic groups.

In some respects human ethnogenesis is comparable to speciation, i.e., the formation of new species among other animals. Frequently, animal populations which are about to develop into separate subspecies and eventually separate species show the most distinct features at the borderline with one another.[5] But, while the distinguishing features of other animals are often linked to their physicality and are genetically determined, for humans – probably more than for any other species – there exist similar processes in the area of learned behaviour. Ethnogenesis is a process which we could call a pseudo-speciation, i.e., a process similar to speciation which, however, is not tied to communities of common descent.

The sixth and last proposition was that ethnic groups are territorial. They strive for a united territory and, eventually, for national sovereignty. However, many ethnic groups feature an occupational specialisation which could not have developed in its current form if they had not cohabited with other ethnic groups. The territorial state, particularly the so-called nation state, is an especially modern development originating in Western Europe. It does not represent a universal development trend. In many places it is only an external structure imposed on an entirely different set of popular self-identifications.

The most successful and usually most brutal form of political realisation of the above six problematic propositions is the foundation of nation states, which ideally are ethnically homogeneous or in which the eponymous national group is at least clearly in the majority. Only a small minority of today's more than 180 'nation' states worldwide, however, corresponds to this picture (Ra'anan 1989). In by far the majority of cases the problem is to deal with difference below the organisational level of a 'nation'. Often this is done by territorial or other group privileges, by ethnic specialisation in occupational niches (thereby avoiding competition but introducing discrimination), and protection of minorities, etc. All the listed forms of dealing with difference share the common feature that individuals are granted rights and obligations by the political system not on the basis of their own merit, but on the basis of belonging to one of the groups constituting the system. The individual is constantly referred back to their affiliation to a group, even if this happens by way of well-meaning measures for the protection of minorities and the administrative promotion of a multicultural, group mosaic. Liberty and rights are granted to collectives, not to individuals.

The first of the six propositions of the 'popular' theory we have refuted above was that ethnicity is the cause of conflict. The other five propositions corroborate the first and add weight to ethnicity as a factor that causes or aggravates conflicts. Against this popular view we insist that ethnicity is not the cause of conflict but rather something that emerges in the course of conflict, or acquires new shapes and functions in the course of such events. The popular theory disregards both micro-level identity changes through which people acquire new group affiliations, and the historical dimension, i.e., larger-scale changes over a longer period, including changes in the cultural content of a given identity, changes in social group boundaries defining an identity, and changes in a given identity's role in broader cultural and economic

---

5.   Examples for this as well as counter-examples can be found in Schlee (1995: 197, fnn. 9 and 10).

contexts. Efforts to integrate cultural differences are largely seen as likely to produce conflict. The possibility that integration at a higher level may be made possible through differences is ignored.

In social anthropology, this perspective is by no means new. In order to distance himself from a scientific tradition which generally assumed the ethnic group as the unit of ethnological research and which tended to view the single culture or the single society as a self-contained universe, Leach presented an entirely different perspective on ethnic differences in *Political Systems of Highland Burma* as early as 1954. He regarded the culturally and linguistically distinctly different valley communities of Burma's mountains as one great social structure, in which the variability of the parts was the construction principle of the whole: 'the maintenance and insistence upon cultural difference can itself become a ritual action expressive of social relations … In this context cultural attributes such as language, dress and ritual procedure are merely symbolic labels denoting the different sectors of a single extensive structural system' (Leach 1954: 17).

Taking liberties in rephrasing Leach, the following can be concluded: the different cultures of Burma's highlands are differentiated by a rich cultural symbolism. The symbols used by some are understood by the others, even though sometimes in a limited range of meaning. So, for instance, elements of traditional costume, which within a culture convey extensive information about the age and status of the person wearing it, might be perceived merely as an ethnic identifier and marker of a social boundary. In the chapter 'Ethnicity Emblems, Diacritical Features, Identity Markers – Some East African Examples' we shall come back to this finding and illustrate it with examples. Although not all intra-ethnic meanings of a symbol may be transported into the inter-ethnic context, there is a level of understanding on which the individual cultures correspond with each other within a common meta-culture. If – in the English tradition of the subject – one prefers to speak of societies instead of cultures, one can differentiate between individual societies and a meta-society. In the terminology of the ethnicity debate, one would speak of an ethnic and a meta-ethnic systemic level. On this superordinate level, the ethnic groups interact through their differences. They avoid competition by integrating different occupational niches and habitats, and by acting according to different norms and values. Each to his own.

Barth (1969) provides similar examples. Among them is an ethnic conversion from one ethnic group to another, in this case from Fur to Baggara Arabs in western Sudan, which was accompanied by a new occupational specialisation (Haaland 1969). Each ethnic group, as it were, had a legitimate claim to their own economic and ecological niche. If one wanted to enter this niche, one had to convert ethnically and adjust to these conditions. So there clearly existed a regulating function via ethnic differences in an interethnic system.[6] Similarly we can view the Indian caste system – which at least partly emerged from an incorporation of ethnic groups into an inter-

---

6.   The later breakdown of inter-ethnic relations in Darfur needs to be analysed in the light of other factors. Nothing in Haaland's analysis points to such a development (see De Waal 2004; El-Battahani 2005, Flint and de Waal 2005, and Prunier 2005 on the violent escalation in Darfur in the early 2000s; Abdel Ghaffar 2006; Behrends 2007a, b).

ethnic, hierarchised system – in its historical development, where a stabilisation and functionalisation of ethnic differences developed historically within a comprehensive system. The Indian caste system may appear to conflict with human rights and not to meet Western ideals of liberty and equality but it can be argued that it was an instrument of a relatively peaceful integration over long periods of its history, and that no constant use of open violence was needed to maintain the system.

If we understand our enemies to the extent that we can engage in meaningful hostile relationships with them, we are part of the same social system. Enemies even tend to borrow from each other culturally or to develop similar cultural forms in response to each other. They develop predictable strategies in dealing with each other 'tit for tat': they engage in arms races and mutual bullying by manoeuvres and parades. Enemies become alike. So sameness combines with hostility and difference with peaceful interaction.

Obviously, there are conditions existent in some parts of the world and non-existent in others which favour a continuation of difference, heterogeneity in a very confined space. If, for instance, we look at distribution maps of languages and dialects – frequently the observable characteristic of different cultures – it is amazing what lies hidden behind them. For example, through West Africa and into south-western Ethiopia, there is a fragmentation belt in which not only many small languages, but languages of entirely different language families, which are as different from each other as English and Chinese, have apparently existed next to each other for thousands of years in a very confined space. Directly north of this belt, we find a spread of Hamito-Semitic languages which runs straight across the entire continent. To the south there is Bantu, a relatively homogeneous sub-subfamily of languages practically covering the southern half of the continent. In between, there are two zones in which hundreds of languages coexist. Why? There has not been enough research on this up to now. Sociologists concern themselves with other areas and topics like Europe and the industrial modernity going out from there, anthropologists with single ethnic groups instead of distributions of this type. But I assume that niche formation and the functionalisation of differences play an important role here.

Apart from these two models – animosity or integration through differences – I want to mention a third one briefly. Surely, there is also the possibility of mere coexistence, where neither one nor the other model clearly prevails. Mutie (2003), in his investigation about the Kamba and the Maasai (see Figure 1, p. 1) in Kenya, took an ecological model as a starting point. Biological species that share the same resource basis cannot coexist. If one species is only marginally more efficient in the acquisition of energy than the other one, it will survive and the other one will be driven out or become extinct. Therefore, special conditions of a limitation of competition are necessary in order to manage coexistence. For the case of the two ethnic groups in which Mutie utilised the biological model, he found a partial overlapping of the resource bases, so that the competitive model was discernible, but not entirely adequate. A restricted exchange took place. This is a case of mutual completion that does not result in a complete integration. One group did a little more farming; the other was pastoral-nomadic. Both competed with each other, had cattle and other things in common, through which a partial overlapping resulted. Violent conflicts did occur but seldom escalated, because mechanisms of conflict regulation are negotiated, individual interests are restricted and compromises made. Occasionally, alliances are formed against a third party, since both feel themselves to be a small, disadvantaged ethnic group within the Kenyan nation state, because both have settled in a semi-arid region, and because both share similar interests in the national framework. In total, this coexistence – a term evoking the cold war – presents itself in such a way that the relationship between Maasai and Kamba is often tense and an annoyance for both parties. Most likely, the Maasai think the world would be a nicer place without the Kamba, and vice versa. A war of annihilation, however, is prevented for a number of reasons. The occasional disagreement continues to be advantageous for representatives of both sides and, in spite of all the opposition, each knows the other very well, and there is always room to compensate and regulate. Once in a while they even pull together in national politics. If there were no Maasai, this would imply some advantages for the Kamba, but also a number of disadvantages, and the same can be said about what a hypothetical situation without Kamba would mean for the Maasai. The profit in the case of the opponents' annihilation is reduced by the loss of the advantages they have provided and to the crucial actors appears so slight that it is not worth the costs and risks of a war of extermination. It is therefore not a matter of love but more a form of continued coexistence. This example represents the third and last possible combination of which ethnicity can be a part. Ethnicity can be (1) an instrument of hostile mobilisation, (2) a vehicle of integration, and (3) a way to constitute an uncomfortable juxtaposition, the mere coexistence of different ethnic groups. It is not always easy to predict what will happen in an individual case, and the precise interests of spokespersons and their followers have to be investigated. But, in any case, we can already abandon theories that demonise or praise ethnic or cultural differences as such. These differences are only the raw material of political rhetoric. What is made of them does not depend on the extent of the differences themselves.

In the following, I will attempt a new start. Popular theories about ethnic conflicts and the clash of cultures are to be set aside. Instead, I want to systematically deduce a conflict theory, starting with basic and seemingly trivial questions. Who opposes whom in a conflict situation? According to which criteria is this determined? Ethnicity and religion will also find their level in this theory, but not as starting points.

Chapter 2

The Question

One type of conflict theory turns its attention to the existence of contested resources.[1] It demonstrates that, behind high and noble war objectives like the implementation of human rights or the political liberation of a people, quite substantial quarrels about mineral resources or occupational niches or positions and salaries are often hidden. One can write books about conflicts and deal with different resources chapter by chapter: one chapter about wars over water, another one about wars over oil, etc. Klare (2001) wrote such a book and named it *Resource Wars*. Here, without denying the importance of these resource-oriented, economically or ecologically inspired theories, I wish to shift the accent from the objects to the subjects of violent conflict. My main concern is the question of social identification and affiliation. According to which characteristics do people group into complex social structures? By which characteristics do they distinguish between friends and enemies? By what criteria do they form alliances or coalitions? Our central terms, therefore, are identity and difference. Both play a role in explaining questions such as 'who with whom?' and 'who against whom?'[2]

If, when talking about conflicts, we think of wars among relatively well-defined European nation states – like the 'Cabinet Wars' (wars between princes) of the eighteenth century or the nationalistic people's wars of the nineteenth and twentieth centuries – then indeed these questions appear trivial. The conflicting parties are common knowledge: Russia, France, England, Austria, and Prussia, later Germany. Likewise the patterns of alliance: the English always striving for a balance of power and forming alliances with the second-strongest continental power against the strongest, which back then was no secret but rather explicit policy. These declared wars between nation states, with a defined beginning and end, with wholly known actors and written contracts of alliance, have become rare, however. In practically all of today's military conflicts, there is at least one, often several non-governmental conflict groups involved, and even states usually do not fight each other directly and openly, but with the unofficial support of a liberation movement directed against the enemy. That the question of the 'who against whom?' is not trivial at all really dawned on me in the case of Ethiopia in the 1990s.

---

1. This chapter utilises paragraphs from my inaugural lecture *Identitätspolitik und Gruppengröße* at the Martin Luther University Halle-Wittenberg, Halle (Saale), 30 June 2004, and passages of Schlee (2004c); for an earlier version in German see Schlee (2000, 2003c).

2. It has become clear from the preceding chapter that identity does not automatically lead to partnership, or difference to hostility. Both identity and difference are part of the explanation of both alliance and enmity.

Back then, in the country's south (and this was only one of several simultaneous and in various ways mutually linked conflicts) heavy fighting took place against the background of a regional reorganisation according to the criterion of 'ethnic' affiliation (whatever might have been understood by that phrase). From a local perspective – which was also that of the simple combatants – the conflict was about pastures and water, and the actors were tribes, as they were called uninhibitedly, i.e., ethnic entities of a medium size like, for instance, Boran or Garre (see Figure 1, p. 1). From the political leaders' point of view, the Boran were part of the Oromo and the Garre part of the Somali, and the conflict was about larger ethno-political entities. To be precise, it was about the formation of the border between Oromia and the Somali region of Ethiopia as well as, of course, about their own sinecures and positions. The political movements in which they were organised showed, apart from ethnonyms, programmatic elements in their names; they were for instance called Oromo People's Democratic Organisation (OPDO), or Somali Abo Liberation Front, so one might surmise that these were groups engaged in a democratic struggle of some kind or other. The fact that the Boran only partly but the Garre in their entirety are Muslims was again used by the latter for a jihad rhetoric. One version was therefore that this was a war between Muslims and pagans. People who didn't know that it was in reality all one and the same conflict might have believed there were four different wars taking place in the same area simultaneously: one between Boran and Garre, one between Oromo and Somali, one between parties with different programmes, and one between Muslims and pagans. From the perspectives of different actors, all these wars did exist next to each other. Which perspectives now depicted the real conflict, and which were an expression of a false consciousness? The question might have to be put in a rather more relativist form and the answer can only be found in an empirical way. In cases like this, one must investigate which interpretations influence the course of the conflict more strongly than others. It may also be the case that these interpretations have effects that cannot be defined separately, because they interact in complex ways and might lead to results that do not comply with the intentions of even one of the parties.

So, empirically, the question of how the lines are drawn in conflict situations does not always seem an easy one. Simultaneously, one must say that it is definitely under-theorised. We know little about the patterns of identification and the ways in which people group themselves, form alliances, and break and regroup themselves in conflict situations. In the trouble spots of the world our predictions about who is going to gang up with whom against whom tend to fail. So the question of the logic of such identifications and the reasons behind them cannot be dismissed as trivial.

One might pause a moment to ask why this rather basic question so often remains without a satisfying answer. Identification processes seem to be shaped by cost-benefit calculations on the one hand and social structures and their cognitive representations on the other. The economically inspired social scientists who deal with costs and benefits and those who deal with social structures and their impact, and the weight of convention, which sometimes silences considerations of cost and benefit, tend to be different people. They are not the same type of thinkers. This little volume is going to explore whether some clarity can be gained by systematically combining these two perspectives.

Considering how and why people take sides in violent conflicts, one can expect two types of reasoning. One has to do with concepts and categories. The way in which people classify themselves and others tends to be of a systematic nature, and employs a certain logic and plausibility structure. Wishing to be or not to be something is not enough; one also needs a plausible claim to an identity or a plausible reason for rejecting it. If plausible alternatives are lacking, one might be forced by one's own logic and the expectations of others to join the fight on a given side. The other type of reason concerns the advantages and disadvantages that may arise from such identifications and such decisions to take sides: in other words with the costs and benefits of taking sides. It is to be expected that the two types of reason interpenetrate each other. Where there is room for identity work, i.e., for people reasoning about their identities and changing them, categories can be expected to be replaced or stretched to fit the needs of actors. These needs often have to do with the size of a group or alliance: one either seeks a wider alliance or tries to keep others out, to exclude them from sharing in certain benefits.

Apart from reasons, one may also look at consequences. Decisions to take sides have consequences both for those who make them as well as those who don't. In the case of the latter, others make the decision for them or the decisions of others affect them. Unintended consequences may, of course, affect later decisions.

One of the most successful explanatory theories in sociology is called rational choice (RC) theory. As at this stage of the argument we have convinced ourselves of the necessity of a decision theory, we might pause a moment to consider to what extent RC theory is suitable for our problem. Is 'rationality' a useful concept? Rationality comes in several ways as humans aggregate into larger units. One may try to join a group for specific reasons. Such an attempt may be rejected on equally rational grounds. A group may increase its homogeneity and the consistency of its aims and strategies by excluding dissidents. Or, alternatively, in the process of accommodating new members it may modify its self-description and aims. People reason about the group boundaries they draw, they invent or select ancestors, and they classify languages and dialects in order to show that these boundaries make particular sense in precisely the way they have been drawn. Smaller units thus delineated are part of larger units, so we find systems of categories and taxonomies.

Neither the cognitive aspects of identification (the logic of categorical inclusion and exclusion) nor the perspective of rational choice in analysing who identifies with whom or what – and why they do so – has been fully and systematically explored in anthropology.[3] Some of the most inspiring works in this direction are already forty years old (Barth 1959, 1981) and little systematic advance has been made since. Much ground remains to be covered.

The emphasis on the categorical framework of identification and the element of choice between options of identification is not meant to suggest that the analysis of human aggregation can be reduced to a combination of cognitive anthropology and rational choice. There are emotional forces at work which are covered by neither of these approaches. If we reserve the term 'identification' for the more rational (or

---

3.   Significant advances in this direction have, however, recently been made by Helbling (2006).

'cognitive') level of categories and classifications, then these may be studied under a label like 'bonding'.

To have options, and to have the time and the emotional freedom to consider them, is not a natural given but a privilege. Identification and bonding often occur in situations of rapid change. We do not need to go far to find drastic examples of this. In the case of the political map of the Horn of Africa, recent change is obvious. But, even where the political map has not changed, as in most of Africa, life has. In the 1960s and 1970s Africans grew up with the certainty that education would be rewarded. African states, many of them newly independent, had to recruit a public sector; they subsequently embarked on the first and then the second 'decade of development'. Many jobs were filled with relatively young people, blocking the way for the next batch of school leavers. Development should have brought economic growth and more jobs, but in most cases it took place neither in the form nor to the extent anticipated. The options facing the younger generation were no longer to become a farmer or go to town to get a job. Market relations and land scarcity made the rural option difficult or unattractive; meanwhile urban unemployment had become high. Other options – like informal-sector employment, self-employment, or crime – came into the picture. Failed development and corruption (which was itself one among the many causes of failed development) had discredited the state and given rise to rival armed powers. The Kalashnikov had become one more alternative way of life. New types of identification and bonding have to be seen in the light of deprivation relative both to the earlier promises of the development state and, of course, to consumption patterns globalised by new media fuelling new expectations.

Exit is a response to this situation that is not much discussed in this volume but should at least be mentioned. Somali flock to Canada. Nuer and Anywaa, from the southern Sudan (see Figure 1, p.1) as well as many from western Ethiopia, are resettled to the USA from refugee camps in Gambela (Ethiopia) by a UN programme (Feyissa 2003; Falge 2006). The Oromo are a global nation. Diaspora communities influence politics back home through flows of money and propaganda. The Internet becomes a battleground.

Withholding loyalty from institutions which do not fulfil their promises is another response. Underpaid state agents resort to corruption or extortion. They might remain loyal to individuals in positions of power who protect them, but they become disloyal to their constitutional roles. Others join gangs or militias, which avoid the state or have turned against it. The state must be able to provide positive incentives for loyalty and negative ones for disloyalty and will disintegrate if this capacity is missing. Gellner (1981: 93f.) stresses the importance of education and the promise it holds out for the development of the modern nation state. Give up your local peculiarities and loyalties, adopt the national culture and the language of wider communication, and you will be rewarded by employment or at least the chance of betterment. If, however, this promise is not kept, people revert to other loyalties.

In a recent conference paper, Simons (2000:7) quite explicitly makes the connection between the decline of the state/the official economy and the rise of other forms of bonding: 'the less the state manages to protect and/or provide for all of its citizens, the more people must turn to those they know they can trust'.

Young males have to be socialised into groups which are coherent enough to offer their members security and to deserve their loyalty and trust. The most extreme form of such bonding is one which entails the readiness to sacrifice oneself. Training to become a fighter in a group of fighters should be a choice topic for social scientists interested in the nature of the social, 'but', Simons (2000: 9) regrets, 'there are few descriptions of training, perhaps because the presumption is that no training takes place or everyone already understands what training involves. Even more is needed than just training; something must be done (or used) to compel fighters to stick together and follow orders.'

Two recent articles allow some insights into the socialisation of fighters. De Silva asks what makes the Tamil Tigers, the 'Liberation Tigers of Tamil Eelam' (LTTE), in Sri Lanka such an effective fighting body. 'The LTTE, which is a very successful organization by its own grim standards, produces battle hardened cadres who have been trained in carrying out the most desperate of actions, including the phenomenon of suicide bombing' (De Silva 2002: 226). To explain this intensity of mobilisation, De Silva points to a variety of techniques in the 'cultivation of hatred' (ibid.). These include keeping alive the memory of anti-Tamil atrocities committed by the government: 'torture, rape, murder and the destruction of property' (ibid.: 227). Public statements by public figures on the Sinhalese side are also instrumentalised for this purpose. Revenge and counter-revenge lead to a perpetuation of the conflict.

Kenney (2002) offers a similar analysis of the role of folk history in maintaining the divisions between Catholics and Protestants in Northern Ireland. The voluntary associations which socialise young Irish into partisans in this conflict might be compared with secret societies, age-grading organisations, and other organisational frameworks for male bonding in Africa.

Emotions tend to be attached in particular to minimal differences. Who cares whether he or she is respected by people who are far away and do not matter? To be betrayed by someone we never had a reason to trust anyhow is a mild form of betrayal. It is proximity that breeds the strong emotions capable of leading to rapidly escalating levels of violence. There are parallels to this in everyday life. The police know about the dangers of proximity: when a married person is murdered, is not the spouse the first suspect?

My own perspective in this volume may be criticised for being too rationalist. To ward off this criticism, I might point to having dealt with 'hatred' and other emotions to some extent elsewhere (Schlee 2002a), but I still must admit my emphasis on rationality and a relative helplessness when dealing with emotions. Suffice it to say here that I am aware of emotional factors and would welcome analytical work on them which is pertinent for conflict analysis, but that, as for myself, I am currently preoccupied with the many aspects of identification in conflict situations which I believe to be open to rationalist explanations and which have not yet been sufficiently explained along those lines. And, when that task has been achieved, when the different individual rationalities behind individual identification and bonding have been explained, what comes next? An obvious question concerns the connections between processes understood at the level of particular actors and the behaviour of large aggregates of people, in other words the micro/macro problem. This remains among the most intractable of social science conundrums.

Looking to political science for assistance, we discover model-building that is more diverse and more refined than in current anthropology. (Though I would hasten to add that anthropology has the edge in some other respects: it collects more varied primary data, and treats them with greater scepticism. Not that I wish, either, to preach political science to those readers who happen to be anthropologists.) However, anthropologists cannot simply apply all these political science models to their data: political scientists deal with a world of states; thus, all the units they discuss share some basic characteristics. Anthropologists, on the other hand, describe a world of complex individual and collective actors, some of which are states but most of which are not. Even if anthropologists may not be able to import political science models wholesale, they can still derive inspiration from them. It is apparent that political scientists face a similar micro/macro problem to anthropologists. War, whether actual or impending, forces people to make up their minds about who are their allies, who their enemies, and why. Therefore, I take my examples from a book about war.

In his overview of theories of conflict, the political scientist Cashman (1993) starts with theories which address the level of individuals (level 1). These examine the personality traits and the psychohistory of leaders. (Psychological interpretations of entire 'nations' like national character studies seem to be outdated among political scientists as elsewhere.) The political beliefs of leaders are studied by the methods of content analysis, and the results are interpreted in the light of psychological theories like the avoidance of cognitive dissonance. At the next higher level (level 2), governmental decision-making, groups and organisations are included. A 'rational actor model' is discussed, and this is contrasted with a 'bureaucratic politics model' which sees government decisions to result from the interplay between the diverse interests and perceptions of sub-organisations. These decisions may be far from optimal for the interests of the whole. Perceptions are also influenced by 'groupthink', the pressure to conform. Interaction between states is introduced at a yet higher level (level 3). Among stimulus-response modelling of escalation, arms races and trust building (graduated and reciprocated initiatives in tension reduction, GRIT), game theory and deterrence theory come in at this level. Game theory is about the advantages that can be gained at the expense of other players and about strategies to minimise these advantages and to build trust. Deterrence theory is about the credibility of threats and their effects on the response of the opponent. Both are rational-choice theories, which start on the assumption that the interacting states are rational actors.

There are potential contradictions in all of this, of which Cashman is also aware. Having been told at level 1 that political leaders are shaped by their psychohistories, and therefore should not be treated as entirely rational decision-makers, at level 2 we learn that how these leaders think might not be all that important after all because decisions have been pre-shaped by organisational considerations or influenced by a supra-individual and not wholly rational groupthink. But, just as we learn not to expect too much rationality, at level 3, where states interact, we are invited to revert to theories based on rational actor models. There are problems of consistency as we move from one level to the other. Not everything discovered at one level can be incorporated into our understanding of the next higher levels, because in doing so our theories would become over-complex. Thus, we must constantly ignore valuable insights to reduce complexity.

I sympathise with the political scientists because I face similar problems transferring insights between levels. I would like to know how far the discourses of intellectuals reflect social identities and how far they actually shape them. I would also like to know how individual experience translates into moral evaluations at the level of collective identities, and to what extent pre-shaped identities influence individual experience. There is much gossip in north-eastern Africa about the personal relationships between different leaders. Are these relations translated into politics? And, if so, to what extent does this happen? Alternatively, are leaders captives of their roles irrespective of their personal sympathies and antipathies? Again one asks, if so, to what extent? And, if collective decisions are not the vector sum of individual decisions, then what are they?

Much empirically informed theorising needs to be done before we can answer all these questions. I do not know the end of the journey, but I know where to start and how to proceed from there: The next chapter will explain how the following chapters tackle the question of how group size relates to exclusivist or inclusionist identification strategies, of which 'cultural' stuff identifications are made and where limits of the freedom of identification decisions are.

Chapter 3

How This Volume is Organised

Chapter by chapter, this volume will attempt a formal description of options of identification in conflict situations, and suggest a decision theory that explains the conditions under which differing types of identifications are preferred (i.e., who takes whose side in a conflict). A systematic outline trying to structure the problem ('A Decision Theory of Identification', Chapter 4) will be followed by an action-theory-inspired look at the rhetoric of recruitment of allies ('The Necessity for Strategies of Inclusion and Exclusion', Chapter 5). This chapter proceeds from a simple model (the genocidal model, which could also be called 'winner takes all') to complex cases where losers can be incorporated and the distinction between winners and losers is blurred. The next chapter (Chapter 6) looks at the conceptual toolkit of discourses on exclusion and inclusion. Economic reasoning, often taken as the underlying cause of identity politics and politics in general, is then brought back in under the heading 'Economics as Sociology – Sociology as Economics' (Chapter 7). A theory that attributes preponderance to free decisions in a somewhat extreme fashion, Elwert's analysis of 'markets of violence' (1995, 1997) is critically discussed and the question is raised as to what extent social structures even steer decisions by the apparently most arbitrary power-holders. The point made at the end of that chapter, Chapter 8, is that a new synthesis of economic and sociological perspectives is needed, rather than leaving the two types of reasoning to be dealt with by two different types of thinkers who communicate little and with little success.

Chapter 9 discusses markers of collective identity from a general perspective. Chapter 10 deals with religion, particularly ideas of ritual purity and their role in claims to power in a number of Islamic and non-Islamic societies. Chapter 11 examines the wide variation in the importance of language for collective identification, ranging from ethnic groups without a common language to ethnic groups in which language is the main or, indeed, almost the only defining feature. The emotional attachments generated by religion and language in some cases demonstrate that both may be more than merely emblems of identification.

The last part of the book, Part III, deals with practice. It consists of three chapters, each of which is inspired by the author's experience with Somali people. The first, 'Conflict Resolution: the Experience with the Somali Peace Process', deals with a very formal setting, an international peace conference. The second, 'On Methods: How to be a Conflict Analyst', is derived from and aims at a more local and regional setting and discusses how to facilitate peace initiatives at the local and community level. This practice-oriented part of the book is not to be read as an attempt to apply a ready-made theory laid out earlier. There is no single, unified conflict theory, and, even if there were one, interacting with people in a conflict situation and trying to help them to cope would always be different from the mechanical application of any one theory. Part III does take up themes such as identification and alliance discussed in the preceding theoretical parts, but its main aim is to give the reader a glimpse of the complexities of conflict intervention from a participant's perspective.

This book pulls together ideas published earlier in scattered places. In the footnotes at the beginning of each chapter the earlier publications from which elements of the text have been taken are listed. In the attempt to fit them into a new synthesis the older fragments have been rewritten to a greater or lesser extent and been combined with new text.

The ambition of the book is to be a step towards a new conflict theory. Ethnographic examples are included for purposes of explanation and illustration. Examples from north-eastern Africa predominate for two reasons, one biographical, the other geopolitical. The biographical circumstance is that north-eastern Africa has been my research area for over three decades. I have spent extended periods conducting field research there since 1974. The geopolitical features of the region that make for compelling examples for this book include weak state control over vast areas of the region and a high degree of local autonomy that encourages fluid and shifting alliances to engage in hostilities. These are fortunate circumstances for conflict research but unfortunate ones for the people involved.

Part II
Theoretical Frame

Chapter 4

A Decision Theory of Identification

At the risk of over-formalisation, one can systematise the questions posed above in the form of a theoretical framework.[1] One would have to distinguish three interconnected domains or levels, A, B, and C.

A. Social Structures and their Cognitive Representations: the Semantic Fields of Identity Concepts

People identify themselves and others using criteria such as language, religion, descent, and other dimensions of identification. The identity concepts found in these different domains, for example ethnonyms, names of languages or religious communities, are not isolated words but form semantic fields. They are parts of taxonomies and defined by contrasts and equivalences with each other.

Social identities cannot be made up at will, because they have to be plausible to others. The range within which identities can be changed or manipulated is limited by the systemic logic of these semantic domains and by social convention.

B. The Politics of Inclusion and Exclusion

Within the range of options of identification, special attention has to be attributed to the size of the groups or categories circumscribed by alternative identity concepts. One can opt for wider or narrower identities within the same dimension (e.g., within the linguistic dimension one can put the emphasis on panslavism or, more narrowly, on being a Croatian-speaker; within the religious dimension one can identify with Christianity as a whole or with just one small elect sect, etc.), or one can change from one dimension to another (e.g., from a linguistically based ethno-nationalism to a religious identification, if the latter offers the wider alliance, or excludes people one wants to keep out).[2]

Group size may only be a first and rough approximation to strength, which may be the real issue. Not all allies count alike. Mere calculations of size may be modified by considerations of economic power, organisational capability, cultural prestige or military capability. Size needs to be weighted.

On the level of larger groups and their interactions, only some members of these groups actively engage in identity discourses. Even fewer are virtuosi in identity manipulation who intentionally succeed in the widening or narrowing of group

---

1. This chapter makes use of passages earlier published as part of Schlee (2003c, 2004c).
2. This process has been called 'switching' by Elwert (2002).

memberships or inter-group alliances. One therefore has to distinguish between people who change identities and those who are affected by these changes.

C. The Economics of Group Size and Social Position

Narrower and wider identifications and those which imply differential access to power or prestige have to be analysed in terms of costs and benefits to those who make decisions about them and to those who are affected by such decisions. To single out the dimension of size: a wide alliance may be useful in obtaining certain benefits, but narrower definitions might be preferred when it comes to sharing these same benefits.

A relevant theorem dealing with the economy of group size is known under the heading of 'crowding'. The example used by Hechter (1988) to explain his idea of 'crowding' is a golf club in the countryside. A large membership in a club reduces the individual's costs; membership subscription can be lowered without the financing of the clubhouse or other conveniences being affected. However, if the crowding gets too dense, the leisure value decreases. One has to wait until it is one's turn to play. In the clubhouse, service takes longer, the noise increases, the atmosphere becomes tense. Many of the better-off members of the club will wonder whether it might be preferable to be a member in a smaller, more 'exclusive' club and in return accept a higher club subscription.

The factor of a sharing of costs favours larger groups until the reverse factor, 'crowding', reaches such a degree that its adverse effects outweigh the cost advantage. For participation in the benefits of an institution, fewer people are preferable, because, this way, more is left for the individual. To illustrate this connection, we leave the distinguished surroundings of the golf club and proceed to the less distinguished one of a band of robbers.

A band of robbers must be big enough to overpower its victims, to defend its territory and booty against other gangs, and to face up to the police. If it is not big enough, the members would do well to join other bands of robbers or recruit members among the sons of peasants not entitled to an inheritance. But, once a gang has reached the necessary size, each additional yokel asking to be admitted to the band is a nuisance. If the band is larger than necessary, the booty has to be shared out among more people than were required to make it. Some individuals may be given a smaller share or none at all. There will be quarrels, which in turn will lead to a splitting (reduction of band size) or maybe even to a gang war (reduction of the total number of robbers). Another possibility is betrayal. A part of the gang gets 'busted', and this way the police are left to reduce one's co-robbers in number.

We will come back to the 'distribution of the booty' as a theoretical consideration further down in connection with Machiavelli (1975 [1531]). As we can see, the two theorems of 'distribution of the booty' and 'crowding' are very similar to each other, except for the detail that in distribution every individual takes his/her share, whereas the 'crowding' is about joint use.

From Dichotomies to Variables

In the light of these theorems, identification with a larger or smaller group, or to seek a narrower or wider alliance, appears to be a conscious decision. The implications for group size and potential benefits are obvious and the identification strategies adjust to these expectations, and aim at targets. Costs and benefits here are the reasons for identifications. There are, however, cases in which people profess or attribute identities for non-economic reasons or simply have no options because their social identities are inescapable. In such cases costs and benefits may be unintended consequences of identifications. This ambiguity means that the relationship between C, 'the economics of group size', and B, 'the politics of size: inclusion and exclusion', needs to be examined. It cannot be assumed that it is one of strict determination of B by C.

In this volume I shall not proceed in this order, from A to B to C, but I shall develop my discussion with reference to texts and case histories which might require that more than one level be addressed simultaneously and which also raise additional questions. One of these will be how to assess gains and losses if the units of reference are groups of people which change their composition.[3] In a later part, the thrust of the argument will be against an overdose of free rational decision-making as an explanation for forms of recruitment. Against such positions (which stress level C) it will be argued that one has to take into account the place of the decision-makers within given identities (level B) and the logic of the semantic fields within which they operate (level A). These might restrict their options.

Thus far the overview has focused on the basic structure of the proposed theory. The reader may have noticed that time-honoured dichotomies like primordialism/instrumentalism which have served as a starting point for dozens of other introductions to 'ethnicity' or 'identity' have not been used here. This is due not so much to a dislike of this particular dichotomy as to a dislike of dichotomies in general. A dichotomy is a variable with two values, and that is both theoretically and empirically impoverished. I prefer a gradualist approach in which variables have many values between the extremes. Explanation is about variation and covariation. If one thing changes, what other things does it affect and how does it affect them? To explain the world, we need to define richly variable variables, not dichotomies.

Let us take a closer look at levels A, B, and C and I will explain how I want to rephrase things as variables. A is about criteria of identification and change of

---

3. Cost-benefit calculations in connection with identification during violent conflicts present complex problems. How is one to assess the gains and losses of war when the losers are adopted into the winners' ethnic group at the end of the conflict? This is in no way a rare case: in some regions of Africa there is much evidence of ethnic groups ceasing to exist when they are numerically no longer able to defend themselves successfully, since they either join with other splinter groups to form a larger alliance or simply attach themselves to their attackers, i.e., to their enemies (e.g., Turton 1994). In this way they would themselves – perhaps later, perhaps only indirectly, but in some form or another – benefit from the spoils earlier taken from them by their enemies. In such a case, an analyst wishing to write up the balance sheet of who did what against whom, who lost, who won, and who lost or won what will have the difficult job of disentangling the strands.

identification. Change implies time. Re-identification can occur at shorter or longer intervals and identity concepts may remain the same over a shorter or a longer period.

In 1989 I published a book, *Identities on the Move* (Schlee 1989a), in which I explained, among other things, that one can often find the same clans in different ethnic groups in northern Kenya. I asserted that many of these inter-ethnic clan identities were the result of ethnogenesis – the coming into being of the present-day ethnic groups of northern Kenya out of earlier formations – occurring across clan lines. Fragments of the same clans ended up in different ethnic groups. This implies that many of these clans must be older than the ethnic groups we find now in the area.

My analysis of inter-ethnic clan groups has been interpreted as an assertion that clanship is the stable and immutable principle while ethnicity is fluid and eminently manipulable. This is only one step removed from saying that I have a primordialist view of clanship and an instrumentalist view of ethnicity. Yet any understanding of my approach in terms of such dichotomies is wrong, and there is nothing in my book which supports such a reading. I only assert that in northern Kenya clanship has changed at a slower rate than ethnicity. I also provide a counter-example: in Rwanda groups that split from each other 200 years ago do not share any clans, so the clans seem to be a more recent development than the major groupings to which they belong; otherwise one would have expected at least one or the other clan to have split along the newly emerging ethnic/regional dividing lines (Newbury 1980; Schlee 1989a: 236).

So in my book there is nothing about the inherent stability of one form of social organisation versus the inherent fluidity of another. In one case ethnic groups changed faster than clans, in another clans changed faster than ethnic groups. The question is why? That clans are relatively stable in northern Kenya seems to have to do with the fact that recruitment into patrilineal clans follows a very easy principle: a child is born into the clan of the father, and the father is the man who has paid the bridewealth for the mother. This is a simple and straightforward rule. Even if isolated individual cases do not conform to the principle and affiliation follows some other reasoning, the group bearing a given name and having other features identifying it as one clan or another will be reproduced safely, many times over, and without much conscious effort by anyone. So there are structural factors at work that limit the scope for change. Ethnic groups in northern Kenya, on the other hand, are political and military entities and as such are subject to security considerations and power politics: they react to changing conditions and thereby change. I do not know why the relation between the rate of change of clans versus ethnic groups is the other way around in Rwanda, but I know one thing: I would not even be able to ask this question if I did not have (1) a gradualist perception of stability over time, (2) a relativist concept: one kind of identification changing faster than another, and (3) an empirical approach: let us find out how fast things change and then find out why they change at different rates.

If I had started as the slave of a dichotomy and had to ask myself whether I want to join the primordialist or the instrumentalist camp even before being allowed on the battlefield, I would not even have got to this point.

The primordialist notion of identity, apart from stability over time, comprises other elements like deep emotional attachment. It is a conglomerate of things that should not be rolled into one concept, but should rather be analysed separately. I have not developed the concept and it is not my job to undo it. I might come back to emotions when it suits me, not when the subject is imposed on me by an inapplicable dichotomy.

Other variables (in the true sense) are mentioned in the brief paragraphs on level A above. For example, the range within which identities can be changed or manipulated can also vary in degree. It may be easier to change one's profession than to change one's gender, and how easily, how often, and across what perceived differences one can change one's religion vary greatly with historical circumstances and the type of society one lives in. Not long ago in the Lutheran social environment where I was brought up it was unthinkable to marry a Catholic and to bring up one's children as Catholics. That surely has changed. Even conversion to Islam at one time not too long ago was much less of a problem than now, after the recent religious polarisation on a global scale. Conversion might be credible once or twice in a lifetime. But how about someone who tries a new religion every other year? This is unthinkable in rural or conservative environments all over the world, but may be possible among postmodern urbanites. So one can, in mental experiments and later in empirical research, test the range in which identities can be changed in different periods, in different social environments, in different conceptual or legal frameworks.

Level B moves on to groups and their sizes. Size in itself is a gradualist concept and a relative approach – larger than (>) and smaller than (<) are needed more often in models of strategic identification based on group size than absolute numbers are. Size does not stand alone in such considerations: people come in different kinds (Becker (1998) would not hesitate to speak of 'qualities'). Whether we consider three rich, eloquent, reliable, influential people (add more positive characteristics if you like) to be as important to have in one's own group or alliance as five or ten or twenty ordinary friends is again subject to a gradualist perspective.[4] In our models, we can incorporate whatever values and attributes we deem necessary to take into account various kinds and amounts of social capital without being caught in any discontinuities or dichotomies.

One more variable mentioned under level B is how actively and skilfully people are involved in the identity discourses affecting their groups (virtuosity). This is an actor-specific variable and corresponds closely to the 'range within which identities can be changed or manipulated' on the side of the 'system' or 'structure'. When we discussed this range (above) we considered the logical structures in which an identity concept was embedded and the social pressures used for keeping an identity stable (or for changing it). Virtuosity, in contrast, is a characteristic of people: some people get away with the most unlikely claims to a social identity, others try but fail, and yet others do not even try to be anything other than what they have been born into and what others assume them to be.

---

4.   In ordinary reasoning such problems tend to be optimisations of more than one value or decisions between alternative or conflicting values. The poor friend might be more reliable, the not so pretty wife more faithful, the fierce loyalty of a hundred tribal warriors might count more than the sophisticated weaponry of an alternative ally, etc.

Under C, it has been stated that there are 'cases in which people profess or attribute identities for non-economic reasons'. Reasons in this sense may include emotions. Not even hard-core rational choice theorists claim that our decisions are entirely or overwhelmingly taken deliberately and on rational grounds. They simply try to model behaviour and have found out that behaviour often looks as if it is guided by rational reasoning. What an organism does tends to be to its advantage, by whatever psychological motivations or other mechanisms the action is achieved. No doubt also our conscious and rational considerations are in many ways influenced by less conscious aversions and preferences. So we may talk about degrees of consciousness, degrees of intentionality, etc.

Contractuality as a Variable

Speaking of the economics of identity change, an important distinction is whether an identity is thought of as natural or as contractual. Contractual elements can be more strongly or more weakly represented, so we can speak of contractuality as varying along a scale.

As far back as Maine (1986 [1861]),[5] and maybe even much earlier, a basic dichotomy has existed in the social sciences between the relationships into which a person is born and those into which he or she enters by concluding a contract.[6] This dichotomy has informed related dichotomies like *Gemeinschaft/Gesellschaft* (Tönnies 1991 [1935]) and traditional/modern (e.g., Weber 1990 [1922] and, following him, the modernisation theorists of the 1950s and since). More recently Fox (1993) has shown in the context of competing ideas about motherhood[7] the degree to which contractual relationships have come to dominate over bonds regarded as natural in the United States. Dichotomies like kinship (presumed to be given) versus friendship (presumed to be chosen) are also akin to the status versus contract dichotomy, even though friendship is often not an explicit contractual relationship but rather one in disguise.[8] We need not go into an extensive review of the literature to see that the

---

5. See also Feaver (1969).
6. This distinction is not as easy as it looks at first glance. The relationship constituted by birth and the contractual ones do not form mutually exclusive categories. A person may be born into contractual relations (he may become part of a long-standing political or military alliance into which his group has entered before his birth, the son of a tenant may succeed his father as the partner of an agreement about land with the owner of that land, and so on). One type of contractual relationship, marriage, even typically translates into kin relationships into which people are born in the next generation.
7. The example is a law case in which a woman had the fertilised egg of another woman implanted. According to the contract she had concluded she should have surrendered the child after birth for a sum of money to the couple who had provided the fertilised egg, and this she refused to do. Fox concludes from his extended case study how pervasive the idea of contract is in American society to the detriment of the recognition of the natural bond which develops between a woman and the child she bears during pregnancy, birth, and nurture.
8. There can be no serious doubt that friendship is based on an implicit contract about mutual support, emotional or material. Often, however, reciprocity does not need to be immediate because the relationship is perceived as long-lasting and trustful, and calculations about the balance of giving and taking are said not to take place because the relationship is depicted as

dichotomy between ascribed (inherited, status) and contractual relationships pervades our entire social thinking. To reformulate this dichotomy as a true variable in one context may therefore have far-reaching consequences in other contexts.

In my earlier writings inclusion and exclusion have been key variables. Certain configurations of interest were shown to lead to exclusive ones. Inclusion could take the form of widening the membership in groups or alliances. In mentioning 'groups' and 'alliances' an important distinction has been made, but it has not been elaborated (Schlee 2004c: 142, 2006b: 43).

In widening the membership of one's group, one includes more people in the category to which the pronouns 'we' and 'us' refer, while an alliance is always about others. Alliances do not abolish group boundaries. They do not even blur them. On the contrary, boundaries are highlighted in the processes of defining partners and concluding, affirming, and reaffirming an alliance. While there may be implicit contractual arrangements in the case of widening the membership of descent groups, on a scale from 'status' to 'contract' one would expect them to be far on the status side. Such an implicit contract may take the form of a veiled threat of expulsion: 'We will treat you as a brother as long as you behave like one.' If the group has a formal character, like a voluntary association, membership is of a contractual type. The duties of a member and the obligation of the group towards its members are defined by the by-laws of the association and accepted by the act of joining it. Group membership may thus comprise contractual elements to a higher or lesser degree, depending on the status of a member and the kind of group. In the case of an alliance, however, the relationship is always openly contractual, involving two or more different parties and the form of cooperation they have agreed on.

A good example of an alliance is a parliamentary coalition. It is also a famous one in political theory, because the theorem of the 'minimal winning coalition' (Riker 1962) is based on it. Coalitions are between different parties which remain separate. They just form a joint committee to agree on a policy and share out positions. Typically, however, they are not based on numerical considerations alone. People with a political conviction generally do not form a coalition with just any other party simply to put them over the 50 per cent threshold (although their critics would accuse them of doing just that). Politicians look for coalition partners of related political persuasions with whom meaningful compromises on policy are possible. Therefore, more often than not, the parties forming a coalition, though remaining separate, have some common denominator. They are part of wider groupings. They are all bourgeois or leftist, belonging to one or the other class-based block. In other cases the moderates of different former blocks, striving for the middle of society where they expect most votes to be, form centrist coalitions against what they

---

'not calculating'. In other cases, as among African pastoralists, there are often different named categories for different kinds of friends. These friendships are initiated by different kinds of rituals and renewed by material exchange, often even involving large stock like cows or camels. In contrast to friendship in Europe, the balance of give and take is talked about and the value of the goods exchanged is taken as an indicator of the value of the friendship. For recent work on friendship see Schuster et al. (2003); Grätz (2004); Grätz et al. (2004); Guichard (2007); Schlee (2007); Schlee and Trillmich (2007).

perceive as the margins: the parties subscribing to more radical versions of their respective political ideologies. In other words, alliances are always between different groups, but these groups may belong to the same or different wider groupings. Even single-issue ad hoc alliances that are immediately dissolved after the shared aim has been achieved might have identity-related aspects that go beyond the purely contractual. One may shy away from alliances with the Mafia or the Gestapo because of contamination by association (loss of reputation in other contexts by association with private or state criminality) or the risk of the exit option being blocked by blackmail. ('We will leak that you have accepted our help if you refuse to continue to work for us.') People with ethical standards might also reject such alliances on purely ethical grounds. A combination of ethical and identity-related considerations helps preserve self-respect and may take a form like: 'I am not like these people. I will never become like them and I do not want to have anything to do with them.'

If difference along such and other lines can preclude an alliance, similarity or sameness by different criteria can be expected to increase the likelihood of groups forming an alliance. Helbling (2006: 513) distinguishes cases in which the options of concluding alliances in tribal wars are limited by considerations of genealogical closeness from cases governed by purely strategic calculations, like assuring a victory at minimal cost with minimal risk without any consideration of similarity with or closeness to one's allies on the one hand and one's victims on the other. He posits a contrast between the 'purely contractual' relationships between groups of Swat-Pathans (Barth 1959), and the Mae-Enga of New Guinea, where allied clans usually belong to the same phratry but belonging to the same phratry in the absence of an alliance is not in itself a sufficient reason to extend military assistance to another clan (Meggit 1977). Helbling (2006: 513f.) goes on to cite numerous cases in which different forms and degrees of relatedness influence the formation of alliances to a greater or lesser extent or do not do so.

To the extent that alliances are not 'purely contractual' but are guided by considerations of social identities and the moral obligations attached to them, one can therefore rephrase the contractual nature of alliances as a question of degree. This is in line with my attempts to rephrase other dichotomies so prevalent in social theory in a gradualist language and to regard them as variables so as to be able to study their variation and covariation and thereby their interconnections. 'Contractuality' as a variable would have to state to what degree an arrangement is contractual and, by implication, to what degree it is shaped by non-contractual elements. On a contractuality scale from 0 to 1 a given alliance may have a value of, say, 0.6, and this would mean that it is primarily contractual but significantly influenced by other factors. These other factors may be:

1. The partners are not freely chosen. The choice of allies is limited by considerations of closeness or similarity rather than purely strategic considerations like optimal group size for the formation of a minimal winning coalition.
2. The context of agreement shows a mixture of strategic considerations with 'culture' and 'custom'.

3. As these factors that interfere with the purely contractual character of a relationship can be of many different kinds, we must be aware that many more qualitative questions may hide behind the seemingly purely quantitative statement that something is contractual to a degree of 0.6.

These are just some variables that would have to be considered by a more developed conflict theory. At the present stage of my thinking I have neither a complete set of variables nor a polished, finalised theory. It has become clear that there are alternative ways to present this theory, instead of focusing on group size 'weighted' in various ways and distinguishing levels of A, B, and C (above) as elements of a theory. For example, I could have grouped variables along a scale from 'system-specific' to 'actor-specific', a framework of presentation that suggested itself when I made that distinction above. At the present stage of theorising also numerical calculations do not play a major role.

A group of scholars at the Max Planck Institute for Social Anthropology, Halle/Saale, is working on refinements and elaborations of this emerging theory (Donahoe et al., forthcoming) and our hope is that the questions raised here will also inspire the work of others and thereby strengthen this line of research.

Chapter 5

The Necessity for Strategies of Inclusion and Exclusion

According to Machiavelli (1975 [1531]: II, §8) there are two types of war.[1] One is fired by the ambitions of the ruler to dominate new areas, the other is fought by entire populations against other total populations when:

> a whole people, with all its families leaves a place, driven thence either by famine or by war, and sets out to look for a new home and a new country in which to live. In this case it does not, as in the previous case, merely govern these, but it takes possession of every single thing, and expels or kills the old inhabitants. (Machiavelli 1975 [1531]: II, 378)

Such wars, which are characterised by a lack of survival chances, are described by Machiavelli as being particularly brutal; in modern-day parlance we would call them genocidal. Machiavelli's examples consist of peoples such as the Gauls, the Cimbri, and the Teutons, who multiplied in their original cold and infertile lands beyond what is today known as the carrying capacity of these areas and who then entered Italy in order to take it from the Romans. They did so, not with the aim of reigning over the Romans, but rather of destroying them and living off their lands. At least this is what happened according to Machiavelli.

Had the Gauls been successful in their conquest of Italy they would have emptied it of all its previous inhabitants and would have appropriated all the natural resources for themselves. Of course this is historically doubtful. Later conquerors from cold lands (also mentioned by Machiavelli), such as the Vandals, refrained from completely exterminating the population despite their total military success. This genocide model, macabre as it may be and rare as historical evidence for it fortunately is, has the advantage of being simple. Thus we can disregard some complications such as the victors having to feed the vanquished and having to give them loans for reconstruction.

Let us then first consider a model in which a conquering group which we shall call Gauls consisting of a certain number of people, 'p' for population, conquers a country which we shall call Italy, 'I' for short. The Gauls completely appropriate all the resources of this country, excluding any other peoples from a share. Let us assume that the Gauls subscribe to egalitarian social values. Thus we would expect that each individual Gaul

---

1. This chapter utilises text elements from Schlee (2000, 2004c) and from my inaugural lecture *Identitätspolitik und Gruppengröße* at the Martin Luther University Halle-Wittenberg, Halle (Saale), 30 June 2004.

would receive I/p as spoils and that Italy would thus be divided equally among the conquerors. If we assume an aristocratic constitution with princes, '*principes*', that is people who receive the first or lion's share of the spoils, then we would expect an unequal distribution whereby, on average, each individual Gaul still receives I/p.

As we know, the real Gauls never conquered Italy. Machiavelli's ancient sources relate that the Romans killed 200,000 of them between Piombino and Pisa. Evidently they were not strong enough. Perhaps they should have tried to win over other northern barbarians as their allies in order to become powerful enough to conquer Italy and exterminate all its inhabitants. However, the allies would of course have demanded their share of the spoils. If we assume once again conditions of equality, this time the equality of the allied ethnic groups, then each individual would no longer have received I/p as spoils, but rather $I/(p + p_1 + p_2)$. The greater the number of conquerors the smaller each individual's share of the spoils.

Clearly in such a model the optimal number of conquerors is just as many as are necessary to make the conquest. In optimising their numbers the conquerors would presumably have wished for a certain margin of safety vis-à-vis the necessary minimal force in order to avoid a change in the fortunes of war and a return tide of genocide against themselves. Beyond this, further allies are superfluous, bothersome, and expensive.

Taking the example of parliamentary politics, Riker (1962) developed this theorem and called it 'minimal winning coalition'. A politician wanting to form a coalition needs 51 per cent of the votes on his side, or maybe a few more, to be on the safe side, because you never know who will be at home with the flu when the vote takes place. To enter into an unnecessarily large coalition, however, would mean wasting ministerial positions on brokers of packages of votes which are not even needed for the ballot.

The principle of the 'minimal winning coalition', however, cannot only be applied to war and politics, but just as well to economy. An entrepreneur has to consider how many partners he wants to grant a share in his venture. If he regards the risk as tolerable and he is sure of his success, he will want to invest as much of his own capital as possible, or, from a manager's perspective, to keep the influence of the organisational areas controlled by himself as high as possible, so that he will have to share as little as possible of the profit.

If one wants to optimise the number of one's own comrades-in-arms (in the literal or in a figurative sense) one must therefore be in a position to reduce or increase their number according to need, which means that social and ideological mechanisms of exclusion as well as inclusion are required. A rhetoric of inclusion along the lines of 'we are all northern barbarians and share the same barbaric values' would be necessary in order to increase numbers against a strong enemy. Exclusion, 'you are not real barbarians', would be appropriate for keeping the numbers of allies low when the necessary force for victory has been reached. Thus we have developed a theory of decision-making that is suitable for explaining the formation of alliances, although the theory remains very elementary in that it has not yet addressed a number of basic questions. For example, who makes these decisions (the question of individual or collective agency) and what is the frame of reference for the cost-benefit analyses which inform such decisions? Is it individual gain, or does group identification have a role to play? And, finally, need we distinguish between the calculations of leaders and followers? As we develop our theory, such complications will have to be included into our still rather simplistic model.

So far we have looked solely at the attackers' side. We may, however, find calculations of the same type on the part of the defenders. When threatened from outside they are surely more likely to be ready to adopt strangers into their ranks; however, if they include too many this can result in overly strong pressure on their resources. They might escape military defeat and immediate extermination, but they would have to deal with their economic decline and perhaps even demographic decline of the original core group. Their friends rather than their enemies would be consuming their resources, but consumed they would be in any case. Thus, being able to encourage as well as limit growth in numbers is equally beneficial for groups and configurations of allies who are intent on defending themselves.

It is therefore a plausible assumption that in situations of relative weakness – if the enforcement of their claims to resources is at risk – people try to construct far-reaching common grounds, open up their own groups for new members, and in addition form alliances by looking for common interests with other groups (coalition) or by denying the different nature of these groups and instead asserting commonality beyond isolated overlapping interests (common affiliation of groups to one big group). Panslavic rhetoric and reference to a shared Orthodox heritage on the part of the Serbians during the 1990s may serve as an example here: the Serbs wanted to assure continued Russian support in a violent conflict.

No less plausible is the assumption that in a position of relative strength and secure access to resources, a group will close ranks and reject further-reaching identifications. Again, we can stick to the example of ex-Yugoslavia: the reason for Slovenia's separation might have been that the economically strongest constituent republic of Yugoslavia refused to continue to share its tax revenues with the other republics.

Whatever the economic motives, how can we compare the Serbian and Slovenian identity discourses conceptually? Both the panslavic appeals for Russian solidarity and the Slovenian particularism make use of the same dimension of identification, namely the linguistic/ethnic one. The Serbs, in courting the Russians, referred to a commonality on a large scale, the Slovenians to their particularity on a small one.

The Bosnian Muslims, on the other hand, would have been ill-advised if they had accentuated their differences in language use and local customs. For them it made more sense to choose another dimension of identity, namely the religious one, and to appeal to the solidarity of the global Islamic umma. Some fighters are said to have come from Saudi Arabia, and they probably were amazed at just how little knowledge about Islam and how little Islamic practice were left among their alleged fellow-believers in these secular surroundings. .

So the factor of 'size' can be changed by appealing to larger and smaller units of the same kind, and by switching from generic terms to subsumed concepts and vice versa (see Table 5.1 for such a taxonomy). Or one can switch to identifications along a different dimension and in this way take up different taxonomies.

Table 5.1 – Classification of the Slavic languages according to Brockhaus Encyclopedia.

Slavic Languages		
East Slavic	**West Slavic**	**South Slavic**
Russian	Czech	Slovenian
Ukrainian	Slovakian	Serbo-Croat
Byelorussian	Sorbian	Bulgarian
	Polish	Macedonian
	Kashubian	

If Irena Weber (personal information) is correct and the language most closely related to Slovenian is Slovakian, then this table is wrong, for here Slovenian and Slovakian are placed in different branches. But this is not important for our purpose. With this table I only want to explain what a taxonomy is in general, and how an identity discourse can be switched. Within such a taxonomy one can choose one or the other level (and with it the degree of inclusiveness), or one can leave aside the entire taxonomy and instead turn to a different taxonomy, for instance a religious one. In it, 'Slavic' would be replaced by 'Christian', 'West Slavic' etc. by 'Catholic, Protestant, Orthodox', and on the lowest level we would find 'Roman Catholic', 'Greek Catholic', 'Pentecostal', 'Methodist', 'Montanist', and many more.

Cost-benefit calculations become more complicated if we leave aside the genocidal model, in which only winners survive (the hypothetical model derived from Machiavelli, above), and look at continuing relations between winners and losers after the war or the raiding. For this, we derive our inspiration from southern Ethiopia and northern Kenya. Here ethnic groups can be considered to be relatively recent political and military units consisting of clans and clan fragments that are often themselves much older. This results in a double taxonomy (Figure 5.1).

Frequently the same clan can be found in more than one ethnic group (Schlee 1989a). Throughout its history, part of this area, the lower valley of the Omo River, has been characterised by its great distance from any form of governmental control as well as by a high frequency of wars and the relatively small size of internally peaceful groups, which were hostile towards the outside world. For the lower Omo valley it has been shown that the 'ethnic' or 'political' groups often consist of clans and families that hold traditions indicating that their origins lie with other, no longer existing, ethnic configurations. Fragments of extinct ethnic groups gather themselves anew to form ethnic groups which include several thousand people (Turton 1994).[2]

Although all kinds of reasons for war can be heard from members of the groups involved, such as ritual requirements or cattle raiding, it is possible to prove that battles are also fought over natural resources. Here famine is just as familiar as

---

2.   Similar patterns can be found in Melanesia. In Harrison's account of the Manambu of the Sepik region, villages take the place of 'political groups' in Turton's sense. They are combinations and recombinations of fragments of clans, which exist independently of these major units into which they combine (Harrison 1993: 46).

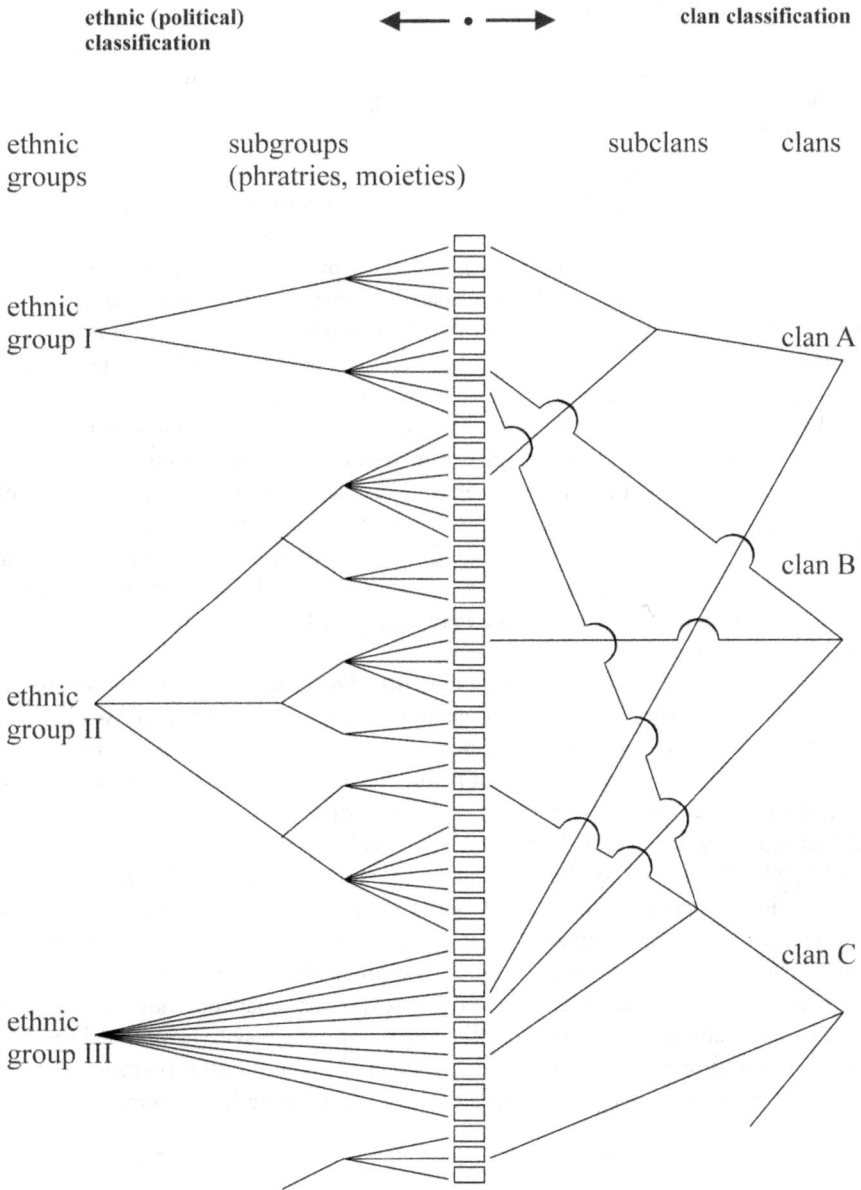

Figure 5.1 Double taxonomy – inter-ethnic clan relations.
The boxes in the middle here stand for small groups (lineages), which can be classified as belonging to major groups by different criteria as we proceed to the left or the right.

abundance. Disputed resources, such as the access to a certain well and the pasture accessible from this well, may be of little significance during times of abundance but they become a matter of survival when the energy expenditure necessary to secure pasture elsewhere reaches a critical level. Thus these groups correspond to Machiavelli's description of people who fight for the same resources at the level of survival. Machiavelli would surely have assumed that wars between these groups should take on genocidal dimensions.

However, this assumption is not confirmed in northern Kenya and southern Ethiopia. No total genocides or expulsions of entire populations are documented. Instead, the predominant pattern seems to be that of regrouping in alliances and the integration of the vanquished. In other parts of Africa and the rest of the world, we may find genocidal wars.[3] The factors that lead to this level of escalation need to be examined further. It seems that agriculture and the concomitant higher population density are significant factors in directing violence at destroying people.

Irrespective of whether the destruction of the enemy goes as far as genocide or not, we can find a variety of strategies of inclusion and exclusion, corresponding to our basic set of assumptions, even within the same pastoral-nomadic forms of production and under the same ecological conditions. For example, the Rendille (see Figure 1, p. 1) and Somali, who both herd camels in neighbouring, even overlapping areas, have quite different techniques of production and organisation, which are connected to mutually incompatible ideologies and have much to do with growth and inclusion or exclusion respectively.

The Rendille keep a breed of small undemanding camels that are only watered at long intervals, for they believe that frequent watering makes the animals weak. They do little to cure sick camels. Likewise people are expected to endure a lot. Herders in the camel camps live exclusively on milk and blood, a rather heavy diet, yet they do not complain of thirst despite the fact that they must be constantly slightly dehydrated. If water is brought to them, they will exchange milk for water at a ratio of 1:1. The Rendille delay the marriage of daughters in one of their age grades and have other practices which have been interpreted as demographic braking mechanisms.[4] They discriminate against strangers and against one another. When they occasionally do integrate strangers, these are often abused for their foreign origins even after 200 years. Their society is characterised by a permanent tendency to fission. It is hard to gain admission to Rendille society and quite easy to leave it. All this can be seen as a form of self-limitation in favour of maintaining the environment. The Rendille are a small society that stays small and adapts to limited resources.

---

3.   Many genocides do not fit the current definitions of war as conflict between organised groups with deadly weapons. The victims are often unarmed civilians. Also the attackers may be civilian mobs armed with agricultural implements.

4 .   Spencer (1973: 35, 143). The practice of delaying the marriage of the daughters of one age set by a full fourteen-year cycle does have a significant demographic impact. It is, however, doubtful that it was adopted as a means to reduce population growth. The Rendille see this rather as an undesirable side effect (Roth 1993). All Rendille ritual and non-ritual practices aim at well-being, growth, and abundance, if one asks for their ultimate reasons. Their effects, however, are often rather paradoxical.

In contrast the neighbouring Degodia Somali keep what are probably some of the biggest camels in the world. Rendille compare these Somali camels to elephants. These camels also endure long intervals between watering, but when this is not necessary the Somali let their camels drink as often as they want to. Their veterinary medicine is highly developed. They marry young and have many children. They are prepared to integrate strangers, and, as long as these convert to Islam, they are assimilated without trace. This can be seen as a strategy of expansion. They use natural resources without constraints and move to new pastures when the old ones are exhausted and their numeric and military strength allows them to do this (Schlee 1988).

The fact that these two differing forms of adaptation to identical ecological conditions exist side by side is of course an affront to any form of ecological determinism. Rather than determining social practices, ecology seems to provide a wide framework for quite distinct patterns of adaptation.

In the case of the Rendille and the Degodia Somali, the balance of energy expenditure seems to be roughly equal for both systems. The low energy intake and low energy output of the Rendille and the high intake and output of the Somali result in roughly the same net return. Were it otherwise, one of these systems of production would have ceased to exist a long time ago. The problem becomes a little more complex when we add the question of interaction to that of coexistence. A conservative form of resource usage can only exist next to another conservative form of production. Where resources saved up for the future by one group of users are immediately consumed by their neighbours whose strategies are less long-term, a host of problems is opened. This has been examined under Hardin's key phrase 'tragedy of the commons' (1968), and invokes the perspective of game theory, particularly through the concept of the 'prisoner's dilemma', because such a situation invites agreements which at least in the short term afford the greatest gains to the one who breaks the agreement first. Therefore such conventions require strong contractual and institutional safeguards and are consequently a preferred topic of 'new institutional economics' (e.g., Anderson and Simmons 1993).

These brief remarks should serve to indicate that strategies of inclusion and exclusion are not carried out by groups in isolation but rather in interaction with the corresponding strategies of their neighbours. Thus, the appropriate unit of reference for anthropological research into such strategies is not the ethnic group or tribe, but rather the region.

The Rendille themselves are well aware of this. When asked why they have discontinued certain rules of their age grade system, which have been interpreted as demographic braking mechanisms, they answer that the neighbouring Turkana are multiplying for better or for worse and that they do not wish to be pushed out by them. Thus demographic pressure is counteracted by demographic pressure, strategies of optimisation are relinquished in favour of strategies of maximisation,[5] and children are raised for future wars: a procedure with which we are familiar from European nation states and which was known there as natalism.[6]

---

5.   Optimisation is maximisation under accepted conditions. These may be the requirements for the sustainable achievement of an aim or the combination of the pursuit of one aim with that of other aims.

6.   Whether this strategy was successful is doubtful. There appear to be no measurable effects of natalist programmes. I thank Georg Elwert for this comment.

These considerations have shown that manipulating the size of one's own group or alliance of groups is of strategic importance. Keeping it small or reducing the size is under certain conditions no less viable a strategic option than the increase and strengthening of alliances under other conditions, though the latter may be the first to spring to mind in this context. In pursuit of these aims, not only biological strategies, in cattle production as well as in the production of human beings, but also various forms of the inclusion and exclusion of adult people are used.

For those who do not conduct research on East African pastoral nomads but rather on modern industrial societies, it may be of interest to pursue these thoughts into the areas of non-biotic systems of production. Successful identification politics among East African pastoralists seem to be directly translated into animal biomass and demographic growth. In modern contexts, there are similar strategies of exclusion and inclusion but one might find it more difficult to define the aim of the game.[7] Without regretting the demise of primitivism, one might say that anthropology sometimes does provide simpler model cases.

---

7.   For an exploration of biological, economic, and social 'rationalities' and the forms of interaction between these (including some dilemmas posed by them), see Schlee and Trillmich (2007).

Chapter 6

The Conceptual Instruments of Exclusion and Inclusion: Social Categories and Their Overlapping Relations

In the following, the categories that are employed in strategies of inclusion and exclusion are to be examined. In the process, their often situational and manipulable character will become apparent, as well as the logic and plausibility of social categories and taxonomies which set limits to arbitrariness and manipulation. In the work of identification, i.e., in the appropriation, elaboration, and contestation of social identities, structure and action clash with one another. The fluid principle, action, bends the rigid principle, structure, or breaks on it. Often a process of mutual modification sets in: a wave breaks on the shore but a long succession of waves, each of them relocating a bit of sand, reshapes the shoreline. Iterative action can modify structure.

For purposes of exposition, it has, up to this point, been assumed that groups identify collective aims, and act collectively to achieve them. In fact, this is an oversimplification. On closer inspection the action-theoretical side is always concerned with individual actors, or possibly the vector sum or some other combined effect of actions of individual actors, and cannot have the collective as its point of departure. We will therefore have to readdress some of the questions, which, for the sake of keeping our models simple, we had set aside above. Among these are the questions of the subject of decisions and the frame of reference of cost-benefit analyses.

First we shall turn to the conceptual and categorical instruments used for the purposes of inclusion and exclusion. Social groups and categories are always named in connection with more or less real or more or less fictional features of groups. For example, we can distinguish local groups, linguistic groups, descent groups, etc., and each of these types, identified by certain dimensions of characteristics, has numerous subtypes. Thus, we can follow various forms of linearity within descent systems, such as 'double unilinear descent' (the coexistence of transmission through the patri- and matriline). When one form of filiation predominates, the other can be understood as a 'complementary filiation'. We can further consider uterine (e.g., belonging to the patrilineage of the mother) and affinal relation sets. Similar things could be said of local, linguistic, and other forms of classification. In short: each type of identification opens up a broad repertoire of possible categorisations, which can overlap with one another in a multitude of ways.

In order to be able to analyse identity and difference in such complex situations, we must first investigate the conceptual sphere in which the actors are located. Since we are dealing with language and with linguistically encoded knowledge, a certain proximity to linguistics cannot be avoided, and this is why I would like to start with a linguistic distinction probably familiar to many readers: namely the one between 'syntagmatic' and 'paradigmatic'.[1]

'Syntagmatic' has to do with 'syntax', i.e., the science of sentences. Let us look at an example sentence (we will stick to the subject of conflicts and include a military commander):

Napoleon needed little sleep.

We read from left to right, and in this horizontal line we find, one after the other, different parts of the sentence, subject, predicate, object, which complement each other and therefore appear simultaneously. The paradigmatic dimension is added if we fill one part of the sentence with a different content, for example if we replace the subject, our military commander, with another commander.

Wellington		
Napoleon		needed little sleep.
Blücher		

Of course, we can also exchange the object for other objects and obtain a funny matrix which we can read in many directions.

Wellington		no emotional attention.
Napoleon	needed	little sleep.
Blücher		fresh quails every day.

The paradigmatic dimension, therefore, is the vertical axis, and on it we find those elements which do not appear simultaneously, but which substitute one another.

Paradigmatic/Syntagmatic

A paradigmatic relation of identities according to the kind of identity (dimension) – for instance, language/religion/class/nationality/age set/clan/past political affiliation – means that one dimension is accentuated at the expense of another; a syntagmatic relation means that they are simultaneously significant. To be a Kenyan Oromo of Christian belief, belonging to a given age set and a given clan, for instance, is an absolutely common combination.

---

1.   On 'alternation/alignment' and 'selection/combination' see Jakobson and Halle (1956: 75), Jakobson (1971: 243–244); on 'syntagmatic/paradigmatic' see Jakobson (1971: 273–274, 524, 719).

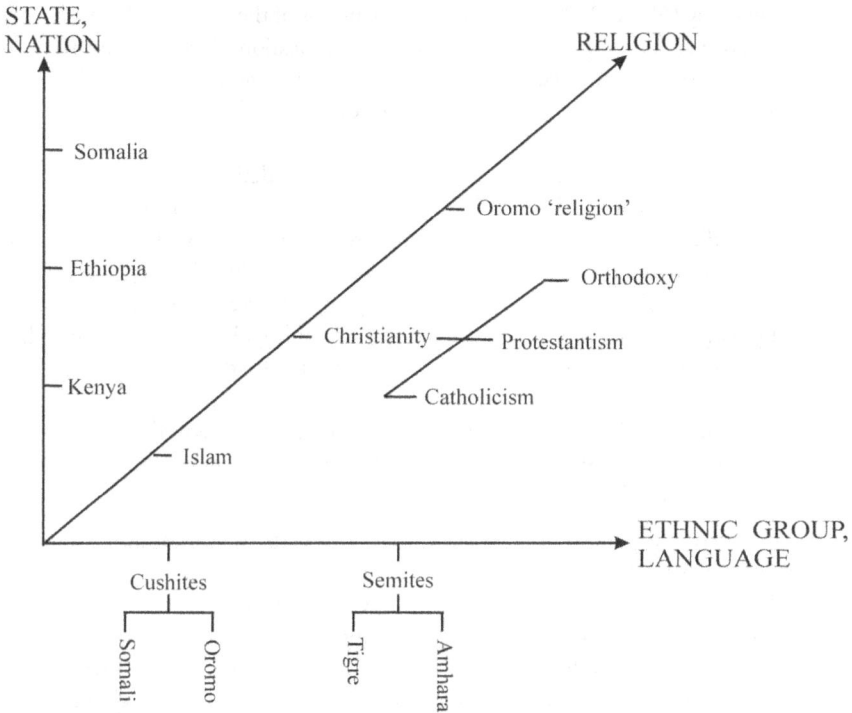

Figure 6.1 Three-dimensional conceptual sphere with ethnicity, religion, and national affiliation.

Unlike in the diagram (Figure 6.1), the number of dimensions is not limited to three. (Only the graphic representation is limited, because human visual imagination is not used to dealing with more than three dimensions.) Past political status can be an important dimension of identity (as in having been part of the Ottoman Empire/the Habsburg Empire, 'former Yugoslav', or 'post-colonial', 'post-socialist', post-soviet, and other 'afterologies'). Quite archaic ideas rise in such contexts, for example, in the 1990s all sorts of rowdies went to Croatia as mercenaries to defend the 'Occident'. Even fictional or rather vague entities from the past can be invoked. A colonial regime which not long ago has been discredited as oppressive may, after its demise, provide the basis for identification: Somaliland bases its separate identity on a British colonial past, Eritrea on an Italian one. The reader can easily add more such dimensions.

Apart from these dimensions, we can distinguish different degrees of inclusiveness within a dimension: sect, church, ecumenical movement, etc., are smaller and bigger entities of the same kind. They, too, have a paradigmatic relation. One can either refer to the particularities of one's own dialect (i.e., the smaller entity) or to a linguistic community (medium level) or to a language family (the most far-reaching affiliation to be reconstructed).

Due to this structure of the conceptual space, each actor has the possibility – without redefining or changing identities – to shift his emphasis to one or the other identification in two ways:

1. Switching (Elwert 2002) between the dimensions of the conceptual space, for instance from a linguistic to a 'religious' identification, depending on what appears to be advantageous in a given situation and without having to lie.
2. Appeals to broader or narrower defined identities of the same kind.

Languages and language families are in great ideological demand. For many changes of borders after the First World War, a language census simply substituted democratic vote (in this village people speak Polish, in that one German …), with language being equated with a predetermined ('ascriptive' imagined) identification. A later chapter, 'Language and Ethnicity', will take this issue up again; here we just point to some interesting paradoxes that can be observed in the area of linguistic classification, which might be amusing if their consequences were not frequently deadly:

- In the Bosnian War during the 1990s, the Serbs succeeded in winning the Russians as their 'Slavic brothers', as if Croats and Bosnian Muslims were not Slavs as well.[2]

- In 1991, when the Ethiopian state was not present in the country's south because the Mengistu regime had broken down and the Tigrean-dominated regime had not yet developed the area, Abdullahi Shongolo and I strolled past the deserted checkpoints into Ethiopia and went straight to the headquarters of the Oromo Liberation Front. There we found OLF strategists bent over a map on a table. They were busy sharing out Ethiopia. They wanted to create a state by the name of Oromia, which later really did come into being. But where were the borders of Oromia to run? Was the territory of the Burji (see Figure 1.1), largely enclosed by Oromo territory, to be a part of it or not? Our interlocutor was in favour of an inclusion. The Burji were not Oromo, he argued, but still Cushites like the Oromo. We were speaking Oromo, but at this point he used the English word 'Cushites'. What had happened? A biblical term, which had found its way into modern historical-comparative linguistics, but had never been significant in local discourses, suddenly served to justify a claim to territory. A harmless linguistic classification had come out of the ivory tower and as an ideological germ had resulted in an infection in the real world.

- Even more tragic was the effect of the pseudo-scientific talk of the Tutsi in Rwanda as 'Hamites'. The somehow vague category of 'Hamite' is no longer in use among linguists. 'Cushites' is maybe the closest equivalent, and occasionally the Afro-Asian languages are also called 'Hamito-Semitic'. The Tutsi, however, speak the same Bantu language as their Rwandan fellow citizens, namely Kinyarwanda, and there are no indications whatsoever that they ever did speak an Afro-Asian language.

---

2. Or was what happened an unconscious mixing of linguistic and religious identifications? Was it the fact that the Serbs are also Orthodox (post-Orthodox?) which made them appear more Slavic to the Russians?

Their own mythological traditions about an immigration from the north, mixed with early colonial speculation that the Tutsi as a master race must have come from the north (because that is where masters come from), have condensed to a Hamite myth. The Hutu deduced from this not only that the Tutsi claim to dominance had to be fought, but also that they were intruders and not real Africans. The genocidal consequences of all this do not have to be discussed here: they are still fresh in our memories.

So we see that, within a pre-structured semantic field, actors make decisions about which categories they will appeal to when describing themselves or others. From a scientific point of view, such ascriptions can be simply wrong, as for instance when Tutsi are described as Hamites, but that doesn't seem to limit their effectiveness. Or maybe it does? Can the provision of knowledge be of any help here? In what way a critique of such identification processes has repercussions on them still needs to be discussed. If simplifications are tolerated to a certain degree, some classifications might bear a historical-linguistic or other scholarly examination, others not. Apparently plausible, consistent identification discourses substantiated by experience have an advantage over pure fiction, but different degrees of plausibility or historical reality surely are not the only characteristics in which identity ascriptions differ from each other. So what are the characteristics we expect to influence the choice of identification?

If we assume that these decisions are interest-controlled[3] (maybe by a group interest, maybe by the interest of who is speaking), then we should not expect every characteristic relevant for a decision to be addressed in the identity discourses themselves. Selfish motives of the speaker are normally not openly addressed in political discourse. We must therefore also consider possibly intended effects which are not addressed, and include non-verbal as well as verbal behaviour in the investigation. We leave the distinction between groups and categories aside at this point and restrict ourselves to groups as alternative options for identification. Such groups can have different prestige; they can be internally structured more or less and in different ways, and also externally have different points to connect to as well as different patterns of interaction. All this can influence identity discourses – their own and the ones about them – just as the factor of group size, which so far had been given priority. Each identification, i.e., each claim to be or not be something, refers to social aggregates differing in their demographic range. The case of two identity constructs resulting in groups of the exact same size and standing is an improbable borderline case. The central question resulting from this for a theory of identification in a setting of conflict is: what effects do the expected characteristics of the group resulting from an act of identification – like group size and social standing – have on an identity discourse and on the choice of cultural features selected or emphasised?

The emphasis on one set of features – say linguistic ones at the expense of religion or the derivation from some medieval empire – does not mean that the other features cease to be of any relevance. One may by the dominant ethnolinguistic affiliation

---

3. This may comprise stronger and weaker forms of control or influence. Habermas's terms (1968) are *erkenntnisleitendes Interesse* (interest guiding insight) and *Erkenntnisinteressen* (interests in gaining knowledge).

connect oneself to certain other groups without forgetting that religious links point elsewhere. One overlaps with different groups by applying different criteria.

Dimensions of identification may have boom periods and periods of decline. Allow history to move on a bit and you see them moving up and down on the scale of acceptability. Many enlightened people before the First World War could not have imagined a war between the European nation states, whose economies were already much more integrated than in later periods, while others, namely militarists, were actively working towards a war.[4] The prevalent discourse of the educated classes was that a war along national lines between the European powers had become unthinkable. The dominant issue was the 'social question', i.e., class. When the war erupted, however, the kaiser declared that he knew 'no classes, only Germans'. The twentieth century then continued to be the century of nationalist wars. The wars ultimately discredited nationalism and ethnicity to quite a degree, while class, which had been temporarily submerged, re-emerged as a legitimate criterion for identification and therefore a legitimate social policy issue. Only later did ethnicity once again became a legitimate issue in the context of migration, minorities and their cultural rights. Religion was out. The last wars said to be religious ones had been in the seventeenth century. The conflict in Northern Ireland, said to be between Catholics and Protestants, was 'really' about class, we all learned.[5] Religion started to enter the public sphere again in the 1980s, but it took the end of the cold war and the search for a new enemy to fully rehabilitate religion as a legitimate political identity and therefore as a potential cause of war by projecting enemy stereotypes onto Islam. Religion ceased to be a private affair; it was, so to speak, 'deprivatized' (Casanova 1994: 5).

On a smaller scale, one can also look at Welsh nationalism. No doubt the Welsh had been economically marginalised by the English. This was an ethnic issue that at the same time was a class issue. But these two components never received equal emphasis in public debates. In some periods the class aspect was foregrounded to such an extent that the Labour Party became the lone home of a Welsh nationalism in a socialist guise; in other periods ethnicity was a legitimate issue, and the Welsh could present themselves as disadvantaged and thereby could appeal to the same universalist values (e.g., 'justice') that were invoked in the class discourse (Dench 1986: 27–31).

We can thus distinguish three types of situations of change in the dimension of identification:

1. Individual (e.g., conversion of a secular nationalist to a politicised religion).
2. Group level (the Welsh cause adopting a class guise or an ethnic guise).
3. The broader public sphere and its preferences (class being a legitimate issue in one period, ethnicity in another).

---

4. E.g., Meinertzhagen (1984 [1957]: 313), who joyfully anticipated the world war already in 1906.
5. This remark refers to the surface of things: dominant discourses, intellectual fashions, and media perceptions. To complete the picture, one may add the constitutional affiliation of Northern Ireland and (anti-)imperialism as contested identifications. Both are, however, related to class. For a recent analysis of language, religion, class, sports, and other elements of Irish identity with a focus on Catholic West Belfast and on representations as well as on what is represented, see Max Planck Institute for Social Anthropology (2005: 132–133) and Zenker (2006).

In social anthropology, the configurations that are created through the overlap of categories belonging to dimensions like clan, ethnicity, language, and religion have been discussed under the term 'cross-cutting ties'. To date, 'cross-cutting ties' have been almost exclusively discussed as factors of social cohesion. Gluckman (1955: 11), who adopts a fairly Hobbesian perspective and sees humanity as constantly caught up in conflicts, argues that such ties make possible a certain measure of internal peace in a society. In this theory then, 'cross-cutting ties' are the very basis of society. Because we use multiple criteria for the establishment of social groups and categories and since these can overlap, we must always be prepared for another person to be our opponent in one context but our ally in another. Consciousness of this prevents us from allowing conflicts to escalate to a level at which they would lead to the destruction of any form of society. Therefore Gluckman ascribes the establishment of social cohesion and the de-escalation of conflicts to cross-cutting ties. To me, this does not seem to be always and necessarily the case. Let us return once more to the notion that it is advantageous for actors and groups of actors to have both means of inclusion and exclusion at their disposal.

I wish to clarify this using the previously mentioned example of inter-ethnic clan relations in northern Kenya.

When a herdsman meets a stranger at a watering hole – the typical trigger situation for violent conflicts – and if he finds out who the stranger is, then the existence of 'cross-cutting ties' opens up the following possibilities to the pastoral warrior: he can either emphasise their difference ('We belong to different tribes, go away before our young men come!'), or he can refer to a shared identity ('Though we belong to different tribes, we belong to the same clan', or 'You belong to my wife's clan', 'to my mother's clan', or whatever the case may be.). The optional character of such references to identity or difference implies that cross-cutting ties can be situationally ignored. They are thus not always present as a binding force. Identity and difference should, therefore, not be considered as resulting from certain criteria, i.e., the presence or absence of certain markers, as factors on their own, which can generate hostility or cohesion. These markers should rather be seen as the raw material for political rhetoric, which can be used selectively to pursue goals of inclusion or exclusion.

However, it is by no means my intention to create the impression that we are dealing with unbounded opportunism and limitless manipulability following purely economic calculations. It is precisely those cases where one becomes a prisoner of one's own logic that are sociologically interesting. If, for example, based on real or fictional common descent in an exogamic clan system, I opt for a rhetoric of brotherhood towards a group with which I come into contact, then I foreclose any possibilities of marriage with that group, however attractive such a possibility may appear to be. All the female members of a group with whom I declare fraternal relations become my sisters and are thus subject to incest prohibitions.[6] Furthermore, fraternity is a transitive relationship. Brothers of brothers are brothers. Thus I am potentially entering into many more ties than I can oversee myself. In less

---

6.   At least this is the case among groups that practise clan exogamy such as the Rendille, who pursue this principle to great depths.

unfortunate cases this may lead to my hospitality becoming overstretched; in more serious cases this can mean that my entire system of alliances and security is overturned and I suddenly find myself on the wrong side in a conflict.

In so far as Gluckman's theory of cohesion and de-escalation is concerned, the case of northern Kenya does not give us any indications that the numerous inter-ethnic clan relations have contributed to the avoidance or de-escalation of violent conflicts. Regarding the connection between cross-cutting ties and the escalation or de-escalation of violence, we must thus consider a kind of zero hypothesis, namely, that there is no relationship between the existence of cross-cutting ties and the frequency or intensity of conflicts between groups who have such ties.

Hallpike (1977) would take this a step further. Among the Tauade of the New Guinea highlands, he found that descent groups distributed themselves widely across local groups. When killings occurred between descent groups the Tauade frequently turned against their neighbours who were members of the clan with whom hostilities had been exchanged and who lived as a minority in their midst and killed them out of vengeance. These neighbours were within easy reach and could be killed with the least risk. Of course, revenge provokes counter-revenge and it is easy to imagine the resulting escalation. Therefore we must also consider the reverse of Gluckman's theory, namely that under certain conditions cross-cutting ties can contribute to the escalation of conflicts.

In another New Guinean case, the Manambu of the Sepik region, Harrison (1993) has shown that cross-cutting ties do not reduce the overall occurrence of violence in any way. Affiliation to the same totemic clan, marriage ties, or trade partnerships might prevent certain people of one village from attacking certain people of another village, but make the latter an even more likely target of other people. Rivalries between inhabitants of one village are carried out by hitting at the partners or relatives of one's rivals in another village. In an indirect way, through their denial, cross-cutting ties can even be said to be the root cause of war. According to one of several systems of norms, namely those postulating the solidarity of the men of one village who are united by one cult, outside links need to be periodically severed by headhunting raids, because otherwise the ubiquity of social ties would blur the boundaries of local groups. In a condensed formula, Harrison presents his findings as: 'In Melanesia it is not so much groups that make war, but war that makes groups' (1993: 18). A radical reading of this formula would imply that without war there would be no groups. A moderate reading would be that that those groups which assert themselves as separate fighting units capable of contesting the resources of other such groups acquire this character by doing just that: they sever outside ties which link some of them to some of their prospective enemies, and wage war together. In the course of war, the composition of the warring parties changes: victims of massacres join larger groups to secure survival, alliances are forged and broken. It is not the existence of groups, but (1) their character as separate fighting entities, which for a time succeed in letting internal coherence outweigh external ties, and (2) their composition which are caused by war.

Generalisations about the relationship between marriage and war remain difficult. For the Manambu even the possibility of village outmarriage is a 'danger to the very *conceptual existence* [emphasis in the original]' of a group, while in highland New Guinea the fighting units tend to be exogamous so that marriage partners are of necessity members of actual or potential enemy groups (Harrison 1993: 137). 'Those whom we marry are those whom we fight' is a saying that applies to many societies all around the world (Lang 1977). In my reading of Harrison's examples, given how easy it is for Melanesians and for many other people with large exogamous clans to combine intermarriage with hostility, it is not so much intermarriage between villages which is a complication for warfare between villages but the presence of people with whom one cannot intermarry because they are brothers and sisters: members of the same exogamous clans among the potential enemies in the other village.

In a case that I have examined in some depth, cross-cutting ties were manifestly unable to prevent a violent conflict between groups. On the other hand they did not contribute to its escalation either. However, they seem to have fulfilled a significant function in coping with the consequences of war.

Two hundred years ago, the ancestors of the Rendille subclan Elemo were captured together with their camels by Rendille warriors. Originally they had been Gabra. Some clan members later followed them voluntarily, since, with no camels from which they might have lived, they had no other choice. In 1992, Gabra people (see Figure 1, p. 1) raided the Rendille and captured a large proportion of their camels. Paradoxical though this may sound, some members of the Elemo sub clan sought refuge from the Gabra among the Gabra and attached themselves once again to their Gabra clan brothers. They also received camels – albeit different camels, not the same ones that had been captured from them – so that they would be able to continue their pastoral-nomadic existence. Twice in their history they had, thus, followed their camels and joined those who raided them. Their clan brothers among the Gabra protected them from attacks by other Gabra. For this they were heavily criticised by these other Gabra.

In this case the existence of cross-cutting ties contributed nothing to the prevention or limitation of the war. Furthermore there can be no general cohesive effect attributed to them. Instead they led to a fission among the Rendille where some Elemo remained whilst others rejoined the Gabra. Cross-cutting ties also led to a division among the Gabra, where a pro-Elemo and an anti-Elemo faction were formed. What these cross-cutting ties did do was to offer several actors options that helped them deal with the consequences of the war (Schlee 1997).

In terms of what has been said above about categories becoming situationally relevant and being situationally ignored, one can say that in this case, at the inter-ethnic level (here meaning the interaction of ethnic groups as entire units, Rendille vs. Gabra), the existence of inter-ethnic clan relationships was ignored. Inter-ethnic clan relationships did not prevent one ethnic group, the Gabra, from raiding another, the Rendille. On the clan-to-clan level, they became relevant again, when the consequences of the raids had to be coped with.

This example suggests that a finer grid of analysis would enable us to see more of the real effects of cross-cutting ties. When we descend from the level of groups to that of individual actors we may potentially perceive differences in the cost-benefit calculations carried out by leaders and their followers. A switch in alliance may have varying advantages and disadvantages for leaders and followers or, rather, for potential leaders and their followers; for it is possible that it is only with a switch in alliance that a leader becomes a follower or a follower a leader.

The Swat Pathans (Pashtuns) of northern Pakistan (Barth 1981) have a segmentary lineage system similar to that of the Somali. Unlike the Somali, however, they do not have a tendency to unite more closely related lineages against more distant ones. The rivalry, particularly over land, is far too great between neighbouring and closely related segments. Instead, the Pathans form alliances with opponents of their immediate relations and immediate neighbours, and, by generalising the principle 'the enemy of your enemy is your friend', all Swat Pathans divide into two factions. Assuming for a moment that social groups may be arranged in a linear sequence, one can imagine that one distinguishes oneself from one's immediately adjacent neighbours while belonging to the same faction as the subsequent ones. Thus, we find an alternating sequence of *a–b/a–b/a–b*. In reality and over space, relations are of course not quite as simple as on this imaginary line and thus there are numerous possibilities for switching alliances. In every given context one group is necessarily stronger than the other, since the liminal case where both are equally strong is extremely unlikely. Correspondingly, the Pathans always call them majority and minority respectively. Such a situation can of course be considered from the point of view of cross-cutting ties: the division into majority and minority overlaps with lineage structure. But these cross-cutting ties, too, are a long way away from producing 'cohesion', at least at the level of the total society.[7]

It is good to belong to the majority. In juridical disputes the majority acquires resources from the minority. The minority therefore tries to persuade members of the majority to join it in order to turn the minority into the majority. An incentive to leave the current group may consist in being offered a leading position in the new configuration. Leaders have privileges and benefits not enjoyed by their followers. For current or potential leaders who are considering a switch in alliance and for their followers whom they would have to bring with them, as they would otherwise be numerically insignificant, the cost-benefit analysis of such a switch or, to put it less politely, of such a betrayal presents itself in quite different terms.

---

7.   In a more recent study of rivalry and honour among the Pashtun, based on the biographies of prominent personalities, Edwards (1996: 157f.) concludes that typically it is patrilateral parallel cousins (sons of brothers) who come into conflict with one another. Here the unquestioning (in Durkheimian terms mechanical) solidarity within the lineage limits itself to full- and half-brothers, to a man's sons. Beyond this the enemy of my rival is more likely to be my friend than a more closely related lineage member himself.

Chapter 7

Economics as Sociology – Sociology as Economics

According to Duesenberry (1960: 233), economics deals with how people make decisions, while it is the domain of sociology to explain why they have no decisions to make.[1] Indeed, *Homo oeconomicus*, the admittedly simplified model of humanity used by economists, appears to be freer in his capacity to make decisions and is thus rather more appealing than the somewhat foolish *Homo sociologicus*, who in the process of socialisation fits into supra-individual units and ultimately meets given role expectations perfectly. However, our analysis of empirical reality should not be guided by such feelings of empathy; rather we must enquire how economic and sociological elements of explanation can best be combined in order to model reality.

As the north Kenyan example suggests, the interlocking of economic and sociological factors may result in actors, in part pushed by pressures of survival, doing the work of identification within a social space which offers certain scope for variation but which is also limited by pre-given options. This applies particularly to one type of actor: the intelligent ones with knowledge of the historical materials of which identity constructs are made and who take liberties in handling them.

The ethnic groups of northern Kenya are ethnic groups in the full, apparently self-evident sense.[2] Each maintains religious and linguistic differences vis-à-vis the others, and they are clearly distinguished by their clothing and habitus. Nevertheless they are linked to one another through a network of inter-ethnic clan relations, which are based in part on splits occurring at the time of the genesis of the present-day ethnic groups, in part on more recent migrations and re-affiliations. It is important for the heads of pastoralist groups to have knowledge of these relations at their disposal. Thus, they can find refuge with clan brothers in other ethnic groups during periods of drought or war. This does not imply an immediate ethnic re-affiliation since they are initially taken in just as clan brothers and may be considered to be guests and not members of the host ethnic group. An actual ethnic re-affiliation may take place at a particular point in time, which is marked by a ritual, or it may drag out over generations and never be fully accomplished.

---

1. Earlier versions of this chapter can be found in Schlee (2000, 2004c).
2. Both in the sense of the popular, enumerating definition of distinguishing features of ethnic groups (language, history, customs, habits, etc.), which is flawed in that in each case different features out of such a catalogue are brought into the foreground or remain unnoted, as well as in Barth's (1969: 9) terms when he speaks of cultural discontinuities. Elsewhere, there are many cases where 'ethnic' distinctions look artificial and invite deconstruction. Not so here. Rendille, Gabra, and Somali look different, sound different, and would be accepted as being 'ethnically' different by most people.

For immediate survival, however, it is in the first instance unimportant whether one finds full cultural acceptance or whether one receives half-hearted hospitality. What can be a matter of survival is virtuosity in finding out and manipulating relationships and appealing to them in order to generate acts of solidarity. This only works when the sense of common membership is also valid and binding for those to whom the appeal is being made.

The one who by means of social knowledge and social intelligence is in a position not to integrate passively into such categories but rather to manipulate them to his own benefit profits from the fact that others dispose of this ability to a lesser degree. Were the virtuosi of relationships, with their appeals to solidarity, always to meet with like minds, equally skilled in finding reasons for rejecting these appeals, the entire game would not work. Thus we are dealing with relationships which to a certain extent are pre-given and fixed and to a certain extent are subject to being instrumentalised and manipulated, albeit only with the requisite knowledge and with a measure of virtuosity. They cannot be used by everybody in the same measure.

So, despite all their constructedness, such social categories, including ethnic groups and nations, are in no way arbitrary. They have a certain reality about them, at least in the sense of having real effects.

This is in part due to the fact that they are not free inventions, no matter how popular the expression has become since Hobsbawm and Ranger's book *The Invention of Tradition* (1983).[3] Instead one should take constructivism in its literal sense and speak of constructions rather than inventions. As in the building trade, which is the source of the metaphor, constructions are not arbitrary but follow the laws of statics, consist of elements which support each other, and make use of local materials. Sometimes old foundations are used, or old building materials are reused. Social constructions, as recent as they may be, by doing all this as well, achieve familiarity, plausibility, and often even a degree of pseudo-naturalness.

But, even where the creation of ethnic groups and nations appears to be artificial and occurs with a visible romanticising ideological effort, it still leads to very real consequences in terms of behaviour. Maybe it is possible to dream up ethnic groups and nations, but when they turn out to be nightmares it is very difficult to dream them away again.

---

3.   One need only think of the numerous book titles such as The Invention of India (used twice), *The Invention of Africa*, *The Invention of Ethiopia*, *The Invention of Primitive Society*, etc.

Chapter 8

Markets of Violence and the Freedom of Choice

Analysts with a sound dose of materialism tend to look first at the contested resources and the economic interests attached to them, when they try to understand a conflict.[1] I do not recommend anything else. Rather than replacing this perspective I want to complement it. Identification in conflict situations is in no way determined by the contested resources. The logic of identification may be the same, irrespective of whether the contested resource is oil, water, cattle, or land. Therefore explanations with an exclusive focus on resources and economic interests may fall short of the target, if they are meant to be an exhaustive analysis of a conflict situation. My critique could be addressed to many authors, but to make it worthwhile I pick out one of the best analysts writing in this field, Georg Elwert.

In 1997, Elwert published an analysis of 'Markets of violence' with the subtitle 'Observations on the instrumental rationality of violence'. As the title and subtitle both imply, the emphasis lies on economic calculation and thus on freedom of choice. In my view the shortcomings of his approach lie in the neglect of the limitations imposed by social structures and the conventional logic of identification, which limit even the rationally acting, radically egoistic warlords postulated by Elwert in the freedom of their choices.

Markets of violence appear in 'spaces open to violence', beyond the reach of state monopolies on violence, and they appear when the market economy expands into these spaces. They are 'a totally deregulated market economy, a radically free market economy'. Extortion and suchlike play an important role.

It emerges from Elwert's own exposition that the 'radically free market economy' is not a further development of the 'free market economy' (1997: 92). On the contrary, it smothers capitalist development at its roots. Portes (1994) makes it even clearer that the origin of the 'free' market economy lies precisely in regulation and not in deregulation:

> This 'triumph of the invisible hand' [here he is referring to Mobutu's Zaire, where everything, even the renunciation of state rules and laws, had become buyable] does not lead to capitalist development, as would be anticipated from public choice theory … the opposite is actually the case. In the absence of a stable legal framework and credible enforcement of contracts, long-term productive investment becomes a near impossibility. (Portes 1994: 432)

---

1. An English version of this chapter can be found in Schlee (2004c), a German version in Schlee (2000). In a subsequent publication Bakonyi and Stuvoy (2005) offer a more extensive analysis of economies of war.

Markets are not formed out of some natural inclination, or on people's tendency, as stated by Adam Smith (1998 [1776]), to send and exchange things. In order for a market economy to be created, there needs to be somebody who is standing outside the realm of competition, 'making sure that property rules are enforced and contracts observed'. Portes, following Polanyi (1957 [1944]) and Everitt (1973), refers to the highly regulated character of markets in Europe at the beginning of capitalist development. There were even bread-tasters and beer-tasters (Portes 1994: 433). Durkheim had made a similar point much earlier and in more general terms, with reference to freedom, not just to the free market. 'Liberty itself is the product of regulation' (Durkheim 1984 [1893]: 320). Someone cannot be called free who can be exploited simply because he is weaker.

Elwert (1997) omits observations from a previous paper with an almost identical title. Elwert (1995) considered markets of violence to be 'a form of modernisation' based on an 'admittedly rather unconventional understanding of modernisation' as the 'interaction of commodity economy and large-scale communication'. Given this definition the attribution is plausible. Commonly, however, one might prefer a notion of modernisation which stands for those processes that have contributed to the enduring preponderance of industrial modernity in processes of globalisation. It then becomes obvious that markets of violence develop rather contrary effects: they destroy bureaucracies and education systems and allow infrastructures to decay. With his focus on 'markets of violence' Elwert expands the analysis of violent conflicts to include those cases in which the state, at least in immediate terms, does not play (or no longer plays) a part. Current theories, on the other hand, assume the presence of statehood, because they postulate the state to be the framework of disputes or the prize for the winner (e.g., ethnicisation as a strategy for appropriating state resources).[2]

---

2.   Wimmer (1995, particularly his decision-making tree, p. 486) provides a good overview of these theories. Another distinction can be made among theories of conflict with reference to the question that they seek to answer. Contrary to Gluckman, mentioned above, who starts with the Hobbesian notion of *bellum omnium contra omnes* and thus considers peace and social integration (in short: goodness) to be in need of explanation, there is another historico-theoretical strand, associated with Rousseau (1999 [1762]), which takes goodness as natural and tries to explain evil. Ultimately we are here dealing with axioms that are difficult to question in theoretical terms. Empirically we can always find examples of both 'goodness' and 'evil' among humans, just as among other closely related species. If one starts with 'goodness' as the normal moral condition, then 'evil' needs to be explained; if one departs from 'evil' (unbounded egotism), then 'goodness' needs to be explained. Such a struggle with the explanation of 'goodness' can be observed, for example, in the sociobiologists' and rational-choice theoreticians' treatment of the 'problem' of altruism (see Gräfrath 1997).

Recently, Helbling (2006: 413–420) has argued that, in his explanation of war, Rousseau was not as different from Hobbes (1994 [1651]) as he himself claimed to be and others believed him to be. Still, their beliefs about human nature may differ, and this difference or similar ones can be followed through the history of ideas. Marx clearly believed human nature to be good and he expected mankind to revert to goodness after the structures which impede goodness (class society) have been abolished (see his idea of alienation in McLellan 2000 [1977]: 83–121). Elias (1997 [1939]), on the other hand, thought spontaneous drives to be rather disruptive and leading to the necessity of external and internal control.

Of course it is precisely in such a surrounding of crumbling statehood that we would expect fragmented social structures and severed bonds and, thus, a broad scope for decision-making or, more precisely, arbitrariness supported by violence among the more powerful. Unfortunately, Elwert integrates the preponderance of the economic in his definition of markets of violence in a rather circular fashion. He writes: 'By markets of violence I understand conflicts called civil wars, warlord systems or thievery, where the economic motive of material profit dominates beneath the surface of ideological and political aims or reputedly traditionally defined battle duties' (Elwert 1997: 87f.).[3] In the following, I do not include the dominance of the economic motive in a definition of the markets of violence. Rather I want to pose the empirical question of how far economic or sociological explanations, i.e., those focusing on actors and decisions versus those stressing structures and givens, are of significance in markets of violence and how they interpenetrate.

According to Elwert (1997), 'not ethnic groups and clans, but economic interests ... are poised against one another in these civil wars'. Here he is making things too simple for himself. Are economic interests not held by somebody? Are they not dependent on existing or nascent 'we' groups, to use Elwert's (1989) own term? Are they thereby not subject to preformed categorisations, i.e., to precisely those ethnic groups and clans to which Elwert here denies any significance? Making reference to them is said to be 'culturalist'. That presumably means that, with culture as an independent variable, other things, such as violence, are to be explained. In 'culturalist' explanations, a culture, thought of as being supra-personal, appears as a means of explanation (*explanans*) and it is this that those who use the term criticise. The term 'culturalist' implies a negative evaluation, as is the case with the terms 'biologising', 'essentialist', 'reductionist', etc. Calling those who refer to clans and ethnic groups 'culturalists' implies that these always consider ethnicity and clanship to be independent variables and assume that clans and ethnic groups simply are the way they are. In the more recent theories on ethnicity and the more recent literature on clans, including Elwert's own work in this area, nothing could be further from the truth. It is therefore unclear which unnamed authors are here being accused of ignorance.[4]

In view of the cruelties inflicted by warlords on defenceless peasants or on each other (e.g., Prince Johnson who had his rival, President Samuel Doe, mutilated and slowly butchered alive in front of running television cameras in Liberia in 1990), it is in any case more comprehensible from a psychological point of view (and in conformity with our own expectations of normality) that one would want to explain why some people commit such atrocities, rather than why other people do not.

One may ask whether the more recent theoretical attempts discussed here can be situated within this dichotomy. Whoever searches for rational reasons behind cruelty and apparent arbitrariness does not appear to depart from the self-evidence of wickedness but rather from the necessity to explain it.

3.   All translations of citations from German into English are mine.

4.   In the discussion of the lecture on which this article is based, Elwert explained that Italian as well as eastern and south-eastern European authors were meant. Indeed it would have been difficult to find such positions in the north-west European/American mainstream. In his essay (Elwert 1997: 86) he attacks anonymous opponents.

Further down he writes: 'The warlords also need trade partners, supporters and neutral forces. In order for them to feel secure it is helpful to let violence follow clear, symbolically pre-drawn lines. Signs of religion, regional dress and accent and similar things serve this purpose and create the impression of ethnic or religious confrontation' (Elwert 1997: 94). This makes it sound as though the warlords were largely free in their definitions of identity – as though they could include in their following precisely those whom they wanted 'in' and could exclude precisely those whom they wanted 'out'. Apparently warlords do not have to put up with the unwanted. 'To put up with the unwanted' means becoming a prisoner of one's own logic: to include individuals and groups in the group defined as 'us' that one would really prefer not to include, being forced to do so by the demands of consistency of, for example, a system of social categories.

For Somalia, one of the most often cited settings of 'warlordism', it was possible to show (Schlee 1996, 2002b) that groups are not fractured and alliances are not formed by the sheer arbitrary will of warlords but, rather, that these processes follow patterns which can already be found in pre-colonial times. The 'total' genealogy (Lewis 1982) encompassing the entire Somali nation may be historically true or it may be fictional. In any case it is a common heritage accepted in many parts and laden with the weight of convention so that an individual cannot change anything at will and certainly not on an ad hoc basis. Thus, if an opponent of the Darood clan family claims descent from Irrir, a clan ancestor of whom we know virtually nothing other than that most non-Darood descend from him, this implies that he must include clans and subclans that claim to descend from Irrir in the definition of the 'we' group, even those that he basically does not like, since otherwise his appeal to pan-Irrir solidarity would become implausible. This means that he must put up with the unwanted. Were he, as was increasingly the case during the processes of fission of political groups throughout the 1990s, to claim descent from far more recent ancestors, he would end up with a much more narrowly defined group that might not encompass many of the sections he would like to pull over to his side. Thus warlords too are prisoners of their own logic; they need to behave plausibly and follow socially accepted patterns, and do not correspond to the type of *Homo oeconomicus*, who ideally makes decisions on an entirely individual and opportunistic basis. Also warlords act within the framework of social structures which are 'constraining and enabling' (Giddens 1976: 121) at the same time. The clan organisation provides them both with the tools and the material of military recruitment and, on the other hand, it limits their freedom of choice in recruiting whom they want. In historical processes, under the influence of repeated action, structures, of course, change (in ways which have been rarely predicted and tend to be explained more or less satisfactorily in retrospect) but for any given actor at any time they are there and need to be taken into account for what they are, with both their restricting and their enabling characteristics.

In his 1995 article, Elwert himself deals more closely with Somalia. Surprisingly, he describes the fight for waterholes as a new phenomenon, although Lewis (1961a: 45) had already pointed out that among the Somali it is not the sword or gun but rather the transportable, wooden watering trough that stands as a symbol for disputes and bloodshed. The 'state courts of law and notaries' who according to Elwert (1995: 132) previously regulated rights to watering places do not according to Lewis (1961b) seem to have been particularly effective even at the height of colonial rule. The 'clan courts' that Elwert mentions in the same context were in reality mediating bodies that debated whether it was possible to pay wergild and thus avoid the need for revenge. Wergild was simply another aspect of violence: open violence was a means of taking revenge, while latent violence served to obtain compensation. In the absence of a non-partisan law-enforcing agency, whoever was too weak to take revenge would also be too weak to enforce compensation payment and would not receive justice from these 'clan courts', no matter how evident the injustice he had suffered. It was thus necessary to belong to a strong community, i.e., to a demographically strong lineage or to one that was contractually bound to other lineages in order to form a wergild community.

This is identity politics of size once more. And again and again we come back to precisely that area of overlap where the issue is to link economic with sociological perspectives.

The simple solution – which is really a way of avoiding the problem – consists either in completely ignoring the existence of social structures and systems and reducing all that is social to the sum of individual calculations or, alternatively, developing pure systems theories that leave out the people. Already in 1979 Giddens regretted that 'those schools of thought which have been preoccupied with action have paid little attention to, or have found no way of coping with, conceptions of structural explanation or social causation; they have also failed to relate action theory to problems of institutional transformation' (1979: 49). And vice versa, one might add, also following Giddens: that other theories unilaterally put the accent on structure and forget about agency. Sociologists have apparently not bridged these discrepancies to their own satisfaction. Twenty years later, in a lecture at Bielefeld, Esser (1999) lamented the fact that large parts of current sociology show deficiencies of these types. In social anthropology there is (or there was before attempts at theory-building drowned in a flood of postmodernism) a parallel discussion. Thus Asad (1972) criticises the analysis of the Swat political system (Barth 1959, 1981) cited above, saying that Barth sees political organisation too purely as the result of a multitude of choices (Asad 1972: 75), neglecting the structures that restrict choice (in this case: class, caste).

More recent trends in economics, such as institutional economics, have followed this linkage between sociological and economic approaches by sociologising themselves. Hirshleifer, undoubtedly an economist and a famous one at that, makes social identity the core question of economy. No economic calculation can do without the question, 'for whom?' Who benefits and within what group boundaries? '[E]fficiency is always relative to the boundaries of the society or group envisioned … We all draw the line somewhere, at the boundary of "us" versus "them". *Efficiency thus is ultimately a concept relating group advantage over the competing groups*' (Hirshleifer in Anderson and Simmons 1993: 8, original emphasis). Elwert and other resource-oriented conflict theorists come from the other side and economise anthropology. In doing so, they enter the very same highly interesting area of contact. What we need is a new synthesis of economic and sociological perspectives. I do not claim to have presented such a new synthesis here in anything resembling a final shape, but I hope to have demonstrated its necessity and clarified some of the questions it needs to address.

Chapter 9

Ethnic Emblems, Diacritical Features, Identity Markers – Some East African Examples

Symbols and Emblems[1]

The term 'emblem' has sometimes been used as a synonym for 'symbol',[2] sometimes for something simpler than a symbol, or, if in the hierarchy of concepts 'symbol' has been used for a more inclusive category, for a simpler type of symbol. 'By "symbols" we mean ... something more than signs. Unlike the latter which may be so, symbols are in principle never fully self-explanatory, self-sufficient or fully autonomous ... They both reveal and conceal, pointing towards, if not fully disclosing, a different order of reality and experience. Symbols are thus by definition mysterious' (Lewis 1977: 1).

This mysterious aspect of symbols is not the topic of this chapter. As symbols tend to be multivocal and represent the same or different thing or things in the mind of different persons, we may very well in the course of this analysis come across phenomena that – for some people in some situations – point to 'a different order of reality and experience', but then we shall regard them not from this mysterious angle but in the somewhat more down-to-earth perspective of how they serve to identify groups of people who use them or to whom they refer. In other words, whatever else such symbols may stand for, I here limit myself to an examination of the way in which they work as simple group identifiers.

An example: in a Christian context the cross is a very complex symbol. It evokes God giving his son to humankind to be killed and may give rise to deep theological speculations about who sacrificed him, to whom, etc. There may be more problems of this type than entire faculties of divinity can answer. On the other hand, a cross worn as a heraldic sign may serve to distinguish the crusaders from the Moors in a battle and thus, in this situation, is a mere group identifier to distinguish friend from foe.

Such different levels of symbolic use also underlie Nadel's classification (1951):

Nadel (1951: 262) indicated three main forms of symbolic behaviour ... The first he cited were 'emblems, badges and other diacritical signs': whether material objects or gestures or other behaviour, their display indicates group membership and other social relationships and provides expectations for

---

1. This chapter is based on Schlee (1994b).
2. For a history of the definitions of these and related concepts the reader may refer to Firth (1973).

corresponding 'real' behaviour. The second category of symbolic behaviour mentioned was 'all forms of social nomenclature,' including, for example, classificatory kinship terminology; from the use of these two, expectations as to other conforming behaviour are derived. Nadel's third category of symbolic behaviour was the 'dramatizations' pervading primitive cultures, instanced by the initiation rites of Van Gennep's classical analysis. (Firth 1973: 174)

These three categories, of course, stand not for different phenomena but for different aspects. A 'dramatisation' may be a diacritical 'badge' if a group is identified or defined by the initiation rites they undergo: all those who perform the *gaalgulamme* ceremony are 'white' Rendille, while those Rendille-speakers who instead perform *ilmugit* sacrifices of the Samburu type are Ariaal (Spencer 1973: 46f.; Schlee 1979: 161f., 224f., 1989a: Ch. 4). The sequence of three categories proposed by Nadel seems to be a progression from relatively simple to complex. To describe the cross on the mantle of a crusader as a group-identifying emblem is indeed simpler than giving a full account of all the theological implications of this symbol. But we shall also see that the relatively modest enterprise we shall undertake has some complications, depending on who identifies whom, and for what purpose.

Inter-ethnic Systems of Meaning

Here I do not want to go into much descriptive detail about the different visible signs by which gender, marital status, age, and age grade affiliation are marked by the Rendille, since I have done that elsewhere (Schlee 1987b). Suffice it to say that these include bead ornaments of all sorts, manipulations of the body like pierced and widened ear lobes, removal of the two central lower incisors, circumcision, hairstyles, and coloured line drawings in red ochre on the face. If one sees a Rendille man with circular ivory ear lobe plugs, red ochre liberally applied to head and shoulders, line drawings on his face, strings of certain oval beads called *ngerinye* across his chest, and his head and neck full of other bead ornaments, one can be sure that he is a member of the warrior age set. A married elder is not necessarily older than this warrior, because there is a substantial overlap of age between subsequent age sets since age sets are recruited primarily on the grounds of generational considerations. But one would recognise his married status by his modest and standardised ornaments: just two strings of glass beads around the neck, no headgear or strings across the chest, small aluminium earrings worn through the widened holes in the ear lobes (see Figure 9.1), which now dangle down, instead of the plugs fitted tightly in the ear lobes until the end of the warrior period.[3] Age grade affiliation is thus marked in a very visible way. There is some ostentation of virility and male beauty in the warrior outfit and a certain soberness and understatement in that of the elders (which reminded me of the grey business suits with a coloured tie as the only ornament, a certain

---

3.   A warrior period ends not in the year of marriage but with the initiation of a new warrior age set, three years later: during these three years warrior ornaments are discarded and those of elders adopted. How fast this takes place depends on individual preferences and pragmatic considerations like the availability of the new ornaments.

(a) The standard aluminium earring worn by elders. Note the plastic pipe inserted into the upper rim of the ear, and topped by a large bead.

(b) A somewhat atypical elder's earring.

(c) A young married man who does not yet have the standard aluminium elder's earrings and wears ornaments he has fashioned for himself.

(d) A nubile girl's ear ornaments.

Figure 9.1 Age- and gender-specific ear ornaments among the Rendille. (see Schlee 1987b: 37)

gender/status/occupation-specific code of dress in Western culture). These symbols (since now we are on the symbolic level and have moved away from mere identity markers) might therefore be not quite arbitrary in de Saussure's sense (1969 [1915]) of a merely conventional link between form and meaning. Rather they visually underline certain age-specific male roles – fierce young men versus wise elders.[4]

But why are *ngerinye* exclusively worn by warriors, forbidden to boys, and not worn by elders? We know the reason as little as Leach knew the reason for certain Kachin hairstyles in highland Burma:

> I do not know *why* Kachin women go hatless with bobbed hair before they are married, but assume a turban afterwards, any more than I know why English women put a ring on a particular finger to denote the same change in social status; all I am interested in is that in this Kachin context the assumption of a turban by a woman does have this symbolic significance. It is a statement about the status of the woman. (Leach 1954: 16)

But it is not only that; it is also an ethnicity marker: it sets off cultures in which married women wear turbans from ring-wearing cultures:

> In the example just given, marriage is a structural relationship which is common to both English and Kachin society; it is symbolised by a ring in the one and a turban in the other. This means that one and the same element of social structure may appear in one cultural dress in locality A and another cultural dress in locality B. But A and B may be adjacent places on the map. (Leach 1954: 16f.)

Ornaments that mark a man as a warrior in a purely Rendille context mark him also as a Rendille in an inter-ethnic context.

Leach stresses that, among the Kachin, identical elements of social structure appear in different cultural dress in adjacent localities and that therefore the boundaries of social systems do not coincide with cultural frontiers there (see Figure 9.2). But, even in cases where the elements of the social structures of neighbouring groups are not identical but only similar enough to be mutually understood, one can observe supercultural and inter-ethnic social systems, the subsystems of which communicate successfully with each other. The Oromo-speaking Gabra, like the Rendille, have age-set systems (three different ones) of the *gada* type (Schlee 1989a: Ch. 4) but do not have a celibate warrior age grade that is formalised and symbolically underlined to the same extent that warriorhood is among the Rendille. Nevertheless, they know very well how the difference between warriors and elders is visually marked among the Rendille and what it amounts to in terms of behavioural patterns and social norms. They know that arrangements for peaceful utilisation of neighbouring pastures and shared waterholes are better arranged through the elders and that a large body of Rendille warriors moving without herds means imminent danger: important cultural knowledge for the successful operation in an intersocietal metasystem.

---

4.   On gender/age roles, see Schlee (1979: 132–168).

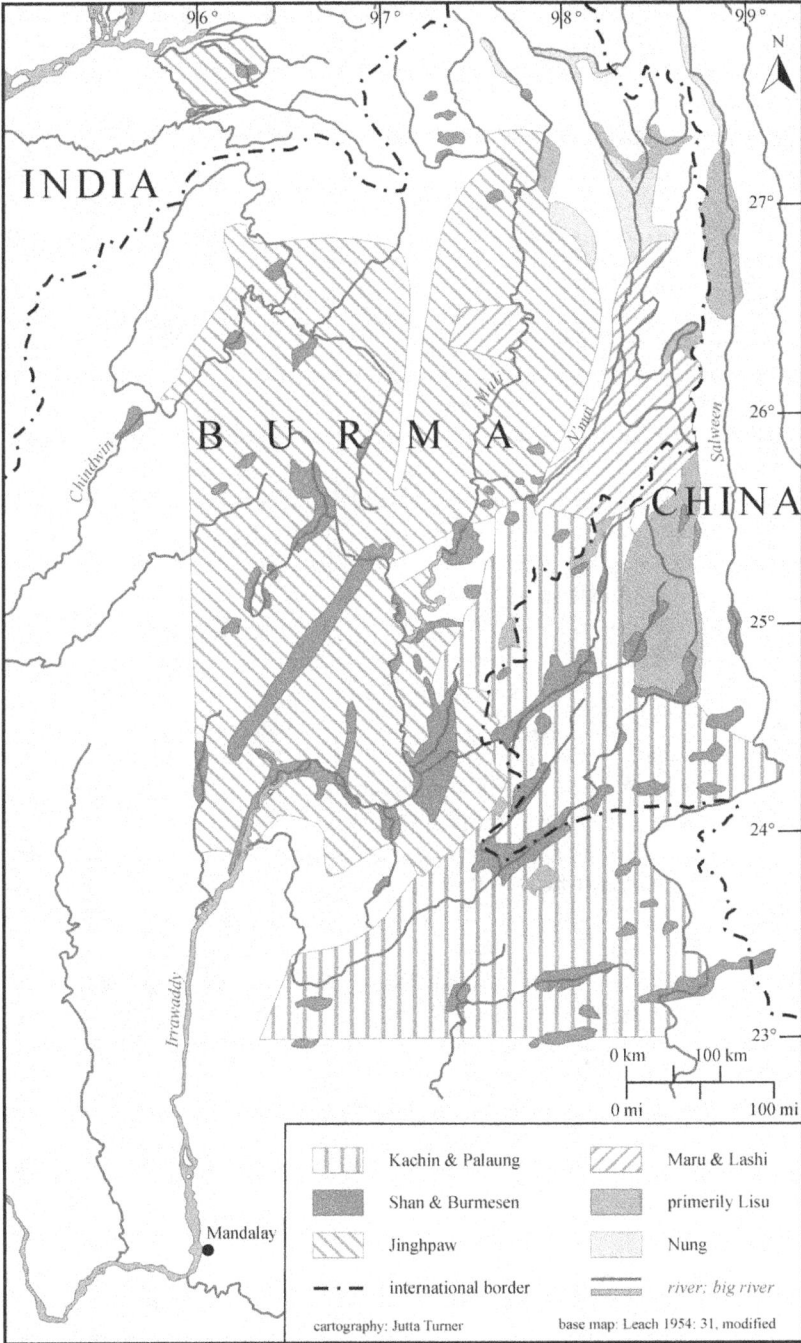

Figure 9.2 The ethnic diversity of highland Burma according to Leach (1954).

The Somali traders in Rendilleland (who do not have age sets) make different use of the same knowledge; they might not hire an elder as a herdsman for their stock because elders have a tendency to stay too close to the settlements rather than looking for faraway good pastures. Or they might try to combine strength with experience in their labour force by hiring both warriors and elders. We might therefore come to the same conclusion as Leach does about the Kachin, namely, that 'in this context cultural attributes such as language, dress and ritual procedure are merely symbolic labels denoting the different sectors of a single extensive structural system' (Leach 1954: 17).

Visibility

The emblems I have so far discussed all share one feature: high visibility. The obvious exception is circumcision, since in public the private parts are normally covered, although by Rendille with less circumspection than by Gabra and Somali. 'There is nothing ugly about a man, so why should a man hide himself?' is a common saying. Among females, modesty is more pronounced, even among the Rendille, and this – in combination with the female anatomy – makes clitoridectomy even less visible, although it is analogous to male circumcision in marking a status difference (in this case, marriageable/married since for women there is no equivalent of the warrior phase).

The Gabra and Somali forms of male circumcision are different from the Rendille form (Schlee 1979: 58ff., 1989a: Ch. 4). Rendille migrants who have undergone simple circumcision in hospitals to avoid ridicule by town women later, at the communal circumcisions, undergo the operation again to be circumcised in the more elaborate Rendille way, which is regarded as the proper form. In the case of inter-ethnic marriages, however, I have never heard it suggested to a circumcised non-Rendille that he should have these elaborations done to himself. His form of circumcision would be regarded as equivalent to Rendille circumcision. Both are equally acceptable as a prerequisite for marriage. If circumcision were more visible than it is, differences might be noted and discussed more often – but this is mere speculation. The Rendille refer to the Gabra and the Boran as *chi ti ilko khabto*, 'the strangers/enemies with teeth', because these northern neighbours do not remove the two central lower incisors. I never heard a Rendille refer to Gabra or Boran as 'the enemies with the funny style of circumcision' or 'with incomplete circumcision'. That teeth are singled out as identity markers may be due to their higher visibility.

Different styles of circumcision – on the one hand by the Rendille, Samburu, El Molo, Maasai, and presumably the Bantu groups referred to as *Massai-Affen* in the early literature, and on the other by Boran, Gabra, and Somali – might therefore be more important to the anthropologist interested in the diffusion of the custom than to the peoples themselves.

Ethnobiological Categories

There are, however, other features, which not only are invisible but lack any empirical basis, that nonetheless are attributed to well-defined groups, and that are, therefore, identity markers. Some of these fall into the domain of ethnobiology. (Ethnobiology, like other ethnosciences, is a curious mixture of an emic and an etic concept. It aims at *their* beliefs and convictions, i.e., at the emic level of description.

But, as biology is a category of *our* culture, an etic category, one has to specify that ethnobiology is what they believe about what we would call biology.) There are no biological differences between Rendille clans because clan exogamy constantly mixes the genetic characteristics of all clans so that no clan-specific gene frequencies or combinations can emerge. Nevertheless, the Rendille are convinced that the junior subclans of D'ubsahai as well as the clans Matarbá, Elegélla, and the subclan Gaalorra of Gaaldeilan, the so-called 'red people' (*'doo 'di gududan*) are biologically distinct from other Rendille, in so far as their daughters have pregnancies of only seven months (counting from the first menstruation that did not occur and discounting the 'waiting period' for this menstruation). The clans Uyám, Urawén, and Tubcha, on the other hand, are *haiyan. Haiyan* are believed to be especially tough and able to stay for ten days without food or water in the bush before they die. Their daughters, as well as those of Rengumo, are said to have long pregnancies, often ten or even eleven months. All other Rendille are 'white people' (*'doo 'di dadakhan*). Their daughters have normal-length pregnancies.

One is tempted to attribute these differences to inexact counting or rather systematically different ways of counting by various clans, but I could not find anything of this sort, and, when Rendille are questioned on these beliefs, they just confirm them as purported facts. The ritual differentiation of the Rendille clans (Schlee 1979) thus finds a parallel in these beliefs about the differences of their biological nature.

Apart from *haiyan*, 'red', and 'white', there are other categories that combine segments from different classes and to which biological characteristics are attached. One such category is the 'K' people (the name 'K' stands for a word that cannot be pronounced without offending the people in question). K people live in enforced endogamy and K men are denied sexual access to non-K girls and women. A child begotten by a K man with a non-K woman married to a non-K man needs to be aborted because it is believed to bring misfortune to its siblings begotten by the husband or other lovers. If she fails to abort and gives birth to a boy, he will eliminate his brethren and remain as the sole heir. The evil force going out from K is localised in their sperm: they are said to have 'bad piss'.[5]

It is difficult to say whether on the emic level such distinctions as K/non-K are ritual or biological because neither of the two terms has an exact equivalent in Rendille, and the relationship between them is not one of clear opposites even in English. By a ritual act the nature of a person can be changed: a 'boy' (who can be up to twenty-nine years old) is believed to be able to beget only a fool, and, therefore, such a child needs to be aborted, whereas a circumcised warrior, as the lover of a married woman, can beget a healthy, normal child.

There are more ethnobiological categories of this type, but rather than enumerating them all I shall limit myself to one central concept in this field of meaning: 'blood'. This category, which is also important in Western folk beliefs, has an important place not only in the reasoning of the Rendille about the differentiations of human nature but also in the corresponding beliefs of the Gabra, Somali, and Boran. Sameness or difference of 'blood' has important consequences for

---

5. The beliefs about blacksmiths are similar (Schlee 1979: 194–215).

those whom one is allowed to kill, and killing is in the core of a cultural complex connected with status achievement, the achievement complex (*Verdienstkomplex*), which is – in some cases closely, in others loosely – interwoven with the *gada* system. To examine the killer complex we must therefore make a short deviation into the *gada* system, to which it is closely related.

Social formations known as *gada*, age-set systems, mainly found among speakers of lowland eastern Cushitic languages, are characterised by generational principles of recruitment and the importance attributed to exact time calculations (Jensen 1936; Haberland 1963) in connection with fixed cycles of years and an elaborate calendar that tends to determine the gada cycles so strictly that little room is left for demographic considerations and adjustment to social pressures. *Gada* systems comprise a hierarchy of ranks, between and within the age grades, and are closely tied to ideas of achievement. This achievement complex can be illustrated by the different material and immaterial goods that are given value in these cultures: wealth in livestock, growing families (i.e., the criteria of success for which one can define 'fertility' as the common denominator), and, alongside these fertility-oriented values, killing as a contrast and complement. 'Whoever has not begotten shall beget and whoever has not killed shall kill' is a much-quoted phrase that seems to have been first recorded by Cerulli (1933: 125f.).

There are different rules to take into account certain species of large game for ceremonially bestowing the killer status on somebody, but in the focus of the killer complex there is the killing of human beings, with which we shall deal here.[6] The connection between the *gada* system and the killer complex is most conspicuous among the Boran Oromo, who, until their incorporation into the modern states, undertook large war expeditions after their age-set promotions so that the same pattern underlay their military activities and (other) life cycle ceremonies with a peak of activity once in eight years (Baxter 1979). According to a sixteenth-century Amharic source on the Oromo ('Galla') (Bahrey, translated by Schleicher in 1893 and quoted in Guidi 1973 [1907]), originally each participant had to slay one enemy before he was allowed to shave his head. The ferocity of these warriors was attributed by Bahrey to the lice that tormented them. Later it was sufficient for the whole party

---

6.   The link between killing and fertility makes it possible to distinguish between enemies who are 'good to kill', because killing them is good for the fertility of the land, the women, and the livestock, and others who do not bring such benefits. This may or may not have to do with those in question having a reputation as good warriors. The idea of a 'good fight' with a 'worthwhile enemy' cannot be adopted unquestioningly as a framework for interpretation, and the killer status should not be confused with being a 'hero'. A penis may count the same, irrespective of whether it has been obtained in a fight with a grown man, by snatching a baby boy or by cutting up a pregnant woman whose embryo happened to be male (Baxter 1979). But, irrespective of notions of chivalry and respect for the enemy, the idea that some people may be better to kill than others introduces ambivalence. Hostility does not always imply negation and rejection. It may also have to do with acquiring ritual benefits from people who are 'good to kill'. For Arbore (Hor) ideas about different kinds of enemies in terms of propitiousness see Tadesse (1999); for those of the Boran, see Haberland (1963: 205–210). I have earlier expressed some scepticism of Haberland's interpretation of Boran ideas about killing and found it to lean a bit to the 'heroic' side (Schlee 1989b: 242f.). On connections between the killer complex and modern Oromo ideas about development, see Zitelmann (1999).

to kill one enemy to fulfil the requirement. Only male victims are counted since penis and scrotum have to be brought back as a trophy. But that does not mean that, among the groups that share this killer complex, women are spared. If there are no political reasons to limit hostilities, damage to the adversary is maximised by also killing women, maybe today more than before because state control, rudimentary as it may be, makes it impossible to keep or sell captured women.

Among the Rendille and Gabra, killing human beings in the context of circumcision, which in the Rendille case is the inauguration into the warrior age set and among the Gabra a precondition for it, has been replaced by killing small animals. Thus, killing human beings, which is associated with the same symbols as among the Boran, has become independent from the age-set cycles and can now be carried out whenever the circumstances are favourable.

'Blood' is the criterion to distinguish between those whom one may kill and those whom one may not. It is not identical with ethnicity because members of other ethnic groups can be regarded as being of the same 'blood'. It is, however, linked to the possibility of admitting strangers to public rituals and therefore has to be examined also in terms of propitiousness/unpropitiousness. There are categories of people about whom it is believed that intermarriage and their integration into domestic and public ritual can contribute to the prosperity of one's own group while others carry the seeds of misfortune and poverty in themselves. I shall first deal with the connections between killing and 'blood' and then with those between 'blood' and fortune/misfortune.

Here is a case history about the connection between 'blood' and the status as a stranger/enemy. In an undetermined, possibly mythical time, a young Boran had the fixed idea of emigrating to the Arsi, another, but hostile, Oromo group. The elders tried in vain to persuade him to give up this idea. When he left, a party of warriors was sent to kill him, because, even if he himself had no hostile feelings, it was claimed that his son might one day come back to wage war against the Boran. The killing should be carried out with spears and the genital trophy should be taken from the corpse. But on the way the warriors had second thoughts because they did not want to shed the blood of a 'brother'. When they caught up with the traveller they killed him with clubs and left the body intact. When they came back without the trophy and reported the way they had killed the dissident, the elders lamented: since they had not killed him like an enemy they had killed him as a Boran, and the killing of an enemy had thus become a murder, the first murder, it is claimed, among Boran. To restore the upset order wergild was then instituted: a compensation in the form of thirty head of cattle was paid to the family of the victim. And this is the topic of the tale: it is an aetiological account of the origin of blood money.[7]

---

7.   Interview with Halake Guyyo, Gabra (Galbo) in Kalacha, August 1980. Also, 'a Boran who was sentenced to be executed was clubbed across the neck and in the groin, but without spilling blood' (Baxter 1979: 70). Although there were executions among the Boran, in Halake Guyyo's narrative the only alternative interpretations of an act of killing were 'killing an enemy' versus 'murder'. I have no definite explanation for this; the story might refer to a specific time frame, when executions did not exist among the Boran; executions may not be talked about; or the matter has been simplified to provide a better narrative. One basic idea, however, is the same in Halake Guyyo's story and Baxter's account of the methods of killing: only the blood of non-Boran can be spilled.

In this episode, the setting apart, the making of a stranger, was meant to be effected by a certain way of killing. Normally, of course, this connection is the other way round: people are killed in a certain way because they are strangers.

Although the Gabra and the Boran speak the same language, have shared a common political system for centuries (the Gabra are often referred to as 'vassals' of the Boran), and are engaged in ritual exchange with each other, their 'blood' is different. A consequence of this is that even today lone Gabra herdboys are sometimes shot from a safe distance because – as the Gabra say bitterly – the Boran need their genitals in order to dance with them in front of the women.[8] From the viewpoint of political rationality this is individual deviance since collectively the Boran and Gabra regard each other as allies.[9]

Mutual raiding is much more frequent between the Gabra and the Somali, unknowingly or knowingly, with or without mistaken identities. About the Somali it is believed, however, that they have the same 'blood' as the Gabra, especially those of the phratry Odoola. It is reported that Somali who have killed Gabra and Gabra who have killed Somali are pursued by misfortune and that their families die out, because they have spilled 'their own blood'. But the Somali are Muslims, culturally rather different from the Gabra, and speak a language that is not intelligible to the latter. We thus have the apparent paradox that a politically allied and culturally related neighbouring group is of different 'blood' and that enemies who speak a strange tongue are of the same 'blood' as the Gabra. This has to do with the inter-ethnic clan relationships, with which I deal elsewhere (Schlee 1989a).

What, then, is the connection between these ideas about identity or difference of 'blood' and categories like propitiousness and ritual acceptability? Gabra and Sakuye pastoralists refuse to marry Boran girls, although these girls stem from the politically dominant group and such marriage would therefore be hypergamous. But the Gabra and Sakuye in this configuration are not interested in 'marrying upward', because, in their view, Boran girls are 'bad for the camels'. Such women would have to be excluded from many rituals because these rituals serve the well-being of the camels; whatever else their object may be, in one way or another they relate to the camels (Schlee 1989a: Ch. 4). Also, to have a Boran mother is a stigma for a Gabra. Elsewhere I have described how the Boran had to be expelled from the holy grounds of the Galbo phratry of the Gabra in Ethiopia before sacrificial ceremonies were held there (Schlee 1987a).

After all these discriminations and segregations, I want to point out some of the consequences of the purported community of 'blood' between the Gabra, Rendille, Sakuye, and Somali. The age-set promotions of the Galbo phratry of the Gabra (Schlee 1987a, b) require the cooperation of a member of the Somali lineage Sheqal, who provides the cloth for the ritual headdress of the elders being initiated into the highest grade. This has happened for generations in a relationship of fixed exchange: the man gets a camel as a payment.

---

8.   See also Baxter (1965: 65).
9.   This text was first published in 1994 and the ethnographic present refers to the 1970s and 1980s. In the early 2000s the patterns changed and there have been many violent clashes between Gabra and Boran.

The woman in whose house the holy drum of the phratry Galbo was kept from 1972 to 1986 was a Rendille and had learned the Boran language, which the Gabra speak, only as a teenager. That the 'mother of the drum', as this woman was called, was not a Gabra did not disturb anybody, since Rendille girls are of the same 'blood' and 'good for the camels'.

The above is certainly not an exhaustive analysis of the 'blood' symbolism of the cultures under study, but I hope to have shown that within the more modest framework of analysis I have laid out sameness or difference of 'blood' is an important aspect of group identity.

Questions of 'Reality' and Awareness

One might argue that these invisible aspects of group identity are not identity markers but parts of the identity that is marked, that they are not symbols but parts of what is symbolised. But where can we draw a line between markers and what is marked? A given clan identity can be made up by a name, clan-specific food avoidances, origin tales, clan-specific songs (micro-level national anthems), a specific house form, girls' ornaments, which, because they are clan-specific, can signify unmarried status or clan affiliation according to the contrasts provided by the situation, clan-specific curse vehicles (persons cursed by one clan are believed to be trampled by a rhinoceros, those cursed by another clan to be bitten by a snake), clan-specific sacrificial ceremonies, purported clan-specific tempers, intellectual and physical characteristics, to list a few. Some of these are permanently visible; others are observable in certain situations; yet others lack any empirical basis, and we can only state that there are such beliefs but we cannot observe what these beliefs refer to. But they all point to each other, and together they form a complex identity. I would, therefore, hesitate to deny the qualification 'identity marker' to elements of the culture that cannot be observed except as verbal statements about beliefs.

Yet there is another prerequisite for qualifying an element of a culture as an emic 'identity marker'. The members of a culture (and/or their neighbours) have to be aware of it. Among the Rendille one can hear *huggung 'ki gaal 'dakhamba a koo kal'dach* – 'the customs concerning camels are all the same'. Those Rendille who share this belief think that there is one proper way to manage camels, including the camel-oriented rituals, which are shared by all camel keepers. That there is not just one proper way can be shown by comparing the Rendille and Gabra with the Somali (Schlee 1988) or by contrasting their forms of management with those employed by the Boran (Baxter 1970). Such a comparison reveals that the Rendille, Gabra, Sakuye, and some sections of the Ajuran and Garre Somali share a complex of rituals and rules for camel management to the exclusion of other Somali and of the Boran. Considerations like which groups in a cluster of neighbouring peoples are more closely related to each other and how these similarities and differences have come about are, of course, not without repercussions on questions of identity, and later educated members of the societies in question might discuss anthropological information of this kind for defining themselves and others. But, as long as the bearers of the cultures under comparison are not aware of these similarities and differences, we would speak, in the tradition of diffusionist anthropology, of such elements as 'features' rather than 'identity markers'.

Increasing distance, of course, makes awareness of cultural similarities more and more unlikely. A Sarakatsani shepherd in Greece, after sexual intercourse:

> must carefully wash his hands before milking sheep and it is generally preferred that the two shepherds of the flock of milking ewes should be unmarried men. (Campbell 1964: 26)

> Women, particularly married women involved in sexual intercourse, or girls during their menstrual periods, do not approach the sheep unnecessarily. A woman is careful not to cross directly in front of a flock, partly for the practical reason that it breaks the smooth rhythm of its grazing but also because her presence in some way affronts the sheep and might cause disease. *A fortiori*, a woman never milks a sheep. (Campbell 1964: 32)

The goats, a less valued species, can be milked by women.

A Rendille who wants to milk a camel with a calf must either be a young boy or an old man, in any case somebody who has not had sexual intercourse for ten months. A sexually active man can milk only a camel whose calf has died because the association of the milker with sex is believed to be harmful to the calves. A woman would never approach the camel enclosure. Less valued species, which are not in the focus of rituals, such as sheep and goats, can, however, be milked by women.

No Sarakatsani has ever gone to Rendilleland. If some Greek migrants went there as traders or water engineers they might wonder about these similarities – the shared opposition between sexuality and women on the one hand and the females of the most valued species of livestock on the other – and perceive a common pastoral ethos with surprisingly similar expressions between their own homeland and that remote place. They and the Rendille with whom they discussed this topic might then develop a notion of a pastoralist 'identity' that links even different continents. But, as nothing of this sort has happened, these corresponding customs are not 'identity markers' but 'features' and pose riddles only to those who are professionally concerned with cultural comparisons, to us anthropologists. Functionalists, diffusionists, environmental determinists have all dealt with riddles of this sort without finally solving them.

'Being aware' thus is a precondition for the use of a cultural element as an 'identity marker'. But one can also 'be aware' of something that is factually wrong, and this does not affect its usability as an identity marker in the slightest way. The Rendille call the Somali *'Dafara. 'Dafar* in Rendille is 'cloth'. *'Dafara* is, therefore, occasionally translated into Swahili as *kabila nguo* – 'the tribe with cloths'. In contrast, the Rendille are *kabila ngozi* – 'the tribe with skins'. (The women wear skin aprons.) This popular etymology of *'Dafara* is probably wrong, although we cannot be sure about this because the first traders who brought cloth to Rendilleland were Somali. In Boran the Somali are called *Safara* (oblique case), and that has nothing to do with cloths. (It has rightly or wrongly been linked to the Arabic *safar*, 'travel', and has been explained as 'travellers'.) Nevertheless, on the emic level the name and the form of dress point to each other and for the Rendille form a part of Somali identity.

Emic and Etic Perspectives: Emblems versus Features

A cultural similarity or difference becomes, as the criterion of 'awareness' suggests, only useful as an 'identity marker' if correspondences and contrasts are provided by their vicinity. Such similarities and differences can, however, also be used to discuss questions of identity without the bearers of the compared cultures being aware of them and without regard to the distance between them. An outside observer might adopt such a position, a third point of reference outside the cultures under comparison. This is what anthropologists often do. Such a perspective is etic rather than emic. In this context we speak of 'features' rather than 'identity markers' or 'emblems'. Comparing features and complexes of features can be, in combination with other types of evidence, useful for 'conjectural history', as this type of exercise has been called by Radcliffe-Brown (1952: 49–89), and to help us, for example, identify related clans in different ethnic groups (Schlee 1989a).

By no means does such 'objective' measuring of cultural similarities lend itself to direct political application. It always leads to etic interpretations, not to emic views of identity. If self-determination is to mean anything, definitions of political identity should be left to the bearers of these identities. In view of actual political power games such a position may sound idealist; but at least we should be aware of the transition when we pass the threshold from anthropology into politics and not just pretend to be still in the field of objectivity and science. Dench writes about the 'objective test of culture' as applied in European history:

> Don't forget Versailles. When the crunch came and western powers needed to operationalize the principle of self-determination, they slipped easily enough from a voluntarist position into using culture as an objective indicator of group commitment. Minorities to be invested with collective rights were identified from above, according to linguistic criteria. Their destiny was defined in terms of history, rather than surrendered to the market. Choices supposedly belonging to individuals were in the event made by powerful groups on behalf of the lesser. (Dench 1986: 159)

There are different methodological standards for working with cultural features, as can be shown by the following controversy. In his book Greater Ethiopia, Levine (1974) lists a number of cultural features that serve to include the Oromo in *Greater Ethiopia* as a culture area. In their criticism of Levine, Baxter and Blackhurst (1978) argue with Graebner's criterion of form (1911), of which, being good British anthropologists, they are of course unaware.[10] It is not legitimate, they argue, to point to circumcision as a common feature of Amharic and Oromo culture, if 'in one case, babes-in-arms or boys are operated on, in the other, political leaders who, symbolically at least, are approaching retirement from active politics' (Baxter and Blackhurst 1978: 163). Circumcision, thus, to the Amhara means something quite different from what it means to the Oromo. 'Some of the traits, such as "hair styles to indicate status", must be near universal among mankind' (ibid.: 164). This criticism implies that Levine is not up to the standards of historical anthropology, and I agree with that.

In addition, it is possible to criticise Levine from quite a different angle, taking the above distinction between 'identity markers' (used by the people under study) and 'features' (used by the outside observer) as a starting point. We may add to Baxter and Blackhurst's criticism of Levine's book that, even if these features were specific and formal enough (which they are not) to justify the postulation of Ethiopia as a culture area (which it is not), this would not justify Levine in giving a title to his book that sounds like a political slogan (Greater Ethiopia). Whether the populations concerned regard these features as relevant to their own identity and whether they want to share a common statehood should be left to them; it is not an anthropological problem to be solved by anthropologists.

Even the relatively simple interpretation of cultural materials as 'identity markers', leaving aside the more intricate symbolical aspects, cannot, I hope to have shown, get around questions like who is to be distinguished from whom and by whom in what situation. The meaning of such emblems varies with each case.

---

10. Other British anthropologists have also come close to Graebner without knowing it. Leach's 'frills' (formal similarities of different cultures that cannot be explained by parallel functional adaptations) are strongly reminiscent of the form criterion. I am too much of a diffusionist to believe that these reinventions are completely independent. But, as *Kulturgeschichte* has not been taken seriously by mainstream anthropologists in Britain since Radcliffe-Brown, these ideas must have travelled to Britain in rather subconscious ways.

From the observer's point of view, actions appear as means to ends, and it is quite feasible to follow Malinowski's advice and classify social actions in terms of their ends – i.e., the 'basic needs' which they appear to satisfy. But the facts which are thereby revealed are technical facts; the analysis provides no criterion for distinguishing the peculiarities of any one culture or any one society. For example, if it is desired to grow rice, it is certainly essential and functionally necessary to clear a piece of ground and sow seed in it. And it will no doubt improve the prospects of a good yield if the plot is fenced and the growing crop weeded from time to time. Kachins do all these things and, in so far as they do this, they are performing simple technical acts of a functional kind. These actions serve to satisfy 'basic needs'. But there is much more to it than that. In Kachin 'customary procedure', the routines of clearing the ground, planting the seed, fencing the plot and weeding the growing crop are all patterned according to formal conventions and interspersed with all kinds of technically superfluous frills and decorations. It is these frills and decorations which make the performance a *Kachin* performance and not just a simple functional act ... In origin the details of custom may be an historical accident. (Leach 1954: 11f.)

Kulturgeschichte would study how such accidents come about by comparing just these 'frills' and trying to reconstruct how these elements have come to have their present distribution.

Chapter 10

Purity and Power in Islamic and Non-Islamic Societies and the Spectre of Fundamentalism

Introduction

The preceding chapters have introduced a perspective which tries to link identifications of oneself and others to perceived aims and the pursuit of advantages. This chapter extends this perspective into the domain commonly called 'religion'.[1] As an analytical concept, 'religion' has the disadvantage of not being a universal category. It is highly culture-bound. The word itself (Lat. *re-ligio* – 'being tied backwards to') suggests a dualism between this world and another world, and a link between the two. In other words: it suggests the existence of a supernatural sphere (and thereby also nature) or a transcendental God (and thereby also a profane world). This is not a universal belief, and it is doubtful how many people beyond the Judaeo/Christian/Muslim cluster share this dualism, which goes back to Zoroastrianism. As a more general category, I have therefore always preferred 'belief system' (Schlee 1979). Some 'belief systems' which are not dualist and do not fit the concept of religion in the original sense have, however, in a globalising world, come under pressure to pose as 'religions' in order not to be second to Christianity and Islam. It is with these that their spokespersons want them to fit into the same category. And it is by this categorisation that competition within a shared framework is established.

Some might think that religion is a sphere where spirituality has a high degree of autonomy. We shall, however, see that religious identification is just as interwoven with economy and politics as we have found ethnic identification to be. In terms of exclusion of competitors it might even be especially effective because of its moral underpinning.

With the field of religion we enter a domain which looms large in recent political ideologies. Towards the end of the cold war, around 1990, there was a time of intense search for enemies. Apparently driven by the fear of a disintegration of NATO from lack of a clear opponent and the structural changes accompanied by this, Islam was

---

1. Most of this chapter is based on Schlee (2003d), which, in turn, goes back to a paper presented at the Department of Ethnology and Cultural Anthropology, University of Ljubljana, May 2003. Ultimately, it has evolved from a contribution to the second international conference on 'Hierarchy and Power in the History of Civilizations', St Petersburg, 4–7 July 2002, and from a report to the German research board from 1999 (www.eth.mpg.de/people/schlee/sudan01/sudanbericht-deckblatt.html). I thank Fernanda Pirie, Krisztina Kehl-Bodrogi, and Bettina Mann for helpful comments.

rediscovered as the adversary of its revived mirror concept, the Christian Occident, which many of us had believed to be obsolete since the era of Enlightenment. The 'West', for a time shorthand for the globalisation of modernity ('the West and the rest'), had found its counterpart again in the shape of the (Middle) East. Since then, our colleagues in Oriental Studies have been fully busy countering the distorted descriptions of Islam in the media.

Needless to say, all this has become much worse since the terrorist attacks of 11 September 2001, when the crusades had a strange revival and quixotic knights in their thousands have started again to defend the Occident against real and imagined Islamist threats around the world. We shall come back to this in connection with the Somali peace process in Part III of this volume. There we shall see that the proximity to Sufi orders is used by today's moderates as a proof of their harmlessness. In the present chapter we shall see that in the nineteenth and early twentieth centuries these same Sufi orders were the organisational framework of militant Islam. That today's militants are tomorrow's moderates might help to put some fears into a more relativist perspective.

This chapter will also show that the link between perfection in religious or ritual performance and claims to power are not specific to Islam and not tied to particular beliefs. To establish this point, we shall start in non-Islamic regions of Africa.

Rendille Ideas about the Power to Curse

The link between purity and power in African systems of ideas can be direct: one may lose one's (ritual) power, for example the ability to utter a potent curse or an efficient blessing, by failing to maintain a standard of purity, such as by violating a food avoidance rule. Social hierarchies between clans with and without specific ritual or political powers and between professional groups of high and low status are constructed along such lines. In other contexts the relationship between purity and power is not direct but mediated by moral notions: ritual compliance is seen as an indicator of a moral standard which qualifies a person for political power. Conversely, non-compliance leads to the exclusion from power. Competition for the forms of power which are legitimised in this way may lead to the rapid rigidification of beliefs and ritual practice. Examples can be found in recent developments within Islam and Christianity. Purity tends to go along with rhetorical exclusion of the 'impure'.

The Rendille live in a state of intermittent warfare with several of their neighbours. One descent group among them, the Gaalorra subclan of the clan Gaaldeylan, has the ability to utter a particularly potent curse against enemies of the Rendille. Or, more generally, they have power over enemies. Gaalorra are not only believed to be able to prevent enemies supernaturally from inflicting harm on Rendille, but also to make them inflict harm on other Rendille. The entire class of subclans among the Rendille who have the power to bless or curse, called *iibire*, of whom the Gaalorra are one, are in possession of particular curse vehicles. One clan is believed to have a ritual association with elephants and, if one is trampled by an elephant, one would attribute it to the curse of that clan. Another clan has a similar relationship with rhinos, a third one with snakes. Gaalorra's curse vehicle is the horse. It might seem strange to find the horse, a domestic animal, in this list of dangerous beasts, but 'horse' here stands for enemy cavalry. In earlier times, the Boran used to raid Rendille camels on horseback, a rather easy method: you gallop through a herd of camels, the camels stampede and run off with the horses. Here, as in many parts of Africa and beyond, the image of the enemy and oppressor is that of the horseman.

The Rendille do not form one homogeneous cultural unit. We find that many cultural traits among them are clan-specific, and so are food avoidances. Gaalorra have more food avoidances than other Rendille and some of them are difficult to keep. The Rendille do not hunt a great deal, but, for example, a giraffe, which in the rainy season has got stuck in the mud, would be slaughtered and eaten by Rendille, with the exception of Gaalorra. They avoid game of any kind. In former times they also abstained from goat meat, although they keep goats like all other Rendille. Goats, just like sheep, are an important source of meat for Rendille, who do not readily decide to slaughter a camel.

What happens if a Gaalorra has succumbed to the temptation and eaten, say, meat of an antelope which has been shot by the police or other poachers? Nothing conspicuous, one might say. He would not drop dead, nor would he become sick. But he would be believed, and he would believe himself, to have lost his ritual power, his clan-specific blessing and curse. To regain it, he would have to be cleansed. His mouth would have to be rinsed with the urine of uncircumcised boys. If people relapse and continue to eat game often, after a couple of repetitions of this cleansing ritual they would rather give up their power to issue a curse.

I take the Gaalorra case as a starting point to move on to wider comparisons and say something general about 'purity and power'.[2] Links between notions of purity and notions of power might exist anywhere on earth, but I take all my examples from Africa, including North Africa, because I am an Africanist and know more about that continent than about other continents. Most of what I am going to present for comparison is material from Islamic societies and deals with purity and perfection in different currents of Islam; but I have consciously taken the non-Islamic Rendille as a starting point, to show that such ideas are embedded in a much wider context and that there is nothing particularly Islamic about the basic idea of attributing power to those who manage to keep certain standards of ritual purity.

The results of the following comparisons are:

1. Belief does not matter. In many cases, at least, the social workings of ritual rules are remarkably uniform, irrespective of the beliefs with which these practices are associated.
2. The relationship between purity and power, or, to put it differently, standards of ritual performance and forms of entitlement, changes little in otherwise quite different contexts.
3. This relationship can be shown to exist in non-Islamic and Islamic contexts, and, within Islam, in Sufi and anti-Sufi currents of Islam alike.
4. It can be accompanied by all sorts of moral reasoning, but this moral reasoning is not essential to it. It can exist also without any moral reasons or theological doctrines attached to it.

---

2.   The phrase 'purity and power' in the chapter title is, of course, modelled after the book by Mary Douglas, *Purity and Danger* (1966), in an attempt at parasitic publicity. It was suggested by Stephen Reyna.

Other Examples from Non-Islamic Africa

The region immediately bordering the northern Kenyan plains, the south-western highlands of Ethiopia, provides more illustrations of how purity is linked to power both in the 'traditional' belief systems and in the branches of Christianity which have come to compete with them.

Braukämper (1984) points to the close links between food avoidances and social status across the entire area. More recently, Freeman and Pankhurst (2001) describe how marginalised groups (craftsmen and hunters or former hunters) are denied commensality by the farming communities around them (ibid.: 5). The pollution emanating from them is believed to have been acquired by them through their dietary habits. They have eaten 'impure' meat, either from hunted animals or from animals which have not been slaughtered in the prescribed way.

For the Maale on the mountain ridge which forms the southern end of the Ethiopian highlands, 'riches and power automatically indexed [ritual] status' (Donham 1999: 114). Ritual status and, thereby, the success in life associated with it, depended on whether or not 'a Maale correctly carried out his or her clan taboos [and] faithfully observed customs' (ibid.: 113).

Such taboos, some clan-specific, others apparently general, comprise:

- Eating finger millet with milk.
- Letting breast milk fall on the grinding stone.
- Eating new crops before they had been tasted by an eldest brother.
- Drinking or any other contact with the milk of a cow in a new lactation period if the cow in question is owned by a younger brother and the eldest brother has not yet performed the appropriate ritual.
- Eating the honey of bees which had first entered a younger brother's hive, before the eldest brother had tasted it.
- Wrongs like theft and murder.

There is nothing in *Marxist Modern* (Donham 1999) that suggests that this list is exhaustive. These avoidances might just be the first examples to have come to his mind. It is, however, significant that all but the last of these taboos have to do with food or rank in the order of eating. Christianity, in the view of converts, was the liberation from these taboos (ibid.: 115–117). This emic view is, however, contradicted by an account of a conversion in which the prospective convert has come to the mission station in order to get medical treatment. He is asked to accept the Christian God first. He does so and is then admonished: 'Don't smoke tobacco. Don't drink beer. Don't drink anything that makes you drunk. Food, you eat food. Don't smoke tobacco. Stay away from prostitutes' (ibid.: 111).

So both the traditionalists and the Christians among them need to keep standards of purity to preserve their status in their respective groups. And status has to do with wealth and power. Donham reports how Christians support each other in land cases and how Christianity breaks up the power of the seniors.

For Christians, too, purity has much to do with things that move through the surface of the body, either by ingestion or by intercourse. But, at least for the Protestant missionaries of the Sudan Interior Mission from Canada, about whom Donham writes in the Maale context, the sinfulness of certain kinds of behaviour is mediated by moral or rational considerations. We assume that alcohol is abhorred by the missionaries because of its intoxicating effect and that prostitution is discouraged because of its adverse impact on public health or on cherished institutions like marriage and the family.

In many belief systems, no such rationalisations or moral links are required. Substances have direct ritual effects. It does not matter whether a Rendille has eaten antelope meat intentionally or inadvertently. Women in New Guinea are expected to go into total seclusion and Muslim women are not allowed to do the ritual prayers or fast while menstruating, without anyone claiming that menstruation is morally bad. A man, incidentally, who is bleeding from a small wound would not be allowed to pray either.

Among the Konso (see Figure 1, p. 1) a little further to the east from the Maale, Watson (1998: 205) has found that the ubiquitous craftsmen (here called *xawuda*) are considered to be unclean by the farmers and are potentially polluting to persons of ritual importance. In addition to this avoidance, ritual importance is surrounded by many other rules. Ritual specialists and people with sensitive political roles like peacemakers are called *namma dawra* in Konso, which translates as 'person for whom things are forbidden' or 'person who is forbidden'. *Poqallas* are the ritual leaders of the Konso communities and the (formerly real, now largely nominal) owners of the land. The powerful among the *poqallas* do not comprise everyone born into a *poqalla* lineage or anyone rich enough to qualify as a *poqalla* but only those who have spirits to help them. These powerful *poqallas* are the typical *namma dawra*. How closely their status is linked to ritual purity and to the taboos which surround them is best illustrated by how this status is undone:

> At the time of the revolution [1974] the revolutionaries cut off all his [a young poqalla's] hair (it was a taboo even to touch [his] hair) and they forced him to break other taboos by eating with other people and to eat and drink polluting substances such as blood. In this way they destroyed his special physical status of poqalla. (Watson 1998: 261)

Konso who convert to Christianity keep new standards of purity and become part of other networks of power. Even Protestants follow the widespread Ethiopian custom of only eating meat of animals slaughtered by members of their own group (ibid.: 255). A butcher of a different religion would be a source of pollution. Protestants tend to withdraw completely from any rituals associated with the *poqalla*. Orthodox Christianity, on the other hand, thought to be closer to local practice and magic, can be combined with participation in traditional rituals and even with the office of *poqalla*. 'In the case of the Protestant Church the *poqallas* who converted have given up their *poqalla* role completely. However, it is notable that those who were *poqallas* have often become quite central and powerful in the church, and hence could be said to have exchanged one set of claims to power with another' (ibid.: 253). Following a *poqalla* or belonging to a church are alternative strategies of access to land.

We may interrupt the description of examples at this point to try and identify some of the emerging patterns. All our examples have to do with people seeking access to a resource: here, mostly 'power', which is the ability to make other people do what one wants them to do. The desired action may be simply an abstention. One might want others to respect one's rights of access to material resources and not to interfere with them. 'Power' in this broad sense includes the Rendille curse, the *poqallas'* land rights, or authority in the new churches. Power is a resource which opens the access to other resources. Between the people and the resource there is the ritual requirement they need to meet in order to legitimise access to the resource. In the title of this chapter we used the shorthand 'purity' for requirements of this type. We can attribute two values to each of these variables (small or high for the number of people, low or high for the ritual requirements, plentiful or scarce for the resources) and combine them in a table (Table 10.1) to help us to speculate about the scenarios which result from the different combinations of these values.

Table 10.1 Explanatory variables and resulting scenarios of inter-group relations.

	Number of people striving for access	Requirements for obtaining entitlement	Availability of resource	Resulting scenario
1	Small	Low	Plentiful	Harmony. No problem anticipated. Probably a small group of people has opened a new niche with abundant resources.
2	High	Low	Plentiful	A bonanza. Many people have access to a resource, which is still plentiful. The situation is unstable, because the resource will be depleted at some point. If the resource in question is power, this means that power will be shared out in smaller and smaller parcels so that ultimately it becomes meaningless.
3	Small	High	Plentiful	Access to a plentiful resource is unnecessarily restricted. This constellation is not expected to occur frequently in reality.
4	High	High	Plentiful	In spite of high numbers seeking access to it, a relatively plentiful resource is protected by high requirements for entitlement. As in case number 2, this is not very likely. Plentiful resources are not normally protected by high requirements for the rights of access, not even if, as in this case, in view of the high number of people seeking access to it, the resource may not remain in rich supply for long.

5	Small	Low	Scarce	The small niche. Few people, who are more or less equally entitled, share a limited resource. Are factors which limit growth at work, like population control?
6	High	Low	Scarce	A small resource base is free for all and rapidly depleted.
7	Small	High	Scarce	A small niche in which a limited resource is surrounded by restrictions of access. The situation is somewhat eased by low numbers of contestants.
8	High	High	Scarce	Intense competition. Exclusivist strategies like rigidification of norms, discrimination or violence can be expected.
9	Constant	Low to high	Total amount constant, but allocated in proportion to which requirement has been met	Within a group of power-holders those who meet the more rigid ritual requirements are those who hold the larger share of power. In a subtype of this scenario the very peak of power-holders are exempt from ritual requirements or the breach of a taboo is even expected of them.
10	Growing	Rising	Constant or decreasing	The number of contestants is rising and requirements become more and more rigid.

Numbers 1 to 8 have either high or low values of each variable as the result of systematic permutation. Combination 8, intense competition for a scarce resource, seems to be particularly frequent in the real world and in this chapter we shall find a number of illustrations for it from the older and recent history of Africa.

The mention of land conflicts by Donham and by Watson suggests that among the Maale and the Konso, both of whom are highland farmers, land is a scarce resource and therefore we can assume that a ritual status which gives power over land is also valuable and surrounded by requirements of qualification. We might regard this as an approximation to case number 8.

One point Watson makes about the *poqalla*s of the Konso necessitates the inclusion of case no. 9 in the above table. Not all *poqalla*s have to meet the same ritual requirements, or the same standards of purity. Those who meet the higher requirements wield more power. She explains:

There is a relationship between purity and ritual powerfulness and the number and extremity of the taboos is proportional to the importance of the poqalla. A local poqalla obeys certain food avoidances but he may grow food himself. At a higher level poqallas may not do so and are only allowed to eat food grown by other members of their own family and prepared by women of their own household. For the more important of these poqallas, it is specified that these women must be virgins, etc. As we move up the scale of power, taboos become more elaborate and more numerous. (Watson 1998: 203)

If we consider cases 1 to 8 as basic types, 9 and 10 can be referred to as combined types. Case 10 is a dynamic model of case 1 or 5 moving towards case 8. We shall come across historical cases of affiliation to a privileged group becoming more contested and the criteria for it more demanding. Looking further afield for comparisons we might find that cases of such correlations between the rigidity of the ritual requirements and the elevation of status only exist up to a certain level. At the very peak of a hierarchy rules might be suspended or the breach of taboos may be permitted or even demanded (e.g., the brother/sister marriage, otherwise forbidden in ancient Egypt, being practised by the Pharaoh, legendary Muslim holy men being married to two wives who are sisters to each other, which is forbidden by the shariah, etc.)

The theory implicit in the above table is rather macroscopic. It is about quantitative distributions and scenarios and does not go down to the level of individual decisions. The micro level of explanation, however, shines through in the left column, where we speak of 'people striving for access' to resources. This alludes to perceptions and motivations. The table, however, remains basically at the group level. A proper decision theory about purity and exclusion would have to be at the level of the individual and would have to address questions like: Under what circumstances would an individual tend to adopt an exclusionist rhetoric? Under which circumstances would s/he lean towards an egalitarian ethos/claim minority rights/resort to violence/turn religious, etc.? It would have to take into account the internal dynamics of a group that does not consist of people of the same kind all basing their actions on the same calculations, but of people of complementary or competing types like leaders and followers, principals and agents, strategists and dreamers, conformists and nonconformists, passive people and enthusiasts, etc.

Whether an individual starts a power struggle or engages in status wrangling, whether in the case of shortness of resources s/he tightens her or his belt or rather snatches the resources away from her or his neighbour, whether s/he rebels or expects a reward for her or his loyalty, depends of course upon much more than the three variables included in Table 10.1: 'number of people striving for access', 'requirements for obtaining entitlement' and 'availability of resource'. Individual dispositions and skills can bring about a situation in which contrary personality types reach similar results via very different strategies. If one wants to do justice to all this on the individual level, one would have to take many more variables into account than the three considered in Table 10.1. The table is an oversimplification in so far as it does not distinguish subtypes that would result from a consideration of further variables. This is what I mean when I write that it is 'rather macroscopic'. The relativisation 'rather' indicates that microscopic elements are also present, that is, references to the calculus of single actors. In the case of many competitors for a scarce resource (cases 6 and 8), there will very probably be someone who formulates exclusive entitlements, discriminates against co-players, and maybe even invents legitimations for the use of violence (case 8). Who this will be, or who in contrast has such a predisposition that s/he will more likely become a follower or a victim, can only be found out through a more fine-grained analysis that includes the differentiation of personality types and forms of socialisation. Nevertheless, one can maintain the assertion that 'exclusivist strategies like rigidification of norms' are to be expected. And that these strategies develop in the heads of single actors and through the communication between them – provided that they actually do develop – should also be indisputable. In this respect this 'rather macroscopic' theory incorporates micro-sociological, or 'microscopic', elements.

The discussion of the relationship between power and resources in the right column of Table 10.1 – containing short descriptions of the 'resulting scenario' – remains a bit sketchy. In case 2 the possibility is discussed that the resource in question is power. In case 9, members of the group of power-holders meet the requirements for obtaining entitlements to different degrees and correspondingly the access to the resources turns out to be different for the individual members of this group. Therefore power here is not a resource but a means for asserting the entitlement to a resource. There are differences in the way sociologists formulate their discussions about power. In decision theories of the rational-choice type, the control of resources is equated with power; yet in the next breath power is discussed as a resource in and of itself. Neither the one nor the other conception of power can or should be done away with. Whoever speaks of power as a resource, however, has to be aware that power is a resource of a different kind from oil or water; it is a resource for gaining access to other resources.[3]

The theory of value implicit in Table 10.1 has also not been elaborated. A resource is not scarce as such, but only with regard to the interest that actors have in it. While the interests of powerless players can be disregarded, the interests of powerful actors have to be taken seriously. Through the interests of powerful players a resource becomes truly scarce and more desirable, not only in its own right but also as a medium of exchange for other resources. In short, in this way the resource attains a high value, and 'powerful' actors achieve their power through the control of further resources. Here the argument becomes somewhat recursive: we come into an infinite loop. What is clear is that power is not an individual disposition (although individual dispositions play a role in the acquisition and maintenance of power), but is the result of interactions.[4]

Different Levels of Rigidification in Islam

I now move on to Islamic societies: first to some examples in which Sufism plays a role, then to modern forms of rigidification of Islam which reject Sufism. I will have to disappoint those who expect new explanations attached to these differences: the basic patterns that I find are the same in Sufi and anti-Sufi and even in Islamic and

---

3.   That resources stand in an instrumental (possibly also mutual) relationship to each other, or, to be more precise, that the control of a resource makes it possible to achieve another one, is nothing unusual. It also goes without saying that power is not only a means for acquiring resources but that the precondition of power is that resources can be disposed of.

4.   The last three paragraphs have been stimulated through comments by Joachim Görlich.

non-Islamic contexts. The rules concerning purity and ritual practice become more demanding as resources (affiliation to a privileged group, political leadership) become more contested, irrespective of the variety of Islamic or non-Islamic beliefs the people in question hold.

The rigidification of ritual requirements for power-holders occurs when potential power-holders become too numerous and an inner circle is defined to exclude some (case 10 in Table 10.1, which in a minimalist version of the table could also have been omitted, because it is really just a transition from case no. 1 to case no. 8).

The term 'rigidification' does not sound like correct English to some of the native speakers of that language whom I have consulted, and cannot be found in smaller dictionaries. My computer continues to underline it as wrong. I mean it as a nominalisation of 'to rigidify', if such a word exists, or 'making more rigid'. Let me briefly explain why I feel the need for this unusual term. Islam has repeatedly gone through phases in which the correct performance of ritual detail was emphasised and in which the religion, for its common adherents at least, was broken down into a set of rules. The keeping of these rules was not entrusted to the individual believer but watched over by the state. A certain selective and scripturalist reading of Islam was thus made to penetrate all spheres of life because rules came to apply to all spheres of life.

This process has, in recent writings, often been called 'Islamisation' of a society. But this term, though mostly used by critical writers of a secularist orientation, inadvertently adopts the perspective of the 'fundamentalists' they seek to criticise. The latter would also say that anyone who does not share their interpretation of the shariah and their practice of Islam is not a real Muslim and needs 'Islamisation'. But as I am not a theologian but a social scientist I do not wish to subscribe to this normative concept, or to suggest by its use that societies which have perceived themselves as Islamic for a thousand years or so are only now undergoing 'Islamisation', or to comment on whether one variety of Islam is better or more Islamic than another. But what I can observe, and what I do not hesitate to state, is that some forms of Islam are more rigid in their dress code and other ritual requirements than others and I therefore call the process that leads to their emergence and growth 'rigidification'. Another term which I occasionally use in this context is 'intensification'. I like it for similar reasons: it is close to the descriptive level and relatively free of normative undertones. The two terms, of course, are not synonyms: the intensification of religious belief and practice may but need not go along with its acquisition of a more rigid or standardised character.

The terms purity/purification and rigidification here, however, are used as near synonyms. This is not arbitrary or coincidental; also in the emic belief systems under study, the ideas of physical cleanliness, ritual purity, and obedience to the law are closely interconnected. From Rahman's instructions about how to be a Muslim (1980: 70–74), we learn that the ablutions are not just a preparation for the prayer but can be regarded as an important part of it. And we have seen above that even the non-Islamic Rendille undo the effects of a breach of a taboo by a kind of washing.

Sufism

As Evans-Pritchard (1954) pointed out in *The Sanusi of Cyrenaica*, Sufism started as a reaction to scripturalist and ritualistic tendencies in mainstream Islam, which left too little room for religious enthusiasm and the ecstatic dimension of religion. It was also from its beginnings influenced by non-Islamic forms of religious asceticism, like that of Christian and Buddhist monks, and possibly by yoga.[5] It is, therefore, no surprise that Sufism is capable of going a long way in adjusting to local cultures and in responding to the spiritual needs of people of different pre-Islamic origins.

On the other hand, Sufi *tariiqas*[6] have also formulated their methods for reaching salvation in mutually exclusive and competitive terms: they have claimed to be the only path to salvation, or at least the one which is a thousand times safer than any other path. Their leaders, especially in nineteenth-century Africa, have demanded an authority which was only short of prophethood in that they did not call themselves 'prophet'. Claiming that title is, according to the teachings of Islam, not possible after Muhammad, 'the seal of the prophets'. Here we find more and more rigour and an increasingly narrower definition of who is a proper Muslim. Obedience to a Sufi sheikh becomes a prerequisite for being a proper Muslim. 'If you have no other sheikh, the devil will be your sheikh,' the saying goes. This development of Sufi movements can be seen as an intensification process, in the course of which they became ritually more elaborate and rigid and politically more demanding of exclusive loyalty.

I start with a short description of a contemporary Sufi community in northern Kenya, which has not gone through such an intensification process: it liberally incorporates pre-Islamic beliefs and practices. Travelling in Sudan and reading about it, I have not encountered there any branch of Sufism which has developed the same degree of syncretism. The closest Sudanese parallels I can think of are the women-dominated *zar* possession cults (Boddy 1989). From this case of a relatively open and heterogeneous community I shall go on to cases where Islam, both Sufi and non-Sufi, has become rigidified.

The Sakuye Case

Ecstatic religion is linked by some theorists (e.g., Lewis 1978) to deprivation. The Sakuye example seems to fit this theory. The Sakuye (see Figure 1, p. 1) were Oromo-speaking camel herders when they were converted to Islam in the first decades of the twentieth century. When the British held a referendum in northern Kenya in 1962 to find out whether its population wanted to belong to Kenya, which was then on its road to independence, or to the newly independent and newly united Republic of Somalia, the Sakuye preferred Somalia, a country of Muslim pastoralists like themselves. Although this was the majority position, that stretch of country was nonetheless allotted to Kenya, because negotiations with the Kenyan delegation in London had, by the time the referendum was over, reached a stage which left no

---

5.   See Schimmel on the influence of Christianity and Buddhism (1995 [1985]: 13) and on yoga (ibid.: 28).

6.   A *tariiqa* (literally 'method') is a religious brotherhood. Purists may forgive the anglicised plural *tariiqas*. The proper Arabic plural is turuq.

room for dividing the territory of the future nation. From the start, after independence and referendum, the inhabitants of the north and their new central Kenyan masters knew what to expect from each other, and a civil war, known as the *shifta* emergency, immediately broke out. The camel herds of the Sakuye were machine-gunned. The remainder of the livestock perished when the Sakuye were kept in camps ('keeps'), the surroundings of which were quickly overgrazed because these camps did not move. There are tales of atrocities and random killings when the Sakuye were marched to the east by their recently created enemies, the loyalist Boran.

In the early 1970s, the impoverished remnants of the Sakuye gathered at Dabel, a group of hills below the escarpment of the Ethiopian plateau on the Kenyan side. There was a little more rain there than in the lower parts of the lowlands and agriculture was just possible, albeit with low returns and high risks. A holy man found underground water and new wells were dug.

Able-bodied younger men earned their livelihood by poaching. Some of them died of thirst on the endless plains, trying to smuggle leopard skins into Somalia. Many young men were unable to pay the bridewealth. Had the parents of Sakuye girls insisted on bridewealth a high proportion of them would have been given to non-Sakuye suitors and many young Sakuye men would have ended in involuntary bachelorhood. To avert this situation, bridewealth was abolished and ethnic endogamy was practised for a number of years.

The camel-oriented rituals, which the Sakuye had previously practised in much the same form as the neighbouring Gabra and Rendille (see Schlee 1989a: Ch. 4), had become meaningless after the loss of their camels. Their still rather nominal affiliation to Islam (to which they may have converted under pressure by their Somali neighbours) did not satisfy their spiritual needs. The gap was filled by the Husayniyya, a Sufi order named after the legendary Sheikh Hussein (Husayn) of Bale in south-eastern Ethiopia (Andrzejewski 1972, 1974; Baxter 1987; Braukämper 1989).

At Dabel, this order was represented by Abba Ganna. This name means 'father of the rainy season': more specifically, of the spring equinoctial rains, the big rains which also lend their name to the 'year', i.e., 'father of wealth, father of plenty'. It alludes to or derives its inspiration from the title of a hagiography of Sheikh Hussein published in Cairo, *Rabii'ul quluub*, 'The Springtime of Hearts'. The souls of saints can travel across time and space and meet other saints, living and dead. This is well known from Sufi legends from all over the Islamic world. In Dabel, however, at least in popular belief, the Arabic concept of *awliya* (sing. *waali* – 'holy man, saint') is mixed with the Boran (Oromo) concept *ayaan* – 'spirit' in general, including 'animal spirit' (Bartels 1983).

When I met Abba Ganna in the 1980s, he was an old man of enormous bodily proportions. He lived in permanent seclusion behind a curtain and was accompanied by a son who held a large umbrella to shield him from the sun and from sight when he left his hut. The number of his wives was kept at the legal maximum: four. When he divorced one he immediately took a young bride as a replacement.

There is a story that once, after the Sakuye had acquired some livestock again, Abba Ganna did not want their camps to move far away from Dabel. Nevertheless, some camps did so and were harassed in the outlying pastures by lions until they retraced their steps. This story is told as proof that Abba Ganna's soul has the ability to communicate with lions or spirit lions.

Abba Ganna's career follows the classical pattern of leaders of possession cults the world over, no matter how diverse they are in terms of religious backgrounds. It starts with his own disease, which was diagnosed as spirit possession at Anajinna, the holy site of the Husayniyya in Bale. He then developed ways of living with the spirits and finally the ability to communicate with them at will. Thus, he also qualified as a healer of others whose diseases were attributed to possession. He became famous, as both a healer and a diviner, and people visited him from as far as Mombasa. In his final years he rarely participated in any healing sessions himself. He had his 'corporals' for that.

The ideas about possession and the practices of its treatment greatly resemble the *ayaana* cults elsewhere in the Oromo-speaking world (see Dahl 1989 on the Waso, 250 km to the south) and the *zar* cults common throughout north-eastern Africa. As with *zar* possession most of the afflicted among the Sakuye of Dabel are women, but there is no preponderance of women among the healers. Dealing with spirits is not a gender-specific affair.

Some spirits demand blood through the mouths of the possessed, which requires the bleeding of domestic stock for the patients to drink. (Before their conversion to Islam, blood taken from stock was a regular part of Sakuye diet.) This is not regarded as a breach of Islamic food avoidance rules, since the spirit, not the patient, is considered to consume the blood. And the spirit may well be a pagan and thus perfectly entitled to his share of blood. The idea that the spirit, and not the patient, consumes the food it demands was illustrated to me by the story of a woman whose spirit had just demanded a huge kettle full of coffee, which she promptly drank. Then the spirit had enough and left her. When the woman became herself again, she was thirsty and wanted to drink more.

The Sakuye also find other excuses for drinking blood. The slightest health disorder is enough to label blood as 'medicine' rather than 'food' and thus render it *halal* (lawful) in the eyes of the Sakuye.

Other spirits demand *hadar* dances, as they are also held on Islamic holidays. These are ecstatic drum sessions in which men and women join after dark in large groups, dancing shoulder to shoulder, with numerous participants, mostly women, falling into trances. It is not regarded as orthodox by bookish sheikhs.

This does not mean that there is little knowledge about Islam at Dabel. One of the sons of Abba Ganna is well versed in classical Arabic, in which he is also able to converse.[7] Other members of the community have travelled far and received formal Islamic education. When I once donated a set of volumes of Bukhari's and Muslim's *ahaadith*, an authoritative collection of tales about the Prophet, to the community, a quarrel broke out between those able to read it. There was even talk of splitting the set and appropriating single volumes individually. What I mean to illustrate here is not the

---

7.   Often non-Arab African Muslims master Arabic only in what Owens (1995) by a computer analogy calls 'the graphic mode', i.e., they reproduce texts without analysing them, and then, of course, they cannot rearrange the words to express ideas of their own.

lack of knowledge about Islam, but the fact that Islamic scholarship and syncretic folk beliefs and practices exist side by side among the Sakuye. In the same family one can find a long-haired mystic with a preference for ecstatic practices and a quiet scholar.

We can summarise that in this setting of relatively new converts to Islam a variety of beliefs and practices exist side by side. Competition over leadership is low. People are free to express different ideas and to gather followers. From this case of non-intensified practice associated with low competition for leadership, we shall turn to intensified and politicised forms of Sufism in the next section.

Sufism and Jihad in Sudanic Africa

Jihad movements, led by Sufi sheikhs who rose through Sufi networks, have occurred throughout the Sudanic belt of Africa from the Senegal to the Nilotic Sudan and beyond to Somalia during the nineteenth and twentieth centuries. They include the jihad of Sheikh 'Uthmaan dan Fodio (Shehu Osman dan Fodio, ibn Fuudi, and other spellings), which led to the foundation of the Caliphate of Sokoto, later incorporated into Nigeria, with its dependency in Adamawa and in what is now Cameroon. This movement later merged with the Sudanese Mahdiyya because of the expected coming of the Mahdi on the Nile and later, after the occupation of the Caliphate by the infidels, the hegira from Nigeria to Sudan in the first decade of the twentieth century. Other such jihad movements include that of the Tijaani Sheikh Al Hajj 'Umar Tall between the Senegal and the Niger. Descendants of Al Hajj 'Umar and his followers are today also found in compact settlements in Sudan and they have preserved their affiliation to the Tijaaniyya *tariiqa* and their jihadist memories. Such movements, which extended their spiritual and military power well into the twentieth century, include the Sanusiyya in what would become Libya and Chad and the 'dervishes' of Muhammad 'Abdille Hassan (Salihiyya) in the future Somalia and Ogadeen.

In the contemporary political situation these movements, often with a political party attached, continue to exert influence. In Nigeria the 'northern' emirs still have much political weight. In Sudan the family of the Mahdi and the rival Khatmiyya are still affluent and powerful religious aristocracies, although now in opposition and partly in exile.[8] The Islamist movement now in power, the National Islamic Front, is not derived from a Sufi order. It would be interesting to see how far it resembles a Sufi order structurally in its cell structure and the highly personalised leader–follower relationships.

The Wahaabiyya of Saudi Arabia is not a Sufi order. It is quite opposed to Sufi practices and to any religious practices that cannot be directly derived from the Koran and be traced back to the time of the Prophet. It is, however, sociologically

---

8. The text here reflects the time of writing. Although that does not affect the present argument, it can be updated: in 1997 Saadig al Mahdi, leader of the Umma party was based in exile and formed an alliance with the SPLA (*Southern Sudanese Sudan People's Liberation Army*) to join the armed struggle against the government of Sudan. Later he struck a deal to return to Sudan as part of the legal opposition. The Umma party then underwent a split and a part of it formed a coalition with the ruling party. Since the 2005 peace agreement also the SPLA is part of a government of national unity.

equivalent to all the Sufi-based movements that we have just enumerated: it is a politicised form of Islam, it has a ruling family, and it was the nucleus of a state. Through Saudi petrodollars Wahaabi influence can be felt and seen in the shape of new mosques in much of the Islamic world today.

I am now going to examine some shared features of these movements. These will be traced in terms of their cultural history, but they also lend themselves to sociological comparison. There are models for establishing holiness and leadership on a competitive basis and ways to make the followers feel themselves among the elect, and to exclude Muslims who do not toe the line of the holy man from the inner circle or even to deny their status as Muslims.

What most strikes the reader who familiarises himself or herself with jihadist movements from Senegambia to Indonesia are the frequent similarities of these movements. These are due to two factors: a common model and mutual contacts. The common pattern on which these movements model themselves is the life of the Prophet. The mutual contacts have mainly been established through the haj, which has united pilgrims from Morocco to the Malay Archipelago on a yearly basis for centuries: an instance of globalisation which predates anything fashionable sociological theorists of 'globalisation', with their exclusive Euro-American focus, appear to be aware of. Wandering saints also spent months and years, often on the way to or back from Mecca, visiting each other and worldly rulers. Often the two socio-types, saint and warrior king, were combined in the same person. These people were linked to each other by the spiritual descent lines between master and disciple and sometimes also by actual kinship resulting from marriages between their families.

There are, thus, two modes of transmission of shared elements (from a common source and from each other), which can, of course, occur simultaneously in a variety of mixtures. But one can also distinguish two kinds of shared features: the direct borrowings and the analogies.

First an example of direct borrowing. When the Prophet had fled from Mecca to Medina, he had two types of followers: the 'refugees', *muhaajiruun*, who had fled with him to Mecca or joined him at Medina from Mecca, and the Medinese helpers, the *ansaar*. Many leaders of later jihads had, at some point in their struggles, to withdraw from one place to some other, and this was invariably called a hegira. Whoever joined the leader on the flight became a *muhaajir* and whoever joined him in the new place a *naasir* (sing. of *ansaar*). This is a direct transfer of names and institutions without much change of meaning.[9]

Borrowing by analogy requires additional steps. Words need to be changed as concepts are taken out of their original context and transferred into another one. What constitutes the resulting analogy is the similarity of the figures of thought in the original and the new context and the identity of a part of the words used, which is sufficient to evoke the original phrase. An example is the description of Ahmad at-Tijaani, the founder of the Tijaaniyya, as *khatm al wilaaya* – 'the seal of sainthood'. This phrase is, of course, coined after the designation of Muhammad as *khatm al*

---

9.   On the hegira of al Hajj 'Umar from Fouta Jalon to Dinguiray in Guinea, see Abun-Nasr (1965: 112); on the *ansaar* of the Sudanese Mahdi, see Holt (1961: 88).

anbiya' – 'the seal of the prophets', meaning the last prophet. A strict reading of 'the seal of sainthood' by this analogy would imply that there would be no saints after Ahmad at-Tijaani. Since later personalities, like as-Sanusi, could not be denied sainthood, this position was gradually modified. Followers of the Tijaaniyya, however, would still regard Ahmad at-Tijaani as the perfect model and complete embodiment of *wilaaya*. Later saints will derive their inspiration from him. 'There may be other *wali*s after him, but none would surpass or supersede him' (Abun-Nasr 1965: 30–32).

Metaphors of sealing and closing point to the exclusivist element of politicised Sufism. Only one way is the true way or at least the best way, so much so that no other way is worth taking. This is also reflected in numerical calculations about the efficiency of Sufi ritual formulas. About one such formula, the *salaat al faatih* of the Tijaaniyya, it is claimed that the Prophet, who appeared to Ahmad at-Tijaani, had informed him 'of its great efficacy in the remission of sins'. The Shaikh of the Tijaaniyya also claimed that the Prophet informed him that the merit of reciting it once was 'equivalent to that of the recitation of all prayers of glorification to God (*tasbih*) that have ever been said in the universe, all Sufi prayers of remembrance of God (*dhikr*), every invocation (*du'a*) long or short, and the [recitation of the] Qur'an six thousand times' (Abun-Nasr 1965: 51). While the numbers involved are reminiscent of astronomy, the type of reasoning resembles business administration. If one is conscious of costs and benefits, why should one recite long texts with little efficacy of salvation instead of short texts with a many times higher salvation impact? All other forms of Muslim piety appear as rather futile in comparison with the irresistible magic of the Tijaani formula, if one accepts these numerical proportions.

As the sheikh was in possession of the right formula for everything, followers had to show absolute obedience and loyalty. It was believed that God through His grace would admit to paradise anybody who followed the saint and would lead astray anybody who ceased to love the saint, so that such a person would die as an infidel and thus go to hell. Deviation from the path prescribed by the sheikh was thus regarded as deviation from the path to heaven. This comes close to the tendency among leading representatives of politicised Islam, even today, of condemning people and making statements about who is going to heaven and who is going to hell, instead of leaving this decision to God, as the Koran would suggest.

This monopolisation of the truth and the exclusion from salvation of everybody who did not subscribe to it as well as from worldly resources was, of course, directed against other Muslims. That non-Muslims would go to hell went without saying. These exclusion strategies against other Muslims, however, went beyond marking them as bad Muslims: they contested their very status as Muslims. One problem, which all saint-warriors of the nineteenth century in the Sudanic belt of Africa faced, was how to declare jihad against fellow Muslims, the normal condition for waging jihad being that it is directed against non-Muslims who have rejected a legal summons to convert.

The commonly held view is that anyone who has uttered the two articles of faith, the unity of God and the affirmation that Muhammad is His Prophet, is a Muslim. By calling a Muslim a non-believer, one might even risk placing oneself outside the fold of Islam, because calling a Muslim a *kaafir* amounts to equating Islam with *kufr*, with unbelief. How did the jihad leaders of the nineteenth century overcome this problem? 'Uthmaan dan Fodio and his son Muhammad Bello set the precedent when they declared war against the sultan of Bornu, Muhammad al Kanemi. They reasoned that al Kanemi supported the Hausa sultans against them. These Hausa regarded themselves as Muslims as well, but the leaders of the Fulani jihad denounced them as unbelievers because they performed certain pagan rites and anyone who supports pagans against a Muslim ruler is to be regarded a pagan himself.

This model was later followed by al Hajj 'Umar Tall when he declared war against Ahmadu Shaikhu, the king of Massina, the Defender of the Faith, the third in a line of Muslim rulers who had fought the pagans. Some of their converts were found by al Hajj 'Umar still to worship idols. As these people had fought against him, he constructed the same case of a Muslim supporting pagans against a Muslim ruler against Ahmadu as 'Usman dan Fodio and Muhammad Bello had constructed against al-Kanemi (Abun-Nasr 1965: 122–124).

Narrow definitions of who is a Muslim were also promoted in nineteenth-century Africa by the practice of slavery. As Muslims were not allowed to enslave other Muslims, large numbers of converts threatened the potential slave supply. The further progress Islam made, and the more people were converted, the stronger the argument became to separate 'real' Muslims by some set of criteria from nominal Muslims, and to declare the latter as unbelievers, and eligible for enslavement (Meillassoux 1986). All these examples from nineteenth-century Africa have shown how competition between different Islamic movements and their leaders, as well as the economic consequences of the spread of Islam, can be linked to the rigidification of ritual practices and distinctions between purer forms of Islam and less pure, which often came to be labelled as non-Islamic.

Glimpses of Egypt and Sudan in the 1990s

Now we turn to quite recent developments in two Muslim countries which are going to show that the links between status competition, political power, and claims to ritual purity are as robust now as they were 100 or 200 years ago. In recent decades, the dominant forms of Islam, which demand strict adherence, no longer have anything to do with Sufism. In Sudan the two parties which dominated politics after independence in 1956 or prevented politics from taking place by blocking each other have been out of power since 1989. Both had their historical origins in Sufi orders and their charismatic leaders. Both are now referred to as the 'traditional parties' and their leaders as representatives of a 'religious aristocracy' which has been overthrown. The new leaders have discarded 'tradition'. Their brand of Islam – and now I am speaking about the ideological level and not that of practice, which sometimes falls short of lofty ideals – can be seen as both minimalist and maximalist. They are minimalist in so far as they want to purify Islam from all historical accretions and go back to a scripturalist reading of the Koran and the Sunna, the practices of the Prophet according to authenticated *ahaadith* (sing. *hadiith*, 'tale, account') as the only sources of the shariah (apart from their own political agenda as an unnamed third source of inspiration). The 'maximalist' element is that there is no limit to the demand of a formalistic form of piety, which penetrates all domains of life, and the shariah is transformed to an all pervading force of regulation. This is a new development, since even in the classical periods of Islam, *qanuun*, the law of the ruler, and *aadat*, customary law, which was acknowledged as long as it was not in direct contradiction with the shariah had substantial roles to fill as well (Rahman 1982: 30).

While in Egypt the Islamist discourse is critical of the government, which is perceived as Westernised and morally depraved, in Sudan the government itself follows the Islamist line of reasoning, as do some of its critics, who see to what degree power has corrupted the Islamist cause and now criticise the Islamist government on Islamist grounds. Since the takeover of power by the present National Islamic Front (NIF) regime in 1989, the NIF has succeeded in monopolising both political power and business. Opponents have been weakened by the destruction of their businesses. Exclusionist discourses in a yet more violent setting, Algeria, have recently been studied by Kaiser (2002).

Enough of high-level politics. In everyday life and in the interaction between the generations within families we can observe status competition and the struggle for spaces of action as well. Just as in the political sphere, these domestic or micro-social forms of competition are also pervaded by ideas of purity and devotion.

While in many Islamic societies, the *Mawluud*, the birthday of the prophet, is an important festival, these modern Islamists (and the Wahaabi in Saudi Arabia before them) reject it. This makes perfect sense in the light of the Sunna: the Prophet did not celebrate his birthday himself, and therefore this practice cannot be commended. In a study about female lifestyles in Cairo, in which Werner (1997) describes the various stages through which young students pass when becoming 'devout', she mentions a discussion about birthdays. A young woman with the intention of gathering strength for becoming more 'devout' wanted to celebrate her birthday. A friend who had adopted a more complete form of veiling and reached a higher stage of 'devoutness' tried to dissuade her from this and to 'convince her to abandon this pagan habit'. Werner goes on to explain: 'In the Islamist camp there is a discussion going on about legitimate and illegitimate feasts. There exists a strong faction whose members vote only to celebrate the original Islamic feasts' (Werner 1997: 132, fn. 128). Of course an Egyptian student would celebrate her birthday according to the universal Christian calendar while the *Mawluud* of the Prophet and all other Islamic festivals follow the Muslim calendar. This marks one kind of event clearly from the other, so that no one would be able to assume that the birthday of an ordinary person could be ascribed any religious significance, which could be construed as heterodox religious practice. But the logic behind this is different: any festivity, no matter how innocent, has to be forbidden unless it is explicitly recommended by Islam. The shariah is not just used to cleanse human lives of everything forbidden, but to restrict human lives to those things explicitly recommended by it. Celebrating birthdays or not is just one indicator of different sets of ideas about the functions of the Law.

Hierarchies are established with reference to standards of moral purity within groups of students and between them. The 'normal' female students, i.e., those who have not adopted any of the more rigid forms of veiling, seem to have the more difficult game to play. They have to balance the requirements of appearing attractive to young men in mixed-gender groups with those of a sexual morality which, even among these 'Westernised' students, appears fairly restrictive if compared with contemporary Europe. Among the women-only Islamist student groups, the direction is clear: one adopts more and more restrictive forms of practice stage after stage, as one feels fit for them. There is no balance to be struck. Qualification for a high status in the mixed-gender groups would appear to require finding something the Islamists would regard as impossible to find: a compromise between the requirements of God and those of the devil (see Werner 1997: 138).

Islamist purity discourses are also used in the competition for authority between generations. The authority of the parental generation, which grew up in a much more secular and liberal cultural atmosphere, is challenged by the students. While lip service is paid to parental authority in accordance with the teachings of the Prophet, wherever the demands of the parents diverge from that of the religiously oriented peer group, they are perceived as conflicting with the will of God. As God's orders overrule those of the parents, this line of reasoning opens new spaces of self-determination for the members of the younger generation by pushing back the boundaries of the domain of parental authority (Werner 1997: 221).

Another field of application of such discourses is in cross-gender strategies. Young unmarried women use Islamic norms to make their boyfriends 'respect boundaries'. In one case the sudden adoption of a complete form of veiling led to a temporary breach in the relationship with a boyfriend who had been too persistent in his demands for sexual favours (ibid.: 135–138). Chastity, to the point of denying superficial forms of tenderness and jocular verbal exchanges, and the religious reasoning behind these forms of restrictive behaviour are used to increase the value of young women, both as respectable persons, and on the marriage market. There are no statistics to show whether this strategy is successful in procuring the type of husband desired. We have seen that the female students frequenting the mixed-gender peer groups pursue a different strategy: maintaining erotic tension without giving in to sexual demands. The strategy of the young women who adopt the fuller forms of veiling, however, poses a clear alternative: withholding and hiding female charm either helps in domesticating men and transforming them into responsible husbands or helps in frustrating them to such a degree that one gets rid of them.

The stages of 'devoutness' through which these young women pass are ordered by them along a numerical scale from 0 per cent Muslim to 100 per cent Muslim. We here, against a rather different theological background, find the same accountant-like attitude as above among the Tijaani of the nineteenth-century, who calculate the efficiency of their prayer formulas. Here is an example by which criteria the young women students locate each other on such a scale: 'While Jihan respected Shuruq's knowledge of Islam, she took the fact that Shuruq didn't wear a *hijab* as a shortcoming, and in a discussion on this topic Jihan evaluated Shuruq's degree of religiosity as only 65 percent (which was still more than the 55 percent rating which she gave herself)' (Werner 1997: 130).

A study from another north-east African capital, Khartoum, provides additional illustrations of these female strategies (Nageeb 2004).

These studies analyse Islamist discourses and their strategic use on the micro level, in couples, between parents and children, and in groups of students on a campus. Werner even analyses the power play within a group of siblings (1997: 117 ff.). This focus on everyday interaction among ordinary people is a necessary complement to our findings about purity and power at the level of politics and the state in the preceding section about the jihadist movements in nineteenth-century Africa, and also to what has been said about present-day politics in the Islamic world, which also abounds with power-sensitive purification discourses.

Conclusion

In the growth zone of the Islamic world, along its periphery, one might observe two phases in the history of interaction between Islamic and non-Islamic cultures. These phases might not always be easy to separate and they might coexist synchronically in neighbouring areas, but it still makes sense to distinguish them analytically as types of interaction where one tends to precede the other in time.

In the first phase of expansion Islam tends to tolerate and even accommodate many pre-Islamic elements. Islam is still weak and needs to pay for being accepted.[10] It comes half the way to bridging the cultural gap between the Muslim minority and the host society. Later, when at least nominal affiliation to Islam has become the rule, more purist and more exclusivist attitudes tend to be adopted. Politically, i.e., in terms of legitimation of claims to power, this makes perfect sense. If everybody is a Muslim, such claims cannot merely be based on being a Muslim. One needs to distinguish different degrees of virtue and claim the higher echelons for oneself.

This, however, is not a one-way road. Where Islam is well established but of a 'traditional', 'liberal', or 'lax' kind (depending on the values of who speaks), some people react to rigidification by complying, others react by resisting. In such settings we almost invariably find rigorists who claim influence or power on the basis of their stricter adherence to beliefs and practices, but these are not invariably liked. People defend the joys of life by passive resistance or even with good theological reasoning ('God cannot have given us life to spend it in sadness and boredom', or the like). Where Islam is new, there may be controversies over whether or not the local beer is to be considered '*hamr*' (literally 'palm wine'), and therefore forbidden; where Islam has long been established, it is generally accepted that all kinds of alcoholic beverages fall under the Koranic interdiction of *hamr*; and where it is undergoing rigidification one finds people who want to extend this interdiction to all kinds of narcotics, including *qat*[11] and tobacco. Other forms of enjoyment can also be more or less severely restricted, and this may provoke resistance.

In Somalia, the edicts of Islamic Courts banning *qat* were unpopular among the general population (ICG 2005: 7). Yet, at the same time, the acceptance of the

---

10. I owe this phrase to Jamil Abun-Nasr, oral communication, early 1980s.
11. *Qat* (Amharic: *chat*; Somali: *qaad*; Swahili: *miraa*; Lat.: *Catha edulis*) is a mild narcotic. Leaves, the softer part of twigs, and/or the bark of the *qat* tree are chewed. Its heavy use leads to long periods without food and sleep and to (mental) health and economic problems (see below Chapter 12).

Islamic Court militias was positively affected by their abstention from *qat*, as a critic of these courts grudgingly admitted: 'People like them because they don't chew *qaad*, they don't rape, and they are more disciplined' (ICG 2005: 20). When the Islamic Courts targeted pornography, this was widely accepted. But when, in 2005, 'they began raiding and closing down mixed-gender parties and cinemas showing "Bollywood"[12] films', they met resistance from angry patrons or armed cinema guards, with the result that Islamic Court militia men were killed or wounded and some of their armed vehicles captured (ICG 2006: 11).

Sufism illustrates the entire spectrum, from a form of Islam that is responsive to ideas and practices from outside, to one exhibiting the most rigid and exclusive tendencies. Theologically it may be a special form of Islam – mystical Islam, as it is sometimes called – but sociologically it is not. We may find the same tendencies of inclusion and exclusion in Sufism and in other streams of Islam. In the Somali case just cited, the Islamists tend to be of a Salafi or Wahaabi persuasion, hostile to all local customs that have developed since the time of the Prophet and which thereby cannot be traced to the Koran or the Sunna. The adherents of Sufi traditions depict themselves as moderates (see above and Chapter 12).

Politics at all levels, from the small face-to-face group to the state and the international arena, seems to be a major determinant of where on a scale of piety Muslims locate themselves or are located. In a wider context we can say that high standards of purity or excellence in ritual matters or the moral field are closely linked to exclusionist strategies in power games not only in Islam, but among adherents of all sorts of belief systems.

The examples we have discussed come not only from Muslim settings. They are not exhaustive or systematically chosen. I took my own fieldwork experience in north-eastern Africa since 1974 as a starting point and then went on to include literature about neighbouring areas and cases further afield in Africa that I happen to have read about. There is room for more systematic testing of the explanations given here. All these examples, however, suggest that standards of ritual purity or morality are density-related. The more people compete for a resource, a status, or an office, the more rigid the standards to be met appear to become. Standards of ritual purity should not be confused with moral standards; they may be integrated into systems of moral reasoning, or not. Obedience to a rule may simply be explained by reference to God or custom as the source of the rule, or by pointing to what is considered proof of its efficacy: one has so far not suffered misfortune while following the rule. The correlation between the ritual requirement met and the status or power achieved exists irrespective of the complexity or simplicity or complete absence of doctrines attached to the ritual requirements. Classical sociologists (Durkheim 1984 [1893]; Weber 1990 [1922]) ascribe a great deal of social and economic force to elaborate beliefs and moral convictions. In the light of the present findings, one might suspect that much of this is based on an over-sophisticated

---

12. Musical films produced in Bombay (Mumbai) target family audiences and are regarded as completely harmless in most parts of the world. Due to the particularities of Indian women's fashion, however, the navel of the dancers is often visible.

model of human beings. If meeting ritual requirements and sticking to rules have the same effects with and without elaborate beliefs associated with these practices, one can disregard the beliefs to some extent, or at least look at their impact on practical life with a higher dose of scepticism.

This finding, that belief does not matter, is not meant to imply that people do not argue in theological terms. Of course they do. And it would be in contradiction to what we have explained above about plausibility of identity constructs as a condition for their acceptance if we assumed that these beliefs do not need to have some coherence and logic (although some theologies tolerate significant departures from logic), or at least psychological appeal and persuasiveness. I am only saying that it is not necessary to determine the degree of belief in order to figure out where rigidification and political exclusion are taking place. Almost always the more easily observable proliferation of rules and ritual requirements is sufficient as an indicator of such a situation.

It is assumed to be universally valid that in cases of variations in rigidity the more rigorous tend to claim moral and political privileges for themselves. It goes without saying that it is not the only sociological factor influencing (and being influenced by) religious developments. Other processes can have very similar effects.

Where law enforcement agencies are absent (as in Somalia), or where their involvement is undesirable because transactions are illegal (as in smuggling), or where transactions are huge and difficult to control (as in high finance), trust is more important than in other situations. The recent rise of more rigid forms of Islamic practice in Somalia has been explained by the circumstance that Somali traders needed to build up trustful relations with business partners in the Gulf states (Marchal 2004: 115). Somalia, stateless as it is, has developed into 'the largest duty-free shop' in Africa (see below, Chapter 12):

> Mogadishu has become a free port for the whole region, where goods are brought from Saudi Arabia, Yemen and Dubai and then re-exported to Kenya, Ethiopia and even Uganda. The Gulf business class has been a source of inspiration for many emerging Somali traders who often become more religious, even militantly so, in order to build the trust necessary to get access to their counterparts on the eastern side of the Red Sea. (Marchal 2004: 115)

It is therefore no surprise under these conditions that the variant of Islam that is dominant in the Arabian Peninsula (Wahaabi) has determined the direction of rigidification.

Trust is normally associated with closeness, although it may also involve the maintenance of distance (no harassment, no exaggerated inquisitiveness, etc.). Another way of managing distance, generally by keeping a greater social distance, has to do with the 'trader's dilemma'. Traders often need to define themselves as somehow unattached to their social environment. They form separate communities so as to protect their profits from demands for redistribution. Conversion to a different religion or sect might be helpful if the traders are not already among the numerous religious or ethnic minorities to start with. On the other hand, to be charitable and supportive to the wider society is also essential here, and protects against discrimination and ethnic violence. Traders need to be distant enough not to have to give credit where they do not want to and where they cannot afford it, and yet they have to be close enough not to be perceived as complete strangers or enemies. Religious prestige helps in striking this balance (Evers and Schrader 1994; Evers and Schlee 1995).

Trust, the management of distance, and the discourse of exclusion based on purity are not incompatible or mutually exclusive explanations. One can easily imagine a case – say of a rich man going into politics – where the three factors combine. Mogadishu before the Ethiopian invasion in December 2006 seems to have been a case where, in the absence of a state, Islamic rigidification and business sponsoring Islamic Courts have produced just such a combination, which seems to have led to a degree of order.

Chapter 11

Language and Ethnicity

Ethnicity is a form of collective identity, and thus belongs to the same class of phenomena as religious affiliation, lineage, clan, or class membership.[1] It is the awareness of belonging to an ethnic group, and the belief that others belong to other groups of this kind. Ethnic groups differ from other groups, like voluntary associations or age sets, by the following criteria: they comprise people of both genders and all ages, or, as Elwert (1989) puts it, entire families. Even where exogamy extends far beyond the nuclear family, ethnic groups comprise sufficient exogamous units to guarantee self-sufficiency in biological reproduction: marriage partners can be provided within the ethnic unit. This means that ethnic groups have the potential to recruit members by birth, and, indeed, that is how they recruit most of their members. It does not mean that this is the only form of recruitment and that there is no ethnic conversion.

The criterion of self-sufficiency in biological reproduction sets the lower limit of the size of an ethnic group. The upper limit is set by the criterion of alterity. As ethnic groups define themselves and are defined in contradistinction to other such groups, an ethnic group can never comprise all of humankind. Ethnic groups tend to be medium- to large-scale human aggregates, typically ranging from thousands to millions. Many ethnic groups, including those which do not have a 'nation state' to their name, exceed many independent states in the size of their populations. 'Ethnic group' and 'nation' form a pair of concepts, the first stressing cultural aspects, the second political ones. 'Nation' includes the additional element of statehood in one or another form. One can say that an ethnic group plus a state in which it predominates or a claim to such separate statehood is a nation. The fact that political rights like self-determination are attributed to nations in the political and juridicial discourse does not help to define which ethnic group qualifies as a nation and which one does not. Any ethnic group can claim to be a nation and become one through such a claim. The only difference between an ethnic group and a nation without a state is that the latter claims political sovereignty and the former does not necessarily do so. This distinction may not be very helpful in solving practical political issues, but social science does not provide a more helpful one.

Ethnicity is a cultural construct and its construction materials are cultural as well. There are other cultural constructs which are partly based on biological givens, like the social category 'gender', which is partly based on biological sex, but, in all cases in which ethnicity claims to be based on biological facts like discontinuities in the distributions of genes (race), such claims can be shown to be without a biological basis. Genes may cluster in different ways, but they never mark ethnic boundaries.

---

1. This chapter is based on Schlee (2001).

Ethnic groups are never based on race, but very frequently on beliefs about race. Another element ethnic groups tend to attribute to themselves, often contrary to fact, is a venerable age, and therefore ethnicity can in some ways be said to be a pseudo-biological category: ethnic groups view themselves as natural and stable in time like biological species. In addition to beliefs about race, other parts of culture play a part in the construction of ethnic groups. These include the reference to real or imagined historical events, peculiarities of customs, and the like. No two ethnic groups have a set of criteria which is alike, but typically ethnic discourses make reference to a plurality of such criteria. If only one such criterion is stressed, like religious affiliation, one would not speak of an ethnic group, but, rather, of a religious one.

For our present topic it is of special importance that language tends to be (but by no means always is) high up in the catalogue of cultural criteria used to mark the boundaries between ethnic groups. This makes the question of the relationship between language and ethnicity appear tautological in some cases. Where language is used as the primary marker of an ethnic boundary (Barth 1969), ethnic and linguistic units tend to be congruent. In post-First World War Europe the language census has in numerous cases simply replaced the declaration of political will of local communities in effecting boundary corrections between nation states (Dench 1986). On the other hand, the school system and the exclusive use of the majority language for administration, national languages, or languages which enjoy a special status in certain areas have been imposed on linguistic minorities (Gellner 1981). Congruence between linguistic communities and ethnic units/nations has thus been promoted on the interstate level by adjusting political boundaries to language distribution areas, and on the intrastate level by extending a language policy to the boundaries. In spite of the fact that these processes have been at work for some time, still only a small fraction of the world's nations are linguistically homogeneous (Ra'anan 1989).

While in some cases ethnic and linguistic units are coterminous, at the other extreme we find ethnic units, well defined by other criteria, which have nothing to do with language. The Garre of north-eastern Africa (see Figure 1, p. 1) conceive of themselves as one ethnic group because of their common genealogy and clan organisation, their shared pastoral-nomadic culture, and their desire, not always fulfilled, to keep peace with each other. The Garre are divided into four linguistic clusters, which cross-cut other criteria of differentiation like clanship. Some of them speak an Oromo dialect close to the one of the Boran, while some speak Af Rahanweyn and yet others Af Garreh Kofar. The latter two are closely related Somali-like languages but are kept clearly apart by their speakers. There are also Garre who speak Somali proper. Oromo is a different language well beyond the comprehension of speakers of any of these Somali dialects. It belongs to the same lowland branch of the east Cushitic languages as the Somali-type languages, but internal differentiation within this branch is high. The fact that the Garre are also divided between three nation states (Kenya, Ethiopia, and Somalia) has nothing to do with this linguistic differentiation, since speakers of all four languages are found among the Garre of all three states. The only language which is spoken exclusively by Garre appears to be Af Garreh Kofar, but to the outside observer it is difficult to distinguish that language from Af Rahanweyn (also called Maymay), which is spoken by hundreds of thousands of non-Garre, namely Somali of the Rahanweyn clan cluster. It does happen that Garre who do not share one of these Cushitic languages are obliged to converse with each other in languages from totally different language families, like Swahili (Bantu) or English (Germanic) which they have acquired at school, an institution frequented by only a minority of them, mostly for short periods.

If there are enough other elements (political, economic, and cultural) on which a feeling of ethnic belonging and commonality is based, such an ethnic unit can tolerate a high degree of linguistic diversity. If these other foundations are absent, no amount of linguistic homogeneity can prevent disruption. Even within a language formerly perceived as one, now three different languages can be distinguished if the political will so dictates. This is exemplified by the split of the Serbo-Croatian language into Serbian, Croatian, and Bosnian.

The close association between a nation and its national language is a fairly recent development of political ideology even in Europe, and more so in other parts of the world to which this idea has been exported. Originally the term mother tongue (*Muttersprache*) referred to the language learned from the mother or wet nurse as distinct from the language of the male sphere, of officialdom and scholarship, i.e., Latin (Ahlzweig 1994). Through romanticism and the evolving linguistic nationalism this term later acquired political overtones. The modern nation states of Europe have, in their formative period, taken little account of the map of language distribution. Personalities claimed in retrospect as forerunners of German, Russian, or other nationalisms in their real lives often preferred to speak French. The ethnicisation of the state, its culturalisation, and its evolving association with a particular language was a gradual process in the development of modern Europe. Linguistic obstacles were sometimes artificially raised between nations. As their national standard the Norwegians have chosen from among their many dialects the one most different from Danish.

Not only languages but also language families have been politicised by identifying them with groups of people who were often ascribed racial characteristics, as a result of which they were either accorded privileges, or denied such privileges and even such basic rights as freedom and the right to live. Nowadays nobody outside the lunatic fringe would use the term Semite, to the extent that it is still used at all, in any other sense than speaker of a Semitic language. But there are other such terms of Biblical derivation like Cushites and Hamites which still continue in political careers which were unforeseen by the late eighteenth-, nineteenth-, and twentieth-century European historical linguists who applied them to clusters of languages they found to derive from shared ancestral forms. One can hear Oromo nationalists in Ethiopia arguing for the inclusion of minority groups and their territories into Oromia on the grounds that, although they are not Oromo, they are also Cushites. Ideologies about the repulsion of Hamitic intruders are at the root of the genocide against the Tutsi in Rwanda, although the Tutsi, in fact, speak the same Bantu language as their Hutu murderers, and historical theories that they ever spoke a different language are questionable to say the least. Ironically, too, the term 'Hamitic' is no longer used by linguists. This may serve as a recent example of linguistic classifications, once they cross the boundaries of the academic sphere, developing a dynamic of their own, and such a dynamic can be quite a murderous one.

Linguistic nationalism often appeals to romantic notions about the relationship between a particular language and other aspects of the culture of its speakers. The language we speak is believed to influence our thinking in a subtle way, giving language a much deeper cultural implication than that of a mere boundary marker between different cultural/ethnic units. Such ideas, which go back to Johann Gottfried Herder (1744–1803), cannot be explained away by pointing to the ways in which they are instrumentalised by nationalists. In Herder's view, a language is the 'collective treasure' of a nation and, since each language shapes the perspective on the world in a different way, the intellectual wealth of mankind consists in the diversity of its languages, i.e., in the number of such treasures (Schlesinger 1991: 12f.). Or, in the words of a modern Herderian: 'It is ethnic and linguistic diversity that makes life worth living. It is creativity and beauty based upon ethnic and linguistic diversity that makes man human' (Fishman 1989: 15). Very differentiated assumptions about the interrelationship between language and thought have also been put forward by von Humboldt (1988 [1836]), while a more simplistic view, basically a linguistic determinism, was proposed much later by Whorf (1962). Whorfians have also claimed the earlier Sapir as one of their persuasion and speak of a Sapir-Whorf hypothesis. A fuller analysis of the interrelationship of language and thought or language and cognition would go beyond the scope of a chapter on language and ethnicity (for a summary see Schlesinger 1991).

The above-mentioned possibilities, that an ethnic group is completely coterminous and identified with the community of speakers of a certain language, and the opposite case, a total lack of such a congruence and the absence of any association between an ethnic group and the language(s) spoken by it, are two extremes of a range of variation. Between these extremes we find language and ethnicity interacting in a great number of ways. To examine how language relates to ethnicity, and which languages/ethnic identifications persist in which functions in a plurilingual and culturally heterogeneous setting, i.e., to study the ecology of languages, the following variables need to be taken into account: demographic variables, like the sizes of language communities and their growth rates, and their compact or dispersed form of settlement, including the forms of mixture with speakers of other languages; political and juridical variables, like the status of a language and the institutions in which it is used, and the presence or absence of ethnic stratification of the labour market with which language status often correlates; ethno-cultural variables, like the association of a language with a group's history or religion, and the potential of a language in terms of range of vocabulary and tradition of writing; interactional variables like communicational mobility and degree of multilingualism of speakers, specialisation of the functions of speech varieties in diglossic and polyglossic settings, and routines of interactions between ethnic groups/speech communities; variations on topic, to explore the influence of different topics on the choice of a language; predominant/exclusive use of a language in the public/private sphere, and the linguistic distance between the languages in contact (Haarmann 1986: 11ff.). This list is not meant to be exhaustive.

Some of these variables are illustrated. In contact situations, languages may undergo functional differentiation. The original language in bilingual communities may become restricted to sacral functions. Ethnicity and language choice should not be studied in isolation from other dimensions of social identity like gender and age. Minority peoples may revert in their old age to the language of their childhood, while their professional lives have been dominated by languages of wider currency (Dow 1991). The past interaction between languages, their differences in potential and prestige in different semantic domains, and the relationships between the speakers of those languages and the cultural values attached to their ethnic identities are reflected by loanwords. Contrary to the widespread assumption that loanwords are typical for specialised concepts, these often extend far into the basic vocabulary and may designate parts of the body or kinship terms (Haarmann 1986: 186ff.; Schlee 1994a). In intensive language contact situations, borrowing is not restricted to the lexicon and there may be light or heavy structural borrowing (Thomason and Kaufman 1988: 74f.).

Written language and writing systems show a stronger tendency to be maintained as sacred, and/or symbols of ethnic identity, than spoken language does. Aramaic-speaking Christians became speakers of Arabic, which they also used for writing and in which they produced a considerable literature, but for a long time they continued to use their earlier Syriac alphabet because they identified the Arabic alphabet with the Koran and Islam. The mirror case is provided by Muslims in the post-*reconquista* Spain who wrote Spanish in Arabic characters. Jews throughout Europe for centuries wrote the respective majority languages of the countries in which they lived, with a sprinkling of Hebrew words, in Hebrew characters. Where the new alphabet, like the Arabic alphabet in non-Arabic countries converted to Islam, is associated with holy texts, the opposite may occur. Many different languages have been written in the Arabic script, and other writing systems, some of them ancient, have fallen into disuse (Lewis 1998).

Linguistic variation within the performance of one speaker in the same speech act can also highlight aspects of language and ethnicity. A narrator may switch in a story back and forth between languages and/or more or less standardised/creolised varieties of these languages to depict characters to whom different ethnic and other social identities are attributed. Also, in presenting themselves, polyglot people, or people who master more than one register of a language, can play with options of identification rather than being tied to one form of speech and the ethnicity or, more generally, the identity it connotes (Le Page and Tabouret-Keller 1985).

Part III
Practical Frame

Chapter 12

Conflict Resolution: the Experience with the Somali Peace Process

Introduction

This chapter is based on practical work as an 'expert' involved in a peace process.[1] It reflects the time of writing, which is 2003, with some additions in 2004 (see also Schlee 2003b, 2006a). Later updates are mostly found in footnotes. History can be continuously rewritten as new events occur, but I decided not to change the text too much. In October 2004 the peace conference described here elected a new president of Somalia, Abdullahi Yusuf, and a new government. Much of the scepticism found in my reports, on which this chapter is based, was justified by subsequent events: the new government was not in a position to assert control over the whole country. It was not even able to agree on a capital where all ministers felt safe (presumably from their fellow ministers). There was fighting about Baidoa as an interim capital with the result that the government could not go there. Then there were two capitals, Mogadishu and Jowhar, situated a short distance from each other without the respective parts of the government being in full control even of these two towns and their surroundings, and without the Jowhar ministers daring to go to Mogadishu or the Mogadishu ministers daring to come to Jowhar for fear (of their colleagues?). Finally the government did succeed in moving to Baidoa but lost whatever power it had had in Mogadishu to the 'Islamic Courts', a more credible authority. It took a foreign military campaign to oust the Islamic Court from Mogadishu and to bring Abdullahi Yusuf to power there.

---

1. See unpublished reports, one 'Consultancy report to the Somali National Reconciliation Conference' for IGAD, the Djibouti-based 'Intergovernmental Agency for Development', dated 15 November 2003; and two for the GTZ (*Gesellschaft für technische Zusammenarbeit*), namely 'Conflict analysis in Bakool and Bay, south-western Somalia. Report on a two-week consultancy in the framework of the conflict resolution and reconciliation component of the Improvement of Farming Systems Project (IFSP), Bay and Bakool Region, 3–17 March 2004', and 'Conflict resolution and reconciliation as a component of the Improvement of Farming Systems Project (IFSP). Report on a consultancy at Dinsoor, Somalia, 6–20 April 2005'. These reports can be accessed under: http://www.eth.mpg.de/people/schlee/pdf/consultancy_report _nov_2003.pdf, http://www.eth.mpg.de/people/schlee/pdf/consultancy_report_mar_2004.pdf, http://www.eth.mpg.de/people/schlee/pdf/consultancy_report_abr_2005.pdf. A version of this chapter has also been published in Schlee (2006a, b).

Now (2007), after Abdullahi Yusuf and his government failed to establish their control over a significant part of Somalia through their own merits, and the Ethiopians, backed by the United States, have had to fight the way to Mogadishu for them, it would be easy, with the benefit of hindsight, to rewrite this account as if I had foreseen this precise course of events. I had not. Rather than changing the text and introducing confusion by mixing up different times of writing, I have chosen to keep the wording of what I had written in my reports at the time. I leave it to the reader to determine to what extent I was right in the light of subsequent events. The present chapter ends with recommendations for two different future scenarios from a 2003 perspective: the success of the Mbagathi peace process, and its failure. A third final section is about 'Actions Recommended Irrespective of the Outcome of the Mbagathi Process'. These scenarios are now a matter of the past. We know that the Mbagathi peace process has had mixed success: the government has been established, but only by a foreign military intervention. Medium- or long-term prospects for peace are as uncertain as ever.

In the final chapter of this book, 'An Update from 2007: Reconsidering the Peace Process', I make a clear cut and a new start. This new chapter provides an opportunity to reflect upon why some elements of the alternative 'futures' of 2003 have materialised, while others have not. This approach, I think, more accurately represents the actual processes of conflict resolution and therefore is more instructive and thought-provoking than would be a harmonised account, written entirely anew from a present-day perspective and with the benefit of hindsight.

The older parts of the following text, however, have not been left completely unaltered: references to earlier chapters of this book, which are meant to link the practical experience gained in the course of this peace process with one or another point of theoretical interest, are recent additions.

This and the remaining two chapters can be read as a contribution to historiography, written from different standpoints in time. In the present context of conflict theory and its practical application, however, they are primarily meant to illustrate the following three points:

1. The theoretical focus on 'who with whom' discussed in earlier chapters is indeed the bread and butter of practical conflict analysis and conflict intervention. The various identifications, which partly contradict each other by territorial or genealogical criteria, are the stuff politics is made of.
2. Due to the involvement of regional (north-eastern Africa) and global (European Union, European countries by themselves, Arab League) actors and the extent to which such processes are donor-driven or influenced by a host institution, there is a need to study the perceptions (identifications) the parties to the conflict have of each other, as well as the perceptions of third parties.
3. The practical work of an anthropologist who is part of a peace process is not limited to applying a conflict theory to a real case. Much of his/her work has little to do with conflict theory or even with anthropology in general or any other academic discipline for that matter. One gets

involved as a whole person with all one's skills and shortcomings. Much of my work consisted of elaborating an agenda for a committee which might have engaged in much lengthier and less conclusive debates without such an agenda. It also consisted in helping people who do not draft documents every day to cast the results of these deliberations into the form of a policy document.

To make room for this focus on the theory and practice of conflict resolution, much detail has been cut out. Those readers who are primarily interested in the case of Somalia for its own sake should refer to an earlier version (Schlee 2006a). For students of law and legal anthropology, Somalia provides a huge and ongoing 'natural experiment'.

Since 1991 urban and rural properties have changed hands by violent means in Somalia on an unprecedented scale, often taking the form of expulsion of entire clan groups from a given area. Recently, since the terrorist attacks in the USA on 11 September 2001, the international community has rediscovered an interest in re-establishing statehood in Somalia. A peace conference, hosted by IGAD (Intergovernmental Authority on Development, a north-east African organisation) and financed by a number of Western countries and the EU, started in October 2002 in Eldoret, Kenya, and has continued since January 2003 in Mbagathi (Nairobi).

My role was that of a 'Resource Person' for one of the committees set up at that conference, namely Committee Three: 'Land and Property Rights'. That committee drafted a fairly uncompromising report which recommended property restitution, or compensation for loss of property. Elements of traditional law with its emphasis on bargaining and compromise are hardly visible in the resolutions. We shall briefly discuss the workings of traditional law and its contexts to find out why this is so. The present chapter further discusses how property issues are interrelated with other elements of the peace process and constitutional arrangements in which the peace process might result. In view of the prominent role allocated to the holders of armed power at the conference and the actual relationships of violence on the ground in Somalia, it also discusses the chances of the resolutions of the Property Committee ever being put into practice.

To avoid confusing readers unfamiliar with the region, it might be necessary to explain at this stage that the peace conference mainly concerned the southern and eastern parts of Somalia. The north-western part, which goes under the name Somaliland, has been de facto independent from the rest of the country since 1991. Although claims to represent the whole of pre-1991 Somalia were numerous during the peace conference, it in fact only concerned Somalia in the narrow sense, i.e., Somalia minus Somaliland. A brief historical note may explain how this came about.

Some days after its independence in 1960, the former British colony Somaliland in the north-west joined the territory entrusted by the UN to the former colonial power, Italy, east and south of Somaliland. This territory had been released from the trusteeship at the same time. The new capital of the unified state was Mogadishu in the south, not Hargeisa, the capital of what used to be Somaliland. People from the north, as they came to be called, former Somalilanders, many of them of the clan family Isaaq, were represented in successive governments in the early independence period, but, especially since Mohammed Siad Barre took power in 1969, they were increasingly marginalised. They formed a resistance movement, the SNM (Somali National Movement).

By 1988, the Siad Barre regime waged a war against the Isaaq, which acquired genocidal proportions. Hargeisa was bombed by the air force and wells were poisoned. The population fled, mostly to Ethiopia. One of the most notorious generals of Siad Barre at that time was Mohammed Siad Hersi, alias General 'Morgan'. He and his like are now represented in the Somalia Peace Process in Kenya, and that is one of the reasons why Somaliland will not join this process.

After the breakdown of the Siad Barre regime in 1991, Somaliland reasserted its independence in the boundaries of the former British colony.

A more recent experience is a two-week consultancy in March 2004 to the European Commission-sponsored Improvement of Farming Systems Project in Bay/Bakool, where I was concerned with the conflict analysis and conflict resolution component and had the opportunity to observe local and regional peace initiatives by people who had grown rightfully impatient with the Mbagathi process. Another visit was paid to Dinsoor in 2005. Some background knowledge is also provided by ongoing research with my wife Isir Hassan Musa, a Kenyan Somali, on the Somali diaspora in Europe (Schlee 2004a).[2]

The ultimate failure of the preceding peace process in Arta (Djibouti) in the year 2000 should be a warning to the Eldoret/Mbagathi process. The Transitional National Government (TNG), formed in Djibouti, did not, when it was transferred to Mogadishu, manage to establish its authority over the national territory or a significant part thereof. One of the reasons for this was the lack of instruments to carry out its policies.[3] Within the first weeks of its transfer to Somalia, the new transitional government about to be formed at Mbagathi/Nairobi will need to show speedy success in establishing peace and justice if it is not again to lose whatever initial legitimacy it might possess. The Mbagathi resolutions about restitution of property, demobilisation, etc. need to be implemented soon and any preparations for this which can be done now need to be done.

The success of development intervention depends to a large extent on its fittingness with the perceptions of the target group. Intervention should respond to the aims and needs of the target group as they perceive them themselves. The chapter first addresses the stated needs of the Somali represented at the Eldoret/Mbagathi conference, and as

---

2.   I extend my gratitude to everyone who dedicated their time and hospitality to me in these different research contexts. My special thanks go to Paul Simkin, Jutta Bakonyi, and Getinet Assefa, who commented on earlier versions of different parts of this chapter.

3.   Or rather: It would not have had the means to carry out its policies if it had had policies. *The European Commission Strategy for the Implementation of Special Aid to Somalia, 2002–2007* states: 'Right from the beginning, it became obvious that the Transitional Government (TG) [= TNG] did not have a clear political agenda for completing the reconciliation process as well as diffused and unsubstantiated priorities' (p. 12). This is the technical aspect of this failure. A more political view of the reasons for the failure of the TNG has been given by Samatar and Samatar (2003b).

expressed in the documents accepted by the conference and derived from discussions with the delegates. From these sources, statements are derived which specify the inputs expected from the international community for the implementation of future Somali government policies, and the measures which the conference has obliged it to adopt. Where such needs have been formulated only in a very general way, I try to specify the questions which still need to be clarified and to list technicalities yet to be specified. Discussions with representatives of various international organisations are then summarised, and project documents analysed in order to see how many of these needs are already being addressed and how supply of and demand for international support for the Somali peace process can be matched better.

The possibilities of future intervention are then discussed in a variety of potential political scenarios.

Background: Recent History and the Current Peace Process

The script of a theatre play starts with an enumeration of the characters, the dramatis personae. I will follow this time-honoured fashion and introduce some of the more relevant 'players' (to switch to a sporting metaphor) in present-day Somali politics, most of whom were represented at the Somali peace and reconciliation conference in Kenya, where I spent many weeks between October 2002 and March 2003. I will write a couple of paragraphs about each of them.

Somali Factions

In discussing Somali politics the emphasis on clans has frequently been criticised by those who propose that the conflict is really about land or really about money or about class. This kind of criticism seems to neglect a necessary distinction, that between parties in a conflict and their contested object.

Let me explain this by a hypothetical animal experiment. Three hungry dogs (or call them tigers, if the comparison with dogs sounds too derogatory) get one bowl of food. None of them wants to share peacefully; each wants more than a third. None of them is strong enough to chase the other two away on their own. Dog One and dog Three bare their teeth towards dog Two. He puts his tail between his legs and clears off.

What part of the conflict have we explained by naming the disputed resource? It was about eating, that much is true. But much more interesting is the problem of the borders drawn between the conflicting parties. Why One and Three against Two? Why not Three and Two against One? Or One and Two against Three?

To account for this problem is an ambitious task. We are not in the least able to predict which two will form an alliance against the third. Even if we knew the story of the three dogs (Are two of them from the same litter? From the same kennel? What kind of experiences did they make in past alliances with each other?), we would not be able to make predictions of this kind if we had not beforehand studied on a broad basis which of the three levels of experience (kinship, origin, social learning) is more relevant for dogs than the other levels in situations like this.

In conflict configurations, we therefore have to recognise two kinds of distinctions: the distinctions between the parties in conflict must be distinguished from those between the conflicting parties and the object in dispute. The latter distinction is not always as simple as in the case of the dogs and the food in the bowl. The conflicting parties and the object of their dispute might be creatures of the same species, for instance, human beings. If two women are fighting over one man, then it is a conflict between two persons, not between three. The third person is merely the object of conflict, much as the cattle snatched by African pastoral nomads, or oil wells fought over by modern states, are not in themselves considered conflicting parties.

This is not as trivial as it may sound. A confusion of these two kinds of distinctions (party vs. party/party vs. object) occasionally leads even noted scientists to make analytical mistakes. Besteman and Cassanelli (1996) deny that the military conflicts in Somalia can be explained by referring to clans and lineages. Class is said to have taken the place of clan membership as the relevant criterion of distinction, particularly in the river oases in the southern part of the country, since the distinction between peasants (in part former slaves) and central and northern Somali, who dominate them militarily, is believed to be a class distinction.

So far so good. A more thorough reading reveals, however, that the peasants in the south are as contested a resource as their land. Northern Somali and central Somali of nomadic origin used to challenge each other's access to the fertile estates of the south, and whoever managed to seize power over these often also made their former owners submit to their will as forced labourers. Besteman and Cassanelli (1996; see also Besteman 1999) in fact stress the peaceable nature of the peasants and the fact that they are victims of this conflict, but not themselves actors in the conflict. Now, northern and central Somali are recruited according to clan membership and alliances between subclans of different clans, regardless of whether the conflict is over camels or airports, and regardless of whether they follow traditional leaders or city-based warlords. These patterns cannot be understood without any knowledge of the combinations of clans and clan alliances. In what respect is class membership considered to have taken the place of clan membership in its significance? The class distinction is that between warriors and their prey, the peasants. If the patterns of alliances and oppositions among the fighting groups themselves are to be explained, one still has to rely on studies of clan structures.

In their rich and detailed analysis Besteman and Cassanelli (1996) rightly stress the importance of agricultural land as a contested resource. They are also right in pointing out that there are other divisions than clanship in the Somali society, namely slave vs. free origin, racial type,[4] and recent forms of class differentiation. What is unjustified, however, are their numerous dismissive gestures about studies of clanship, like the regret they express at the 'neglect' of the 'significance of land', which they attribute to 'the preoccupation of foreign scholars and Somalis themselves

---

4.   'Bantu', a fairly recent but fast-spreading appellation applied to people of a more pronounced African type with 'hard hair', is the name of a language family, but in Somalia it is used in a racialised sense. '[O]nly one so-called Bantu community, the Mushunguli people of the lower Jubba valley, actually uses a Bantu language' (Menkhaus n.d.). So what Somali mean by 'Bantu' is not speakers of a Bantu language but people who look as if they spoke one.

with the politics of clan and nation, which, fascinating as they are, have obscured the underlying roots of conflict in the modern history of Somalia' (Besteman and Cassanelli 1996: 14, 201; see also Schlee 2002b: 269). If the conclusion from the empirically rich regional studies presented by these two authors is that we have talked too much about clans and too little about land, this would be misleading and falls short of what could be derived from the argument they present. The question is not about having talked too much or too little about one or the other, but about how these things are interconnected. In fighting about land, people recruit supporters along clan lines. So how can one overstress the importance of clanship in analysing problems of 'land rights' or rather problems arising from forceful land appropriation? It is also wrong to assume that an adequate analysis of class relations requires neglecting clan affiliations. Agriculturalists were often reduced to serfdom and appropriated along with the land, and the people who fought about them were the same people who fought about the land, and they were – once again – organised along clan lines. The process of subordination of these lower agricultural classes itself has often taken the form of affiliation to a dominant clan of agro-pastoral or pastoral ('proper' Somali) origin.[5]

There is much agreement that in the first wave of violence the agriculturalists played a passive role. The 1991–1992 fighting in the Juba/Shabelle area was not a class struggle but a struggle within a class about people of another class. The fighting was within the dominant, partly economically advanced, formerly state-connected pastoralists or former pastoralists, Darood and Hawiye in clan terms, and it was about the appropriation of the land and the labour of Digil and Mirifle and the Bantu associated with them.[6] De Waal (1996) explains that it was two categories of people who fought with each other about the farmlands and the farmers. These two categories are the 'landowners' and the 'liberators'. Both designations are only used in inverted commas, for good reason: the 'landowners' are the allies of the old regime who grabbed large tracts of land when their protectors were in power and the

---

5.   'These associations with Somali lineages can range from minimalist (mainly ritualistic acknowledgement of a sultan) to substantial (*diya*-paying obligations) and can shift significance over time. Where Bantu communities are integrated or affiliated with weak Somali clans, such as Digil-Rahanweyn, they are essentially a minority, doubly disadvantaged as a group occupying the bottom rung in a Somali social hierarchy which seems far cry from the egalitarian, "pastoral democracy" so often invoked in describing Somali political culture.' (Menkhaus n.d.)
        All this is fully supported by Besteman and Cassanelli's own work.
6.   The Rahanweyn (Digil and Mirifle) got themselves organised and armed to a significant extent only in the mid-1990s. The Bantu successfully asserted their political identity even more recently. Factors which may have contributed to arming these latecomers to the active engagement in the fighting may include 'the excellent 1994 harvest' (US Department of State 1996), part of which was sold to the World Food Programme (University of Pennsylvania 1995) and the proceeds of which may have been used to procure arms. (No blame on WFP for this; to buy cereals locally is the right thing to do for the revival of agriculture.) The Somaliland government also supported the Rahanweyn Resistance Army against Aidiid as a retaliation for Aidiid's interference in Somaliland affairs (UNHCR Somalia 1996). Ethiopia is likely to have been another source of arms.

'liberators' are those who wanted to conquer these areas for themselves.[7] Both groups comprised modernised elites who, however, in the recruitment of their forces still had to take clanship into account. Clanship here certainly is not 'traditional' in the sense of something which disappears in the face of modernity. With modern forms of competition having been added to the old ones about pasture and water and the episodes of establishment of a degree of statehood (the late colonial and early post-colonial periods) being a matter of the past, clanship is as important as ever in Somalia, or more so.

For someone who wants to investigate the actors' logic of action, the patterns of identification behind the opposing fronts, and the calculations on which alliances are based, the question of the contested resource is of rather secondary importance. Whether solidarity on a larger scale is oriented towards religious affiliation, language, nationality, or province, or whether (on a smaller scale) I prefer to rely on my brother instead of my classmate, sometimes has very little to do with the object of the conflict for which those alliances are instrumentalised – be it a bank robbery, an election campaign, a war over oil, or a war over arable land. The answer to the question of what a conflict is all about therefore only partly explains this conflict. The entire field of problems regarding the opposing fronts, who is facing whom, what criteria are used to define friend and enemy, is at best touched by it, but not explained.

And, since – as explained in a previous chapter – even for the warlords, with their allegedly arbitrary power, there is no escape from clan logic when recruiting their following, in order to do justice to Somali reality we cannot avoid mentioning clan names.

The Transitional National Government (TNG)

The Transitional National Government (TNG) was set up at Arta in Djibouti in 2000. It was based on a formula called 'four point five', which meant that the four big clan families were represented in equal shares and all the small groups, the so-called minorities, got half a share. Put with more mathematical clarity, this means that the big clan families got two-ninths each and all the minorities combined one-ninth. In Table 12.1 the big clan families are the ones in the left column. The right column comprises some names of major clans which form part of these clan families, without any attempt at being exhaustive.

Table 12.1 Clan structure according to the '4.5' formula.

Big clan families	Some names of major clans
Dir	Isaaq, Biimal
Darood	Majerteen, Dulbahante, Ogadeen, Marrehan
Hawiye	Abgal, Habr Gidir, Saad
Digil/Mirifle (formerly Rahanweyn)	Digil, Mirifle
Minorities	Benaadiri, Jererweyn

7.   'Much of the land seized by various militia had previously been appropriated by well-connected politicians during the Siad Barre years. In addition, small farmers lacking security of land tenure and without the means to defend themselves suffered in the scramble over the rich agricultural lands of the Juba and Shabelle valleys. The widespread looting of water pumps further restricted agricultural productivity.' (Longley et al. 2001: 4)

In spite of its broad clan base, the TNG, once established on the ground in Mogadishu, could secure control of only a very small territory. If members of the parliament constituted at Arta and then transferred to Mogadishu ('the TNG parliament') ventured outside the area under TNG control into other parts of town, or even dared to visit their rural constituencies, they would be kidnapped, to be released on ransom.[8]

Adversaries of the TNG came to depict it as just one of many factions, the 'Arta faction' (Lewis 2002: 5).

The TNG agreed to come to Eldoret with a number of delegates equal in size to the umbrella organisation of the opposition, the SRRC (Somali Reconciliation and Restoration Council). In fact both the TNG and the SRRC had an allocation of sixty-five delegates (actual numbers were always contested and inflated), but the TNG had some quite plausible complaints that groups which had originally been comprised within the fold of the SRRC started to get separate allocations of seats, so that, as a part of the whole, the weight of the TNG was diminished. On 4 November 2002 the TNG complained in a position paper: 'The SRRC has been broken down, for the purpose of delegate collection, into RRA [Rahanweyn Restistance Army] (28), Puntland (28), SNF [Somali National Front] (14), Benadir (2), SDU [Somali Democratic Union] (2) and another bloc of 65 delegates, which comes to a total of 139 delegates.'[9]

In frustration about what they perceived as marginalisation at the conference in Eldoret/Nairobi, some TNG members favoured a boycott of the Nairobi conference and wanted to set up a rival conference at Mogadishu.

The logic of the '4.5' formula, developed at Arta and adopted at Eldoret/Mbagathi, reflects the interplay of local structures (clanship) and global discourses (minority rights, proportional representation). To be recognised as a minority is an interesting special case of the size factor in identity politics, discussed in Part II. One needs to be a rather big dwarf. If a minority is too big, it does not attract minority protection because it is not weak enough; if it is too small, it does not represent a factor to be reckoned with and an attractive coalition partner (see above on Riker and the 'minimal winning coalition'). So the best thing is to be a vocal minority of just the right (the optimal) size. Numerical formulas for minority protection would be an interesting subject for international comparison.[10]

The number of delegates allotted to each group was the main bone of contention at the conference, and not only because of the conflicting formulas resulting from the promises made when the different factions were persuaded to join the conference. In addition, the IGAD (Intergovernmental Authority for Development) front line states

---

8.   One such case is a kidnapping in Tieglow, Baqoor Region, by RRA, the Rahanweyn Resistance Army (André Le Sage, oral communication, 6 February 2003).

9.   Transitional National Government, Position Paper on the National Reconciliation Conference in Eldoret, Kenya, 4 November 2002.

10. In Russia there is a population limit of 50,000 to qualify as a 'small people of the North'. This entails privileges like hunting rights and thereby encourages identity games like group fission so that the resulting groups remain under the limit (Donahoe 2005; 2004; Donahoe et al. (accepted by Current Anthropology); Sokolovski 2005).

and other international players had their favourites among the Somali and wanted to increase the representation of some groups at the expense of others.

The SRRC – the Somali Reconciliation and Restoration Council

The SRRC was founded in Awasa, Ethiopia, in March 2001.[11] This was a time when Ethiopia also made efforts to militarily unite the factions it armed and supported.[12] Its chairman became Hussein Mohammed Aidiid, son of a pretender to the presidency of the 1990s, a minor Mogadishu warlord. It included also 'Osman Ali Atto, Muuse Sudi Yalahow, and Mohammed Siad Hersi, better known as General Morgan, as well as Abdullahi Yusuf, the president of Puntland'.[13] Hussein Aidiid at the time of writing (May 2003)[14] is still the chairman of the SRRC, although there is no reason to assume that he is a particularly strong player. When the SRRC was founded, his military clout was already greatly reduced as he had suffered an earlier defeat at Baidoa (Baydhaabo) at the hands of the RRA (Rahanweyn Resistance Army) and the Ethiopians. This defeat made him change sides and join the winners. Hussein Aidiid only controls a couple of blocks around the former presidential palace in Mogadishu, but he has procured himself some money by getting 30 billion Somali shillings from the British American Banknote Company, a subsidiary of Quebecor, Montreal, Canada. He was not alone among his warlord colleagues in having Somali shillings printed abroad, either to be spent in the country, where they caused rapid inflation,[15] or to be converted into hard currency for arms purchases (Schlee 2006a: 122f.).

Since 11 September 2001, the terrorist attack on New York, a new source of finance has opened for Hussein Aidiid and other faction leaders: Western intelligence agencies flock to them and pay them substantial sums for questionable intelligence about international terrorism (United Nation Security Council 2003: 46). When I visited Hussein Aidiid with a German diplomat and a former member of the Saxon *Landtag* (State Parliament) at his residence, Soy Lodge near Eldoret, he appeared free from financial worries. The forms of address used by the Member of the State Parliament, 'Mr President' and 'Your Excellency', may, however, appear as an exaggerated courtesy.[16]

---

11. Somaliland Net (http://www.somalilandnet.com/warya/2001/april/37286.shtml).
12. Somaliland Net (http://www.somalilandnet.com/warya/2001/april/37331.shtml).
13. Somaliland Net (http://www.somalilandnet.com/warya/2001/april/3269.shtml).
14. An update: a year later, in May 2004, Aidiid was still regarded by the Kenyan hosts as indispensable for the peace conference. Mohammed Affey, Kenyan ambassador to Somalia, and the conference chairman Ambassador Kiplagat intervened on his behalf and got him released when he was jailed for defaulting over paying back a 15 million Kenya shilling loan (*Daily Nation*, 21 May, 'Aideed sent to jail over Sh 15m debt', 26 May, 'How Aideed secured his freedom', Nationmedia.com/Daily Nation/NEWS).
15. According to Little (2003), this caused an inflation of about 25 per cent in one year. Otherwise, the Somali shilling has been remarkably stable, as used currency notes drop out of circulation. It is one of many examples in history where currencies remain in use without a central bank.
16. In the meantime, however, Hussein Aidiid has done well. At present (January 2007) he is deputy prime minister in the Ethiopian-promoted government.

The SRRC is a loose umbrella organisation, comprising factions of warlords who are very much at odds with each other. Even during the peace conference, and after the ceremonial conclusion of a ceasefire agreement, fighting continued or even intensified between some of them.

During the conference, a number of factions which had originally come as parts of the SRRC started to be treated by the Technical Committee of IGAD (see below, the host organisation) as separate entities, and were allotted seats without reducing the number of remaining SRRC delegates accordingly. As explained above, the TNG understandably complained about this, because this was a shift in numbers to the detriment of its own relative weight. The new units appearing on lists of delegations comprise Puntland, RRA, SNF, and minor groups.

Puntland

Punt is the ancient Egyptian name for the land where incense was collected in antiquity. A territory inhabited mainly by the Harti subgroup of the Darood clan family at the extreme point of the Horn of Africa, in the north-eastern corner of Somalia, has adopted this name. 'Hartiland' would have been more descriptive. The Harti comprise, among others, the Majerteen and the Dulbahante. The dominant element in Puntland are the Majerteen. Many Dulbahante live in the neighbouring Somaliland to the west. On the basis of the affiliation of the Dulbahante to the Harti, the easternmost regions of Somaliland, Sool and Sanag, are claimed by Puntland.[17]

The claim to Sool and Sanag is based on the clan affiliation of (a part of) the population, not on their political will. This is illustrated by a press release by the Puntland government of 26 April 2001, signed by 'Abdullahi Yusuf Ahmed, State President of Puntland', where the attempts of the administration of the then president of Somaliland, Mohammed Ibrahim Egal, to hold a referendum there were branded as 'unwise and provocative'. The clan territories which Puntland claims to follow in the delineations of its boundaries are attributed an older age than the colonial boundaries on which Somaliland is based. Somaliland's claim to 'Hart[i]/Darood territories' like Sool and Sanag and the district of Buhoodle is therefore perceived as an aggression against 'the territorial integrity of the state of Puntland'.[18]

Puntland claims to be a separate state with a president (or two rival presidents)[19] of its own. Unlike neighbouring Somaliland, however, it does not strive for international recognition. In the Puntland case, the claim to statehood in its own right seems to be an instrument in the struggle for power in Somalia as a whole.[20]

---

17. For a recent study about Somaliland with special emphasis on the contested areas, see Höhne (2006).
18. Somaliland Net (http://www.somalilandnet.com/warya/2001/april/3765.shtml).
19. At the time of writing, 2003, the elected president, Jama Ali Jama, still refused to give up his claim to his predecessor, Abdullahi Yusuf, who had not honoured the results of the election. In the end, Abdullahi Yusuf prevailed. He only had to give up the Puntland presidency to accept that of Somalia in October 2004.
20. In view of later events, one of the two rival Puntland presidents of 2002/2003, Abdullahi Yusuf, having prevailed and now being the President of Somalia, whatever that means in practice, this strategy appears to have been successful.

Both Somaliland and Puntland are examples of rival identity discourses (see above, Chapter 5, about the ups and downs of 'religion', 'class', and 'ethnicity' as 'legitimate' identifications). Both use names that are not ethnonyms or clan names. Somaliland, suspected of being dominated by the Isaaq clan, makes a point of not being based on clanship (although belonging to one of five 'resident' clans is a relevant consideration for citizenship), and of granting fair representation to non-Isaaq clans. In asserting its different political identity, it has recourse to its British, rather than Italian, colonial past and the administrative and legal heritage of that past. In setting itself apart from the rest of Somalia and deriving its claim to sovereignty from having been a different political entity in colonial times, Somaliland resembles Eritrea (Schlee 2003a: 348). Puntland, on the other hand, bases its separateness and its territorial claims on clanship, despite the fact that its name does not reflect its association with a particular clan (Harti). This could be seen as gesture to the taboo imposed on speaking of clans that came into existence and was even legally enforced during the Siad Barre regime (1969–1991), even though (or perhaps rather because) that regime was based on a clan alliance.

In different ways, both entities and their identity politics reflect the ambiguity of clanship. Clanship continues to provide the social structures on which power is based (either by the dominance of one clan or clan alliance, or by an equilibrium struck between clans), but it has also acquired many negative connotations in recent Somali history.

A peaceful agreement on a boundary between Somaliland and Puntland (being a part of Somalia) is unlikely for two principal reasons. First, the government of Somalia refuses to recognise Somaliland and is supported in this attitude by the international community. Secondly, the different logics on which the two entities base their boundary claims are incompatible. Somaliland cannot claim all territories belonging to the former British colony without impinging on Puntland's claim to comprise all lands inhabited by members of the Harti clan.

The RRA – the Rahanweyn Resistance Army

The RRA is one of those groups which, according to the TNG (above), were originally included in the SRRC quota of delegates, and then managed to get a separate allocation of seats. The Rahanweyn are the bulk of the more sedentary and more agriculturalist population in the area between the rivers Juba and Shabelle in southern Somalia. Since 1991, they had been victimised by Hawiye and Darood militias, and their stated aim was to defend the component parts of the Rahanweyn (not a clan but a federation), namely the Mirifle and Digil, against these invaders from the north and east. The RRA is, however, mainly composed of Mirifle. Digil present at the conference did not feel represented by them and complained about not having been given an adequate voice.

Peace conferences can lead to increased warlike activities. Just as in Puntland, where the question of territorial representation at the peace talks might have intensified the fighting between two pretenders to the regional state presidency, Abdullahi Yusuf and Jama Ali Jama, in the south-west there was also fighting between militias of the RRA chairman, Hassan Mohammed Nur 'Shatigaduud', and his vice chairmen, Sheikh Adan Madoobe and Mohammed Ibrahim Habsade.

Shatigaduud lost the town of Baidoa (Baydhaba) to his deputies on 31 July 2002.[21] Immediately after the ceasefire agreement at Eldoret on 27 October 2002, fighting around Baidoa intensified, as if the two main antagonists, Shatigaduud and Habsade, both of whom were signatories to the ceasefire, wanted to prove to the world that they had mobile phones and were still capable of military action. In the subsequent period Shatigaduud's forces were pushed back further and further and Madoobe emerged as the Rahanweyn strongman.

When I visited Huddur in the Bakool region in March 2004, there were still tensions between the three rivals for RRA leadership. Sheikh Adan (clan: Hadama) and Shatigaduud (clan: Hirin) both enjoyed the support of Ethiopia. The vicious fighting between their two clans, which had escalated in spite of this shared alliance, had subsided a bit and there was a level of understanding between the two. The third pretender, Habsade (clan: Leisan), locally represented by Saransur (Hadama), was rather alone in cultivating links to the TNG in Nairobi.

The pro-Ethiopia warlords wanted to meet with the Majerteen warlord 'Morgan', a former general of Siad Barre[22] whose notoriety as a war criminal surpasses that of most of his warlord colleagues, while his independent power base no longer does. He manages to stay on stage as an Ethiopian mercenary and clansman and ally of Abdullahi Yusuf, the 'president' of Puntland.[23] Habsade was strictly opposed to Morgan and his militia coming to Huddur for a meeting. But Saransur, his man on the ground, and his militia were in the end outnumbered and local elders persuaded them to stay in Saransur's compound to avoid bloodshed.[24]

This part of RRA politics is not without repercussions on other regions. If internal peace in the RRA and in the Bay and Bakool region is maintained by agreeing to allow Morgan to move through the area, he might well go straight to Kismayu, the coastal port from which he was expelled in 1999. The price for peace in one region might be war elsewhere.

---

21. UN SOMALIA Press Releases 2002: 'RRA faction imposes condition for attending conference', Nairobi, 14 October (IRIN). www.somaliuk.com/News/archive.php?month=10&year=2002.

22. The late Mohammed Siad Barre was also his father-in-law. For more on personal and clan relationships see Schlee (2002b).

23. Later that year to be elected 'president' of Somalia by the Mbagathi peace conference.

24. One year later, in April 2005, when I made another visit to the RRA-controlled area, this time to Dinsoor in Bay, the new government formed in Nairobi had just announced its plan to transfer itself to Baidoa (Baydhaabo), the capital of the Bay region, because it still considered Mogadishu unsafe for many of its members. This plan was supported by those leaders of the RRA who held positions in the new government, namely Shatigaduud and Sheikh Adan Madoobe, but not by Mohammed Ibrahim Habsade, who just like Madoobe was a vice-chairman of the RRA but had not become a minister. In order to show the new government that they had nowhere to go, he allied himself with Hawiye forces from neighbouring regions and captured Baidoa. Many people in that situation had an interest in demonstrating that Bay was unsafe, either because they were against the new government and wanted to spoil its plans or because they just favoured another town or city as the interim or permanent capital. That such a point could be made by shooting at Europeans was an eventuality which worried project workers in the region, including myself, to quite some extent.

Digil and Mirifle clan elders have long tired of the warlords instigating clashes between their respective factions and clan militias. They have started to exert pressure on militiamen and militia commanders at the lower level, compensation payments for killings and wounds have been paid, and there is a tendency for elders to assert their authority over the militias. They cannot be said to be in command, but they have certainly gained a degree of moral authority which is sufficiently high for even the warlords to pay them lip service. An important forum for this is a regional peace conference, largely organised and funded by the local population themselves, which started in Baidoa in October 2003 and was then transferred to Waajid (Schlee 2004b).

A Conspicuous Absence

Somaliland

Since it reasserted its separate status in 1991, the former British colony Somaliland rejects the dogma that national unity needs at all costs to go along ethnic lines. In July 2002 the president of Somaliland, Dahir Riyaleh Kahin, explained to me that the former General Secretary of the United Nations, Boutros Boutros Ghali, an Egyptian, had stressed to him the importance of Somali unity. He, so he told me, replied in the form of a question: What has become of the United Arab Republic which once combined Egypt and Syria? And how about the unity of the Arab nation in general? Especially representatives from the small emirates on the Gulf find themselves confronted with such questions, if they exhort the Somali (fellow members of the Arab League) to maintain or restore their national unity simply because they are culturally similar and speak dialects of one language.

The Somaliland position on the Somalia Peace and Reconciliation Conference in Kenya is that it might be good and useful for southern Somalia. Somaliland itself, so they claim, has had its reconciliation and is peaceful already. This claim is not unfounded. In Hargeisa there are no militia fights, no kidnappings, no robberies. No woman is afraid of parading her golden ornaments.[25] NGOs reschedule their meetings and relocate their activities to Somaliland if the security situation in the south does not permit their undisturbed movement there.[26] Many foreign governments extend a good deal of de facto recognition to Somaliland. The only taboo for the international community seems to be formal diplomatic recognition.

Somaliland has had one peaceful presidential succession already, when the late President Igal was succeeded by his vice-president Dahir Riyaleh Kahin from the smaller Gadabursi clan. In April 2003 Somaliland held presidential elections, and the GTZ (Gesellschaft für Technische Zusammenarbeit) provided material and organisational help to this end. This is interesting because it somehow contrasts with the official non-recognition of Somaliland. The outcome was a narrow and contested victory for the incumbent.

25. There is a price Somaliland pays for internal peace. In the mid-1990s there has been heavy inter-clan fighting. To mollify former fighters, Somaliland employs them or gives them pensions. Somaliland 'is a prisoner to its peace and around 60 per cent of its budget is spent on clan militias or the army' (Paul Simkin, personal communication).
26. One event was relocated there from Baidoa during my visit in July 2002.

For the international advisers like myself and the representatives of the front line states, it was a taboo to discuss the possibility of Somaliland remaining or officially becoming an independent state. On the other hand it is clear that a forceful reincorporation would lead to disastrous results. Anyhow, there is no military power in view which can control even the south alone, not to speak of a reunited Somaliland. When asked about my views on this issue (informally, because it was not part of our committee work), I tended to advise my interlocutors to create social, economic, and political conditions in the south which are so attractive that Somaliland will wish to join. The response tended to be slightly embarrassed laughter, because that is a rather remote possibility. Still, insisting on Somaliland being invited (although it had been invited repeatedly) and complaining about its non-participation were always a position with which one would find consent, and it may also have been a means to shift guilt from oneself during the conference if things did not go so well.

TNG insisted on Somaliland's participation. Although Somaliland had not been represented in the earlier Arta peace process, from which the TNG emerged, the TNG as the only Somali government recognised by anyone (United Nations, Arab League) had to insist on speaking for all of Somalia if it did not want to become like any other faction. The TNG topped the list of eleven signatories in an appeal to the IGAD Technical Committee and seven other international and foreign bodies dated 23 October 2002, in which 'international, regional and sub-regional organisations' were reminded of their resolutions to respect Somali sovereignty and territorial integrity, and were called upon 'to urgently communicate with the northern regions delegations, representatives of the civil society, who are willing to fully participate in the Eldoret Somali peace process' and to provide transport for them. This was just one example of appeals for Somaliland participation, or, in this case – circumventing the Somaliland government – of calling for participation of anyone from the north who wished to participate.

In the presence of the then Kenyan President Daniel arap Moi, Abdullahi Yussuf (the one of the two pretenders to the Puntland presidency who had gained the upper hand by then) at the celebrations of the ceasefire agreement at State Lodge, Eldoret, on 31 October 2002, said that he was the first person who, many years ago and for legitimate grievances against the Siad Barre regime, started the Somali civil war. He now wanted to end it. Anything which would happen in the future would not be his fault.[27] With this he shifted the blame for his subsequent actions from himself onto others. He interrupted his stay at the conference, and a little later hostilities flared up in the Sool and Sanag regions at the easternmost end of Somaliland at the border with Puntland. These regions are, as has been explained above, claimed by Puntland on the ground of their clan composition. In an almost comical inversion of who had invaded whom, Puntland claimed in a press release on 9 December 2002 that the movement of Somaliland forces into Sool and Sanag, which are not regarded as part of Puntland by anyone except Puntland, constituted a violation:

of the territorial integrity of the state of Puntland. We therefore call on the Eldoret Somali conference, the IGAD Technical Committee and the

---

27. Eldoret, 31 October 2001 (field diary: 23).

International Community to condemn in the strongest terms the hostile action of the leadership of the Northwest Zone (Somaliland) and to take all necessary steps to penalise the aggressors and require them to join the peace process from now on.

That the international community could be persuaded to such a course of action or that the Somaliland government could be forced to comply was, of course, entirely implausible. That Abdullahi Yusuf did not want Somaliland to join the conference is clear from his statement. He only wanted to shift the blame for the non-participation and the blame for the hostilities with Puntland to Somaliland.

The Leaders' Committee, i.e., the representation of the warlords at the conference, proposed to allocate, according to an announcement by Abdullahi Yusuf, fifty seats of delegates (there were about 400 delegates at the time) and five seats in the Leaders' Committee (hitherto twenty-three) to Somaliland. Somaliland promptly rejected this proposal. It is unlikely that Somaliland will ever agree to be represented by anything less than one-third of the whole.[28] The plans for a joint parliament before unification in 1960 were thirty seats for ex-Somaliland and sixty seats for the former Italian Trust Territory. The southerners then increased their seats to ninety while the northerners only received three nominated members in addition to their thirty. This proportion of thirty-three to ninety remained until Mohammed Siad Barre took over in 1969. The north, as an Isaaq Minister of the TNG explained to me, was thus cheated out of proportional representation. A number of business people of the majority clan of Somaliland, the Isaaq, are quite influential in Mogadishu and there is one group within the TNG which, for the sake of unification, considers offering the presidency of a reunited Somalia to someone from Somaliland or even transferring the capital to Hargeisa, as least for as long as the security situation in Mogadishu is not conducive to effective work of any kind.[29] Many Darood, however, would never accept an Isaaq president. Suggestions to interrupt the conference and to send a delegation to Hargeisa, as well as most accusations against the IGAD Technical Committee for not having undertaken sufficient efforts to secure Somaliland participation, do not appear sincere. Some might be regarded as diversion of attention from the failures of those who levelled these accusations.

The issue of Somaliland participation might seem a strange priority in view of the problems continuing in the south and the fact that fights between the followers of warlords represented in the peace conference continued to flare up. The position that the south is called upon to solve its own problem first has some plausibility against this background.

---

28. Sources: ICG (2003: 13f.); list of composition of Leaders' Committee as reproduced below.
29. Conversation with a TNG minister, Eldoret on 2 November 2002 (field diary: 35f., 40).

IGAD Front Line States

Djibouti
Djibouti was the host country of the Arta process, which resulted in the formation of the TNG, and Djibouti continues to support the TNG. Arms shipments reached the TNG via Djibouti.[30]

Ethiopia
Since 1996 Ethiopia has repeatedly intervened militarily in Somalia. The first invasion was directed against Al-Itihaad, an Islamist organisation to be discussed below, and ever since then the links to international terrorism attributed to Al-Itihaad have been a convenient excuse for Ethiopia to interfere in Somalia, either directly or by supporting and arming a number of Somali factions (United Nations Security Council 2003).

Also at the Eldoret conference, before and after its transfer to Nairobi, the Ethiopians abstained from diplomatic restraint and played rather open power politics. Others perceived them as pushy. On one occasion I heard an Ethiopian diplomat complain to another member of the Technical Committee that a certain Somali 'leader' had become a 'victim'. What was meant by victimisation was that his delegation purportedly had been unfairly reduced. The other member of the Technical Committee at first did not quite understand, because the person in question was a notorious mass murderer, before and after the fall of the Siad Barre regime. He was commonly known as 'the butcher of Hargeisa', for the role he played in the air bombing of that city in 1988. The word victim does not combine easily with that sort of personality, and that was what caused the incredulity on the side of the interlocutor of the Ethiopian diplomat. Anecdotes of this type can be told by many people who were present at the conference.

Kenya
Kenya has an obvious interest in restoring peace in Somalia, because it has to handle a substantial refugee problem, and has experienced incursions across its eastern boundary. As the host country it chaired the peace process.

Other Regional Forces

The Arab League
The Arab League had sponsored the preceding Somali peace process at Arta in Djibouti and continued to sympathise with the government which resulted from that process, the TNG. Its resolution to financially support the TNG's efforts to restore peace and stability in Somalia (involving pledges which have not been completely fulfilled) gave a number of individual Arab countries the justification to support the TNG bilaterally (United Nations Security Council 2003: 31).

---

30. United Nations Security Council (2003: 27–30).

The 'International Community'

Italy
Italy plays a leading role within the European Union in matters concerning Somalia. Also her financial engagement is substantial. Somali tended to suspect Italy of advocating Italian economic interests too strongly.

The European Union
The European Commission has a delegation in Nairobi (the equivalent of an embassy) and within this delegation there is a Somalia Unit.

Many development activities in Somalia are coordinated by this institution. The EU also played a major role in funding the peace process and was a keen and critical observer of the financial conduct of the conference administration.

The USA
The leading role of the USA in the 'war on terror' is obvious and the connection between the renewed interest in Somalia with the terrorist attack against the USA on 11 September 2001 has been outlined above.

American diplomats showed a continuous presence as observers of the conference and in the group of representatives of the international community which regularly used to meet the chairman of the peace process.

Minor Players

There were visits by Norwegian diplomats, at one time representing the EU, at other times Norway, in addition to a Ugandan minister, a Canadian observer, and many others.

Germany covered a major part of the expenses of the conference in the Eldoret phase (€900,000) and German diplomats felt that German support for peace in Somalia should also be made visible in the shape of a person. That may have been one of the reasons for my appointment. When I enquired whether there was a German policy towards Somalia, I was told to do what I thought to be right, as Germany did not have material interests in Somalia.

After introducing the 'players', a short chronology of the events that led to the recent peace process seems appropriate. Since the American-led UNOSOM (United Nations Operation in Somalia) intervention had ended (it had basically failed in 1993 and then dragged on in a reduced form until March 1995), UN sub-organisations and international NGOs continued to work in the disintegrated country, often intermittently, or wherever the security situation permitted. Technical aid continued in a very much reduced form. In the political sphere, however, there was hardly any interest left in the fate of Somalia in the period from 1993 to 2001. The world did not seem to care. Political observers, used to a world of states, sometimes wondered how life went on without a state, but soon lost interest again. Then there were the terrorist attacks in New York and Washington of 11 September 2001. International terrorists, so it was suspected, might hide in some wilderness beyond the reach of statehood. Statehood therefore had to be restored in places where it had faded away. Money was suddenly available again for peace initiatives for Somalia.

The organisation which was suspected of being the Somali branch, partner, or equivalent of Al-Qaida is called Al-Itihaad, 'unity'. It had operated in the Somali region of Ethiopia (formerly 'Region 5') and been decimated at the hands of the Ethiopians. It had suffered defeats by the forces of Mohammed Farah Aidiid (USC (United Somali Congress), forces recruited in the Hawiye clan, mainly Saad) in Kisimayu in 1991 and against the Somali Salvation Democratic Front in the north-east of Somalia (now Puntland) in 1992. It finally got a foothold in the Marrehan area along the Juba, but, due to Ethiopian incursions into Somalia since 1996 and Al-Itihaad's involvement with the Ogadeen National Liberation Front (ONLF) operating in 'Region 5', which did nothing to endear it to the Ethiopians, Al-Itihaad finally gave up independent military activity. In the Ethio-Eritrean war in 1999-2000, Eritrea briefly supported the ONLF and Al-Itihaad in opening a second front against Ethiopia (Le Sage 2001). Thus it became part of a temporary alliance of Eritrea, the OLF (Oromo Liberation Front, which had been operating in southern Ethiopia from northern Kenya and had been expelled from Kenya), and the forces of Hussein Aidiid (Schlee 2002b: 264; 2003a; Schlee and Shongolo forthcoming).

Al-Itihaad and its sister organisation Al-Islaah are also engaged in entirely peaceful occupations like running orphanages, schools, and health centres (Marchal 2001: 9). Al-Itihaad may be less of an actual terrorist threat to the rest of the world than suspected. The bombings of the American embassies in Dar es Salaam and Nairobi and the bomb attack against a Mombasa hotel frequented by Israelis in recent years have raised the suspicion that non-Somali terrorists and their weapons could easily move through Somalia (United Nations Security Council 2003: 32), but no significant links of Somali with international terrorism have been identified so far.[31] More recently, Al-Itihaad has moved into business, and its activities certainly deserve to be monitored. There are no doubts about its Islamist orientation. So far, however, I have not come across any solid evidence for its terrorist links or inclinations. If there are agencies which possess such evidence, they have not disclosed it.

'Local' (meaning Somali) NGOs are also adapting to the anti-terrorism discourse. By way of an example I want to talk about the Ahl as Sunna wal Jamaa', an alliance of 'Islamic scholars' who like to emphasise that they represent the 'traditional' Islam. By 'traditional', the Somali Islam influenced by Sufism is implied, in contrast to Wahaabite modernisations and radicalisations. Leaflets publicising this movement recommend the Ahl as Sunna as a safeguard against hardliners and terrorists (see Schlee 2004a: 155f.). They denounce the TNG as a network of extremists. They also suspect schools of being in the hands of extremists. To the extent that schools operate in Somalia at all, these might, in the absence of state funding, indeed depend on donations in the name of Islam. Ahl as Sunna's special concern is the youth, although in their description of misguided youths they conflate stereotypes of Islamic extremists with 'gangsta rappers' in their baggy trousers. The Ahl as Sunna is undoubtedly a conservative force that presents itself as moderate.

---

31. In the London Underground bombings of 2005 one of the perpetrators was a Somali. That man, however, has spent most of his life in Britain and his terrorist leanings may have little to do with recent events in Somalia.

Other delegates conjure the danger of terrorism just as much as the Ahl as Sunna wal Jamaa' in order to obtain support from representatives of Western countries. A Somali interlocutor from Finland explained to me that the EU should carry out the disarmament of the militia in Somalia in their own interest, even at the expense of a large-scale military action. For, if they did not succeed in establishing state order in Somalia, terrorism could spread from Somalia, via the numerous new mosques and Koranic schools, to the European Somali diaspora. One wants to counter by asking among which type of Somali a radical Islam is expected to spread in Europe. Among the Westernised youths with their computer games and their pop culture? Among his own children, who – as he was lamenting himself – have long since become Finns and are not interested in Somalia any more? Or among his own generation with all their vehement anti-terror talk?

In this way, the concept of the 'enemy Islam', originally assigned rather to the conservative (post-) Christian camp, in the new structural conditions of reward and revenge became an instrument of Muslims polemicising against one another.

In the Somali framework one can therefore safely say that Al-Itihaad is a minor player. Its role in international terrorism is more difficult to assess, because of the inherently secret nature of this type of activity. Doubts about its importance may be justified. The most dramatic historical effect that Al-Itihaad has so far had is that, by being associated with the spectre of terrorism (be it in reality or in the perception of others), it has contributed to the motivation of the international community to resume diplomatic activities in Somalia and to dedicate substantial means to a renewed Somali peace process. The money flow was not as steady as the Kenyans might have liked, but that also has to do with insufficient accountability. By November 2003, a close observer (Paul Simkin, personal communication) estimates that by then 80 per cent of the funding had come from the EU, and that, apart from limited funding from the USA, the rest had come mainly from Italy, which in addition to payments through the EU engaged in bilateral funding, and the Nordic countries. Apart from these funds for the direct sponsoring of the conference, many countries rededicated parts of their regular development aid budgets to conflict resolution in the aftermath of 11 September 2001. Supportive activities like my own role in the conference were not paid from the conference budget but from other sources, in my case the GTZ.

In Eldoret on 27 October 2002, Phase One of the fourteenth Somali Peace Conference was concluded, with a ceasefire. The signatories to this agreement were the 'leaders', as they came to be known in diplomatic parlance. Most of them are otherwise known as 'warlords'. As explained above, in the section about the RRA, for some of them the signature to the ceasefire agreement was mere lip service and their respective militias resumed hostilities a couple of days later.

The organisation of the conference in 'Phase Two' consisted of the Technical Committee, basically a seven-member steering committee manned by the IGAD front line states which hosted the conference, and a 'Leaders' Committee', composed, apart from the TNG prime minister and a member 'on behalf of the Civil Society' basically of people who would fit the description of 'warlords'. Lists of the members of both committees with their institutional/organisational/clan affiliations can be found in Schlee (2006a: 134–136).

Apart from the Technical Committee and the Leaders' Committee there were six committees which dealt with technical issues, namely:

1. Federalism and Provisional Charter.
2. Demobilisation, Disarmament, and Reintegration.
3. Land and Property Rights.
4. Economic Recovery, Institution Building, and Resource Mobilisation.
5. Conflict Resolution and Reconciliation.
6. Regional and International Relations.

These committees were to draft resolutions to be discussed by the Leaders' Committee and the Plenary Assembly. Resource persons (international experts) were attached to the committees in order to provide the guiding structure.

The 'Proposals for the Process and Structures of Phase Two', dated 1 November 2002, stated that 'the technical, practical and political arrangements must be in place *before formalizing power sharing arrangements*' (emphasis in the original). That makes perfect sense. The constitutional institutions needed to have been outlined, the regional and administrative units defined, and the basic content of the peace agreement stating how the future government was to create a just post-war order needed to be established before power sharing could take place. In other words: powers needed to be defined before they could be shared.

In fact the haggling in the Leaders' Committee (although no formal decisions were taken) then went on parallel to the work of the six thematic committees. The latter, which were composed of the more qualified among the Somali delegates assisted by non-Somali academics, thus were left with the impression that whatever they decided might be of little importance to the parallel deliberations of a group of twenty-three 'leaders', mostly only qualified by the firepower they could mobilise. What if the division into regional states proposed by Committee One should differ from a bargain the warlords had in the meantime struck among themselves? What would happen to the elaborate rules for restitution of property devised by Committee Three if the warlords said that they would not dream of surrendering their loot?

Warlords are people who use arms to acquire loot, to extort money from legal and illegal businesses, citizens and foreigners, or to defend an illegal source of income like payments for dumping waste or selling fishing rights[32] which are not theirs. This illegal wealth is then used to acquire yet more firepower, to play the same game on a larger scale. Invitations to join the peace conference as a 'leader' were on the grounds of military power, i.e., they were awarded to the most successful players of this game.

It is correct to say that the earlier Arta process had largely failed because its results were not accepted by the warlords and that a peace process has to involve the powers that be. But involving them could have taken a different form. Instead of warlords holding court in posh country residences surrounded by their own retainers, graciously

---

32. For some pre-war perspectives on the potential of fisheries for Somalia, see Janzen (1991); Mohamed and Touati (1991).

giving audiences to long successions of diplomats and international journalists, who then proudly enumerated how many warlords they had spoken with, instead of making them feel like the grey eminences behind the peace process, they should have been dragged to the fore. They should have been made to explain their deeds to the mass of the delegates, to the mothers of their victims, to human rights groups. That would have been a meaningful involvement. It would have meant making them part of the peace process by putting them under pressure to accept its results, not by surrendering the peace process to them as a new playground for their power games.

As peacemakers the warlords had poor credentials. An ICG (International Crisis Group) report summarises on 6 March 2003: 'leadership at the conference was awarded to the same faction leaders who had failed to implement previous peace agreements' (ICG 2003: 3). They had not honoured their ceasefire agreement this time either.

Lacking legitimacy, these figures might have been poorly qualified to make peace even if their intentions had been sincere. The TNG shows no effective presence as a government in its own capital, Mogadishu, nor do any of the minor warlords there fulfil that role.[33] The Juba Valley Alliance (JVA), which rules Kismayu, is perceived as an occupying force by the local population. Various factions of the Rahanweyn Resistance Army (RRA) fight each other in Baidoa while their leaders enjoy each other's company in Eldoret/Nairobi. Puntland has no legitimate president but is ruled – if at all – by force, since Abdullahi Yusuf's democratic mandate expired in July 2001 (ICG 2003: 3).[34]

The sincerity of the commitment of these 'leaders' to the peace process can also be put into question by citing the following warlike actions and atrocities, all committed during the peace conference, often while the chief instigators were sitting together, and after they had signed a ceasefire agreement. As mentioned above, in December 2002 Abdullahi Yusuf had to leave the conference temporarily, just in time for the subsequent clashes in the Sanag region of Somaliland (own notes). In June 2003 'clashes between the militias of the rival RRA leaders Shatigudud and Habsade degenerated into a series of reprisals involving abduction and rape of young girls' (Menkhaus 2003: 32). Armed conflict continued in the Medina District of Mogadishu between the militias of Omar Finish and Musa Sude (ibid.). Puntland, often praised as a place with a relatively high level of law and order, was found to have a particularly poor human rights record in terms of arbitrary arrest and detention (ibid., 34) while the conference was going on. This paragraph is not meant to single out individual 'leaders' as particularly bad, but to underline the doubts whether the international community was really dealing with the right set of people, and whether, if dealings with them were inevitable, they should have been given such a prominent role.

A basic shortcoming of the peace process was that Committee One on Federalism and the Provisional Charter, also seen as the one concerned with constitutional

---

33. The present tense refers to the time of writing, 2003, and so does the expectation that the Arta-elected Transitional National Government had a role to fill.
34. ICG (2003: 3), and own conversations.

issues, had controversial discussions and came out with two competing drafts, one of which was hardly federal at all but called for a strong central power. This is especially unfortunate since it would have been useful for all other committees to know more about the regional and constitutional framework within which the activities they planned would take place, be it property restitution or demobilisation. How can you plan arbitration bodies and coordinate them with the administration and the juridical system if you do not know how many administrative units there will be at which level and what types of courts will be established? How can you plan demobilisation if you do not know whether there will be federal or state police, army, or navy of a type and size capable of absorbing a part of the demobilised militiamen?

The preference for a more federal or more centralist model might reflect the interest of the warlords behind the delegates in the committee. Those who feel strong might favour a higher concentration of power, because they speculate that this power might become theirs. Such a line of reasoning would harmonise with the theorems about dividing the loot and the 'minimal winning coalition' cited in Chapter 5, above. Why should you share power more widely if you can keep a higher proportion of it in your own narrow circle?

It is difficult to say to what degree there were connections between the work of the thematic committees and what was taking place in the Leaders' Committee, or whether there was any active warlord interest in what the committees were doing. This may have to do with a general warlord disinterest in legality and other such niceties. People actively involved in the work of drafting resolutions also tended to be more educated than at least some of their political 'leaders' and compensated for the reality of their oppression with attitudes of intellectual superiority.

A Somali lawyer who contributed substantial amounts of text to one of the drafts at one point introduced the author to someone whom he referred to as his 'boss'. Later the author asked him who the man was. He responded with a dismissive gesture and said that the man spoke neither English nor Italian and was of no importance at all. He was deputising for the warlord to whose delegation the lawyer belonged. The warlord, a particularly notorious figure, had gone back to Somalia to practise his profession as such.[35]

In July 2003 the resolutions of the Committees Two to Six were accepted by the plenary session. Discussions about the draft federal constitution, a unified version of two competing drafts devised by Committee One, was only then started and continued into August. It has already been pointed out that the chronological order would have been better the other way round, and that the work of the other committees would have profited greatly if the one on the constitution had advanced faster. Even then, for fear of putting the agreement on a unified document at risk, many problems were set aside rather than solved. The draft (The Transitional Federal Charter), for example, states that federalism will be based on the existing states (Art. 88.0, §1, 41: 'The existing states and regional administration [sic] shall be part and parcel of the Transitional Federal Government of Somalia'). No observer of Somali politics can fail to notice that it is not clear how many such federal states exist. Some

---

35. Eldoret, 3 February 2003 (field diary: 41).

of those which appear to have a kind of existence tend to be engaged in violent boundary clashes with each other. In other words, there are no existing federal states with accepted boundaries which can be used as ready building blocks for a federal system. The entity which most resembles a state, Somaliland, did not participate in the conference, and the other entities still either have to emerge or have a long way to go to become states.

Ambassador Kiplagat, the senior Kenyan diplomat who took over the chairmanship of the conference in January 2003 after many issues had already gone off on the wrong track, and the reputation of the whole exercise had suffered from mismanagement and corruption, demonstrated great skill in making the best of an ill-fated process. It remains to be seen whether the process will come to a conclusion and whether a transitional constitution will be accepted in addition to the five policy documents, whether a parliament will be formed and a transitional government be elected. If that happens, the government will be part of the same peace agreement as these policy documents and will be bound to implement them.

Even in the case of a successful completion of the peace conference, there are many imponderables for the time immediately following. Will the government be able to establish its authority in Somalia? Will it, once elected, honour all parts of the peace agreements? It is common wisdom that we always have to be prepared for the worst case. The worst case is that the peace process evaporates and Somalia stays as it is or further deteriorates, if there is room for further deterioration. But should we not also be prepared for the best case? What if in the not too distant future there is a Somali government, based on a fairly broad consensus, willing to implement the policies outlined in the Eldoret/Mbagathi peace process? It would be a great shame for the international community if they then did not have their tools ready to assist in this implementation.

Personal Experience with the 'Committee on Land and Property Rights'

I was appointed at short notice as an expert to the Somali peace conference at Eldoret in October 2002. I was the 'Resource Person' for Committee Three, 'Land and Property Rights', for which I drew a problem outline and sketched an agenda which is by and large reflected by the document produced by this committee in the subsequent months. The work also comprised identifying questions which had remained open, and discussing problems of harmonisation of the Somali and English versions of the document. From January to March 2003 I was supported in this task by a student assistant, Hege Magnus from Norway. Our work at Eldoret, and later Nairobi, was paid for by the GTZ.[36] My appointment was in response to an initiative by the GTZ representative at the IGAD head office in Djibouti. The IGAD proposal to appoint me was endorsed by the German Embassy in Nairobi and finally the Kenyan Ministry of Foreign Affairs.

The perspective of this section is shaped by my experience with the Committee on Land and Property Rights. The following quotations stem from a summary of the

---

36. GTZ, *Gesellschaft für technische Zusammenarbeit*, the publicly funded German development corporation.

report of that committee which I gave to the Technical Committee on 7 February 2003. In the ensuing discussion the Somali chairman of the Committee on Land and Property Rights insisted that this summary reflected positions agreed on by the committee 'word by word and paragraph by paragraph'. Here a summary of that summary will have to suffice (see Schlee 2006a: 141–144 for the full text of the summary). The report stressed the principle of restitution of property or compensation for the loss of property. Rather than forgiving and forgetting, justice was to be the prerequisite of reconciliation. Alienation of land and other forms of property was put in historical perspective. Injustices during the colonial period were recognised; post-colonial laws were likewise recognised, but transactions that were illegal in terms of the law of the day were not. This established a distinction between nationalisation proper, and private appropriations by powerful individuals in the guise of nationalisation, with an emphasis on the period since 1991, which, as the summary notes:

> has seen land and other forms of property changing hand by force on an unprecedented level. Unlike thieves, who hide what they have stolen, today there are people in Somalia who have acquired land or other properties at gunpoint, by all sorts of human rights violations, who have subdued the former owners of their farms and reduced them to forced labour, and who enjoy the properties they have unlawfully acquired openly; in open defiance of the principles of justice; in open defiance of the teachings of Islam; and of any form of human decency. These people will have to give back what they have taken by force.

This assessment of the situation leads to the recommendation that a number of special committees be set up at local and national levels to deal with the issue of contested property, because the ordinary judicial system will not be able to deal with the high volume of cases. Issues specifically addressed include government assets such as public buildings, national reserves, ships, aeroplanes, and government industries that have now fallen into other hands. Another issue involves regions where the local inhabitants have been expelled or marginalised and intimidated. Locally recruited committees in those cases would only represent the winners, because the losers are no longer around. In such cases the federal government has to establish institutions to deal impartially with these matters. 'All militias who hold occupied territories by force shall be ordered to withdraw, so that evidence on rightful ownership can be gathered without intimidation.'

A report of the International Crisis Group which appeared a month later, though fairly critical of the peace conference in general, found some kind words for the work of Committee Three but also put the finger on some remaining problems. It is quoted here at some length, with comments inserted.

> Wisely, the Reconciliation Committee for Land and Property approached its work by attempting to categorise the various types of land and property disputes and the possible mechanisms for their resolution, rather than passing judgement on which historical period to consider.

In fact, the question of the time horizon was high up on the agenda, which I had drafted for the Committee. The Committee not only agreed to take the Siad Barre period into consideration as well, but wanted to address property issues since 1912, the beginning of colonial rule.

> Focussing exclusively on disputes since Barre's fall would appear to reward those who had profited from the old regime, while punishing the 'liberators'. Extending the remit to cover disputes since independence might appear more even-handed but would also require more cumbersome bureaucratic and legal machinery for investigating titles under previous governments. (Much pre-war documentation has been lost or destroyed, and land titling was extremely politicized during previous governments.) Extending the committee's horizon further back to, say, the clan zones demarcated by the colonial powers – as some members of the Committee have suggested – would risk opening a Pandora's box of irreconcilable claims and counter claims.

That is one of the reasons why one does not find the names of clans in the whole of the report. Existing levels of agreement on the principles of land ownership would never have been achieved if the official report had attempted to attribute any form of collective guilt to any named clan group, or to point to territorial gains by any clan at the expense of any other, even if phrased in a way which sounds morally neutral to outsiders. For a Somali reader it is clear, anyhow, to which cases the various sections of the report refer.

> Somewhat more problematic is the system of national and local level committees it proposes, which would require the leadership of a fairly robust and impartial central government. However, with further deliberation, a more pragmatic system that gives greater responsibility to local authorities might emerge.

That indeed might emerge. It needs to be explained, however, that it was the task of the Committee to design a policy which would be implemented after the government that was formed as a result of the peace process had moved to Mogadishu, and even to schedule the actions to be taken during the first or second months after its formation, etc., without the slightest idea of when or what type of government there would be. After all, Committee One on constitutional issues was working parallel to the work of our committee and on a lower level of internal agreement, so that for us the shape of a future government, whether more centralist or more federal, was not even vaguely discernible.

> The committee's boldest – and potentially most controversial – assertion is that all militias occupying areas by force should withdraw prior to negotiation or arbitration. Although no specific cases are mentioned in the draft, this recommendation has greatest import for the Habr Gidir militia strung out between Mogadishu and Kismayo, and its Marrehan partners in the Juba Valley

Alliance. Difficult as it may be, the issue may be squarely addressed now that it has been tabled. The Lower Shabelle and Lower Juba are unlikely to know lasting peace as long as their leaders impose themselves by force. And now that Somalis have spoken clearly, the international community – which has for too long resisted taking position – should feel emboldened to do likewise.

The Stated Needs: What Somali Expect from the International Community

This section is based on an evaluation of the reports from 2002 of those committees which dealt with policy issues, namely:

Committee Two: Demobilisation, Disarmament, and Reintegration.
Committee Three: Land and Property Rights.
Committee Four: Economic Recovery, Institution Building, and Resource Mobilisation.
Committee Six: Regional and International Relations.

The report of Committee Five, 'Conflict Resolution and Reconciliation', has not been available at the conference secretariat.

What is extracted from these reports are the demands for technical assistance in the implementation of the policies elaborated by these reports. Additional sources are notes taken from discussions with Somali delegates. Wherever these needs are clearly enough articulated on a general level, but not broken down into more detailed steps of technical implementation, more specific questions will be raised.

Demobilisation, Disarmament, and Reintegration.

This report (2002) is the shortest of the four available reports and is correspondingly general in its statements. It asks for the assistance of the international community in two fields. First, it encourages the presence of international observers to implement the United Nations Security Council resolution 733 (23 January 1992) and 1407 (3 May 2002) to stop the flow of weapons into Somalia. It secondly asks for international military advance forces to establish a secure environment for the new government. These forces are to be stationed at government headquarters and at strategic points like airports.

I will come back to the theme of 'Demobilisation, Disarmament, and Reintegration' under the heading 'Ongoing Activities in the Field of Technical Assistance'.

Land and Property Rights

This report addresses among other things the contested regions, where large segments of the population have been expelled by militia from other areas. In order to ascertain collective rights (like pasture rights) in these areas, certain types of evidence are to be considered. As this evidence might be found in archives abroad or in university libraries, needs for research can be identified. The types of evidence mentioned include: historical books, maps, and other documents relating to the contested regions, and documentation about boundaries between the Somali communities drawn by the colonial government and other colonial documents. Expert advice is also requested.

The restitution of agricultural properties to previous owners will leave large numbers of illegal occupants without a livelihood. Many of them stem from pastoral areas. To enable them to engage in productive activities, the areas to which they resettle will need development programmes like restocking, a range management package, a livestock marketing programme, small-scale irrigation, or the establishment of crafts and industries. When it discussed the role of the international community in the reconstruction of Somalia, Committee Three (28 March 2003) drew the attention of the future government and the international community to these inevitable social consequences of the process of re-establishing rightful ownership.

Committee Three also discussed environmental issues like the misuse of the open range and the territorial seas of Somalia for dumping toxic waste. In connection with the protection of the marine environment and the control of the use of marine resources, it stated:

> as there will be no tax income in Somalia in the initial phase of the new government, sources of funding and expertise [have to] be identified. (p. 32)

> The Committee Three on Land and Property Rights would be grateful for any expertise which can be provided on the following issues:
> − Planning and budgeting (including matters like the number of boats required and their prices).
> − Experience, which can be shared by other countries dealing with similar problems. In addition to training of personnel and technical assistance, equipment and instruments to measure radiation and other forms of toxicity are required. (p. 33)

The report of Committee Three, which has been summarised at some length in the above section on 'Personal Experience', stresses the restitution of property and also clarifies some procedural questions. It remains, however, silent, on a number of more detailed technical questions:

1. How are land rights to be recorded and where are these records to be stored? With modern technology like GPS, describing a location and measuring a surface have become much easier, but still such records need to be made for future reference. We shall come back to this under 'Ongoing Activities in the Field of Technical Assistance'.
2. Who is going to enforce the decisions about property restitution by the arbitration committees and later by regular courts? In Kosovo this has been left to the local police and they often have not done anything.[37] Will

---

37. I thank Daniel Lewis, UN-HABITAT, for sharing his experience with me.

there be special organs of enforcement like bailiffs? There must be an institution which is *obliged* to enforce decisions on property restitution, to monitor deadlines, and to carry out evictions. Non-compliance with eviction orders must be regarded as a criminal offence, trespassing, and punished. Orderly evictions require manpower and material resources like holding pens for livestock vacated from a property, and storage facilities for mobile belongings of evicted people.

With proper documentation of decisions and their enforcement these activities need to be done in a consistent fashion. What must be avoided is that they are done in some cases and then the respective programmes run out of funds. This would undermine the credibility of the entire property restitution process. Justice ceases to be justice if it is done in some cases and not in others.

Much more detailed research and planning is required for the smooth implementation of property issues. Statistics about the number of expected cases do not appear to exist. How is the effect of precedent to be assessed? Will one model case settle dozens of similar cases because illegal occupants give up their claims? Or will procedures at least be sped up considerably by precedents? Or will each case be fought out with the same tenacity? Experience from other parts of the world would certainly be welcome here.

Economic Recovery, Institution Building, and Resource Mobilisation

In connection with pastoralists who will have to evacuate agricultural lands which they have occupied by force, the need to rehabilitate livestock production and marketing stated by the Committee on 'Land and Property Rights' corresponds well with the actions and investments recommended by the Committee on 'Economic Recovery, Institution Building, and Resource Mobilisation'. The first four of the recommendations refer to livestock production, namely:

1. Establishment of veterinary services including certification for livestock exports.
2. Encouragement of the export of meat and animal by-products.
3. Development support facilities such as holding grounds, stock routes, quarantine stations, and animal feeds, involving the private sector.
4. Improvement and conservation of rangelands.

The report also goes into some detail with regard to fiscal policies. As revenue and finances affect all sectors of government and economy, we shall come back to this below under 'Cross-cutting Issues'.

Regional and International Relations

In the report of the Committee on 'Regional and International Relations', the importance of the integration and active participation of Somalia in regional and wider international organisations is stressed. This is a means to reduce tensions and the danger of conflict, as consultations will be possible as soon as problems are articulated.

In terms of capacity building it is suggested that Somali delegations visit national and international institutions to see how parliamentary work or the activities of governments are carried out elsewhere. The lack of qualified personnel in the field of diplomacy is identified as a problem for Somalia.

Ongoing Activities in the Field of Technical Assistance

Demobilisation, Disarmament, and Reintegration

There are some differences between the resolutions of the Eldoret/Mbagathi process and what seems to be the prevailing expert opinion on 'demobilisation, disarmament, and reintegration' (DDR). The resolutions of the peace conference give chronological priority to disarmament, because 'the new government will not have the ability to fulfil its duties as long as the weapons are in the hands of the people'.[38] Also Committee Three, 'Land and Property Rights', argues with some plausibility that arbitration about areas occupied by force cannot take place before the militias occupying them have withdrawn (see report of Committee Three, 'Land and Property Rights'). All this gives the impression that not much can be done in terms of government activities while the arms are about. On the other hand, a policy document by international experts[39] states under the heading 'Lessons learned' that 'Peace and the existence of an effectively functional authority is a pre-requisite for the conduction of a DDR exercise.' This turns the chronological order around: it states that a functioning state is a prerequisite for disarmament rather than disarmament having to be completed before the state can take up any functions. Also 'Land Commission' is found here among the prerequisites of DDR (see report 'Demobilisation, Disarmament, and Reintegration'). That means that conflicts about land must be defused before disarmament can take place. The chronological order of these processes or how they can mutually further each other if carried out simultaneously appears to need further discussion.

An intermediate position would claim that not necessarily a functional government, but surely a sincere and binding peace accord is a precondition for DDR. This also implies that DDR cannot be the first step in de-escalation. There are examples of disarmament with undesired effects, and certainly unbalanced disarmament in situations with a sustained potential for violence needs to be avoided. In 1993, the fact that the Americans and Belgians disarmed Ahmad Omar 'Jess' in Kismayu and thus enabled his rival Mohammed Sa'id Hirsi 'Morgan' to occupy the town did much to antagonise Aydiid, an ally of Jess, and may be one of the causes of the subsequent UNOSOM disaster (Schlee 2002b: 265f). Knighton (2003) describes how disarmament programmes have rendered the Karamojong of Uganda defenceless against plunder and rape by government forces. No one can be asked to surrender his gun in a situation of ongoing insecurity. A certain level of law and order is a prerequisite for DDR and only then can DDR contribute to the further establishment of peaceful and just conditions.

---

38. Somali National Reconciliation Conference, 'Disarmament, Demobilisation, and Reintegration', draft report, 3 December 2002.
39. UNDP Somalia, Somali Aid Coordination Body/Governance Working Group 2001.

To shift our focus from the national to the provincial level, the peace negotiations between different Rahanweyn clans and their militias at Waajid do not aim to disarm the militias but to bring them under the control of the elders. There had been ugly clan clashes, like the ones between Hadama and Harin, which had led to atrocities like killings and mutilations of women, and clashes between Eelay and Tunni among others. Delegates from the peace conference went there and called upon the offending party to give *sabeen*, the propitiating gift which opens the way to negotiations about compensation.

In the many undeclared wars in Africa, ways of regulation which work well at lower levels of escalation are suspended when violence assumes large proportions. If killings become numerous and anonymous, say by the use of automatic weapons, then they are not discussed in a legal setting. As among European nations, killings in a war are not individually prosecuted. That negotiations about compensation are initiated in this Rahanweyn case is an indicator of a positive development for two reasons: the cases are not too numerous to be dealt with individually, and the will for reconciliation is there, because the alternative to accepting compensation would be vengeance.

These negotiations about compensation put the perpetrators, militiamen and their lower-level commanders, into a position which makes them answerable to the elders. The internationally visible figures, the 'warlords', have so far managed to stay out of this process, which would seriously infringe on their de facto powers, but they could not help paying lip service and praising the peace efforts of the clan elders. What happens here at a local level can be compared to the transition which repeatedly took place in Europe when an army was given a role within a democracy after the abolishment of absolutism and dictatorship, when it was brought under the control of society.

Rahanweyn elders do not wait for a result of the peace conference at Nairobi.[40] They try to stop bloodshed, to abolish roadblocks, to guarantee safety to traders within the reach of their own influence. Among the government functions they assume is legislation. There is a discussion about the reformulation and unification of customary law (*xeer*), the body of knowledge primarily concerned with compensation. There are different rates for killings and injuries depending on binary inter-clan agreements. The compensation for killing a man, which would be 100 camels at northern Somali rates, can be as low as forty-four or twenty-seven.[41] There are discussions under way to raise the blood-wealth for killing a man generally to 100, to raise the threshold for potential killers. The culprit will be shot if his group refuses to pay.[42]

The GTZ International Services (GTZ IS) 'Improvement of Farming Systems Project' also organises village workshops as part of its 'Participatory Integrated

---

40. The time of writing here is 2004. In the meantime the results of the Nairobi peace process have come to them. There was fighting between forces opposed to the plans of the Nairobi-appointed government to establish Baidoa as the interim national capital and those in favour of it in 2005 (Schlee 2005).
41. Interview Mohammed Ahmad Yare Dheere, Huddur, 6 March 2004, in the appendix to Schlee (2004b).
42. Interview Sharif Yusuf Sharif Ahmad, Waajid, 8 March 2004, in the appendix to Schlee (2004b).

Community Development Process' (Muchoki et al. 2003). In at least one case, the delegates most urgently wanted to discuss revisions of customary law. Regulatory powers finally seem to revert to the grass roots, as higher political levels remain dysfunctional (Schlee 2004b). What the GTZ project does, both at Waajid and in the various villages, is to facilitate the discussions by providing food, transport (in addition to many resources generated by the local people), and some other material inputs, without setting the agenda or trying to influence the course of the discussions. Local Somali need to have a clear sense of 'ownership' of these processes. As soon as these processes start to be associated with foreign influence, they lose their plausibility and sustainability, and might even become mere façades for aid attraction like many other local 'NGOs'.

Land and Property Rights

The view of Committee Three that injustice in matters of land rights did not start in 1991 and its insistence on addressing property issues since the start of the colonial period are supported by recent scholarship. In a monograph on Geledi (Afgooye), Luling (2002) concludes the section on 'Land and Land Holding' with the following paragraph:

> Behind all these changes force, or the threat of it, was present. The takeover of the land by the Italian colonialists had been based on overt military force, albeit translated into treaties and agreements. The second land grab of the Siyad Barre years proceeded under legal forms, but force was clearly behind it. With the breakdown of state institutions in the early 1990s, the land grab was continued by naked force, and the militias of different clan groupings competed for control. In Afgooye and most of the lower Shabelle it was the Habar Gidir who were in control, and were experienced as the new 'colonists'. (Luling 2002: 163)

Reconciliation between Somali and Somali, as well as between Somalia and other nations, has to be based on truth. It cannot be based on covering up the past. Even in those cases where old land claims can no longer be enforced because they have been superseded by subsequent legislation or by irreversible realities, it is important to bring to light what happened to them. More historical research is needed to set the moral record straight and thus to build a basis for forgiveness.

With regard to all those generally more recent wrongs which can be rectified, the international community has a clear policy. There is broad agreement that lasting peace can only be built on finding out the truth and re-establishing justice, not on some foul and transient compromise between a larger or smaller number of predators who happen to be powerful at a given moment. 'UN development agencies and international NGOs have increasingly embraced a "rights-based" approach to post-conflict development in Somalia' (Menkhaus 2003: 37). No one's property is safe as long as his or her life is threatened and there are no institutions to appeal to in case of infringements on rights referring to one's body, one's dignity, or one's material belongings. Property rights have to be embedded in a wider legal order, and it is on this order that any prospects for deriving prosperity or development from a property regime depend. 'A rights-based approach to development will only have meaning if socio-economic and civil and political rights are addressed simultaneously' (UNDP 2001: 182).

Committee Three on 'Land and Property Rights' has suggested the creation of a number of arbitration committees which will deal with contested properties for a limited period. The remaining cases will be addressed by regular courts, to which appeals can also be made if the results of arbitration are not accepted. This presupposes the existence of judiciary institutions. Recent surveys, however, show that this existence cannot be simply assumed. We shall deal with this issue below, under 'Economic Recovery, Institution Building, and Resource Mobilisation', since judicial institutions are not just relevant for property rights but for the framework of societal and economic development in general.

On a more technical level there are a number of ongoing activities which deserve attention. A UNDP Somalia report with the title *Capacity Building for Governance* from June 2001 addresses many of the problems identified above, in the section on 'Land and Property Rights' under 'Stated needs' (UNDP Somalia et al. 2001). It recommends cadastral surveys, which map each farm in agreement with its neighbours to avoid future conflict. A land database will also serve land management. Pioneer work in this field has been done in Somaliland (see below, 'Learning from Somaliland').

A whole section of the above-mentioned document is devoted to 'Capacity Building for Land Dispute'. The special dimension which the problem of land alienation has reached in southern Somalia is reflected by the insight: 'In the case of Southern Somalia, a large-scale bird's eye view of surveyed farms would be an indispensable tool for the future resolution of the widespread and complex problems of land dispossession in the inter-riverine agricultural areas. Aerial photography cannot, of course, pick out unmarked boundaries.' (UNDP Somalia et al. 2001)

Economic Recovery, Institution Building, and Resource Mobilisation

Between the documents of the Eldoret/Mbagathi process and the programmes of organisations for technical cooperation, there seems to be a high level of agreement with regard to the importance of livestock production and marketing, a functioning infrastructure, and many other issues. Beyond the recommendations made by the committees at Eldoret/Mbagathi, the important field of municipal administration has been addressed by the UN sub-organisation UN-HABITAT (United Nations Agency for Human Settlements).

There seems to be, however, one type of institution which has been given inadequate attention, namely the judicial ones. As has been described above, Committee Three on 'Land and Property Rights' more or less assumes the existence of legal courts to which one can appeal if one does not accept the results of arbitration and which will take over the work of the arbitration committees after the span of the latter has expired. It is therefore worthwhile to have a look at the current state of jurisdiction in Somalia.

The *Human Development Report, Somalia 2001* describes Somaliland and Puntland as the most advanced areas of 'Somalia' (in the wider sense). Still, what is reported about the state of jurisdiction in these two regions is not encouraging:

Only 19 out of 35 judges in Somaliland possess law degrees, the rest having some education and practice in administering *shari'a*. Most district judges read only Somali and Arabic so cannot administer civil and criminal procedures written in English or Italian. There are few complete legal texts available and offices are generally under-equipped. Remuneration for judges is extremely poor, equivalent to UD $4–5 per month in 1999 ... Puntland likewise suffers from a lack of qualified judges. Only 18 out of 44 judges possess law degrees from reputable universities. Most have knowledge of *shari'a*, but no experience in judicial procedure. (UNDP 2001: 176)

I was told in Hargeisa in July 2002 that many people preferred the shariah courts to the ones set up by the state, because the former delivered their service (a verdict) while the latter dragged on endlessly. Elsewhere, the elders took over judicial functions again. About Afgooy we read: 'After the breakdown of the Siyad Barre government, the traditional system remained as chief support of law in a lawless time' (Luling 2002: 200).

A warning is in order here, however, against romanticising the traditional Somali forms of conflict resolution and crediting them with establishing justice and harmony. A close reading of Lewis (1961a, b), no doubt an advocate of doing things the Somali way, shows that the law based on compensations (Arabic: *diya*, Somali: *mag*) is in no way blind[43] to the social standing of the litigants, but that it is highly power-sensitive. There is a catalogue of blood-wealth payments, with 100 camels for killing a man or boy and fifty for a woman[44] at the top end and fixed lower payments for all sorts of physical injury. But whether or not these compensation payments are ever carried out depends on a number of considerations having to do with demographic strength and fighting power. A large *diya*-paying group can arrange these payments in such a way that individual contributions are rather small and the threshold of the use of violence rather low. They can easily afford to kill a member of a rival clan from time to time, for example during the typical dry-season clashes over whose herd has precedence at a well, and thus keep other clans at a distance, reserving the best pastures and the strategic wells from which these pastures are opened up for themselves. The *diya* payments do not hurt them, and the economic advantages brought about by aggressive conduct outweigh the occasional payment of such a fee. On the other hand, if they are strong enough, they do not even need to pay the *diya*. The purpose of *diya* in Somali customary law is to avert vengeance, and a group to whom harm was done has the right to retaliate if they have not been offered *diya* or have not accepted such an offer. The right, however, does not automatically entail the capability. In pre-colonial Somali society (and in many places now again) there are no law-enforcing agencies independent of the clans and *diya*-paying

---

43. As the blindfold of 'Iustitia' in allegoric depictions is meant to symbolise in the European tradition.

44. These numbers refer to a variant of customary law widespread in the north and the centre of Somalia. Among the Digil and Mirifle in the south there are inter-clan agreements with different rates. We shall come back to these local forms of *xeer* (contract, customary law) in the section 'Demobilisation, Disarmament, and Reintegration' under the heading 'Ongoing Activities in the Field of Technical Assistance'.

groups,[45] i.e., the litigants. Whoever is denied compensation and retains the right of retaliation will have to carry this out by themselves. This implies that a strong group, if they are sufficiently sure that their adversaries will not dare to avenge themselves, might not see the need to offer compensation in the first place. Adding insult to injury, their position might be: 'Avenge yourselves if you dare!'

A part of a *diya* payment may be waived as a sign of brotherliness and readiness to reconcile. This rule, meant to give room to noble attitudes like generosity, can easily be misused by strong groups pressurising weaker groups into waiving a part of their claims. The argument would go like this:

> If you (being poor and not numerous) now demand the full amount of diya from us, what would happen in the inverse case, when one of you has killed one of us and we demanded diya from you? (A rather hypothetical case, because the weaker group would not dare to attack the stronger one in the first place.) Would you then be able to pay 100 camels? Better treat us in a brotherly way (a formula adopted whether the two groups are related or not) and accept a lower payment, just as sabeen (reconciliation gift, prior to or in cases of waivers instead of diya payments) or for cooling your pain!

A case history illustrating this line of argument can be found in Schlee (2002b: 259f.).

Enabling legal institutions to work faster and better (taking into account that the often idealised customary law does not always lead to desirable effects) should be high on the development agenda.

Regional and International Relations

The needs addressed by the Eldoret/Mbagathi Committee on 'Regional and International Relations' are to some extent reflected by the emphasis of UNDP and European projects on capacity building for governance. These, however, have no special programmes for the training of diplomats and the raising of awareness of the public and of representative bodies about the role of regional and international institutions.

Learning from Somaliland

Since its devastation by the Mogadishu-based military dictatorship in 1988, Somaliland has managed to attract many international organisations to assist in its rebuilding. It is not recognised internationally and cannot meet its own budget requirements, but, compared to the south, it offers relative peace and security. For this reason it qualifies for the 'peace dividend', the principle according to which aid and development projects are given to relatively safe areas. This not only is in the interests of the project workers, but also provides incentives to other areas to become more peaceful.[46]

---

45. A *diya*-paying group may be a segment of a clan or it may be composed of genealogical subunits of different branches of a clan or even different clans which are bound to each other by contract.
46. The policy of the European Commision states: 'The Commission will globally continue to adhere to the *peace dividend approach*. Its proactive application will form the guiding principle with respect to all administrative and government institutions'. (EC 2002: 19f.)

Lewis (2002) attributes the fact that the Somalilanders were relatively successful in sorting out their differences to the fact that they were left to do so by themselves, while in the south the most warlike and obnoxious elements of society were over and over again rewarded by the international community by inviting them to peace conferences, paying for their air tickets, and covering their hotel bills.

The scarcity of means, which did not prevent Somaliland from doing relatively well, is stressed by the literature. One UNDP report states: 'It was noted that NW Somalia should be commended to demobilise with limited resources.'[47] Elsewhere we read: 'Though it continues to be plagued by serious problems of disputed authority, corruption, and weak administrative capacity, Somaliland enjoys governance of higher quality than any other part of Somalia.'[48] And this is so in spite of the fact that 'civil servants are paid so little that they must work other jobs during the day'.[49]

The relative peace has allowed many studies to be made and much practical experience in institution building to be gathered, from which the south, when similar conditions prevail, will later be able to profit. In the field of demobilisation and reintegration a substantial study by Odenwald et al. (2002) shows the interactions between traumatic experiences and long-term *qat* abuse in the development of psychic disease, which has become a mass phenomenon among ex-combatants and leads not only to human tragedies but to an enormous strain on the families of the affected and has become a burden on the overall economy.

An important model project for the security of land rights is the cadastral survey carried out under the guidance of John Drysdale in Gebiley. Here it can be learned how advanced surveying techniques in combination with computer based data banks can provide solutions to some of the problems outlined above under 'Land and Property Rights' in the section 'The Stated Needs: What Somali Expect from the International Community'. In the wider context of urban planning the European Commission in cooperation with UN-HABITAT has a programme in the framework of which a Consultative Forum on Urban Strategy and Governance, Somaliland, was held in Hargeisa, 30 and 31 August 2003, which I had the opportunity to attend. It emerged from this meeting that there is a hitherto untapped potential to increase the effectiveness of municipalities by letting them learn from each other in the organisational framework of a Somaliland Municipal Association. Also twinning with cities on other continents may provide intellectual stimuli for and material inputs into municipal development.[50]

Cross-cutting Issues

All committees working on the different technical issues in the Eldoret/Mbagathi process were asked to develop a time frame and a budget for the activities they proposed in their resolutions. So they did. There was little concern where the money

---

47. UNDP Somalia, Somali Aid Coordination Body/Governance Working Group (2001: 19).
48. UNDP *Human Development Report*, Somalia (1998: 87).
49. UNDP *Human Development Report*, Somalia (1998: 91).
50. From Atkinson and Couté (2003) insights about the possible future course of EC activities in the field of urban development can be gathered.

in question would come from. It was implicitly understood that it would have to come from outside donors.

In the Committee on 'Land and Property Rights' I could not gain acceptance for my proposal that a part of the costs of adjudication should be paid by the losing party, so as to discourage upholding evidently unjustified claims and to provide some revenue. This will give even the richest warlords the opportunity to litigate in defence of their loot at the expense of others, presumably the international community.

The heavy reliance on outside finances has been a prevailing feature of the Somali state in the different periods of history. No state in Somalia has ever been able to finance itself from locally collected revenue.[51]

Paucity of revenue will probably be a birth defect of a possible re-emerging Somali state, not only in its initial phase. But, unlike the 1980s, there are now no blocks of nations led by rival superpowers competing for influence in the Third World. The *Human Development Report, Somalia 1998* (UNDP 1998) predicts that those who expect outside finance will be disappointed:

> Like a post-Cold War cargo cult, Somali political leaders continue to believe that if they can cobble together an internationally-recognized state, funds will flow again into the coffers. Few have fully grasped the changed nature of international politics since the end of the Cold War and the failed intervention in Somalia. Few understand that, for the first time in history, the Somali state will have to rely primarily on resources generated internally. (UNDP 1998: 28)

Since that was written (1998) the situation has changed again. In the aftermath of 11 September 2001, the international community tries, in the name of anti-terrorism, to abolish statelessness, and money for rebuilding and maintaining a state in Somalia might be available to some extent. But a situation like that in the 1980s is unlikely to recur.

The report of the 'Committee on Economic Recovery, Institution Building, and Resource Mobilisation' of the Eldoret/Mbagathi peace conference asks for an 'effective and operative federal fiscal structure' which defines the powers to levy taxes at various levels of government and provides a formula for sharing the revenue between them. In the field of fiscal policies, as in that of monetary policies, assistance is sought from outside agencies ('the Swiss authorities, and/or the World Bank and IMF').

At present, many individuals and institutions like schools are supported by remittances from the Somali diaspora, which may amount to US$550 million to US$1 billion per year. Much disarray has been caused by the ban of Al-Barakaat, a major transfer bank, for its alleged links to Al-Qaida in November 2001. Since then successor firms have come up. Some hopes are attached to the continuous flow of these remittances (which is not very likely in the long run, because the second generation of diaspora Somali tend to lose interest in the country of their origin and a renewed flow of remittances would require fresh waves of refugees). On the other

---

51. UNDP (1998: 26, 57 quoted in Schlee 2006a: 157f.).

hand the development world hopes for a return of human capital, and a partial return of the diaspora would, of course, also diminish the remittances.[52]

The international community shares the perception that in this field assistance is needed. Good governance, transparency, and accountability are high on the agenda of many development assistance policy documents. Fiscal institutions need to collect, store, and retrieve vast amounts of data, a feature they share with other branches of government. The vagueness of many of the policy documents produced by the Eldoret/Mbagathi process speaks for itself. It is obvious that statistical data and other types of policy relevant information are missing. 'One of the tragedies of severe internal conflicts is the destruction of public sector institutional memory located in staff and information centres. ... The Somali governing authorities face several challenges to effective policy formulation. First, there is dearth of data and information to provide a rich basis for policy alternatives' (UNDP Somalia et al. 2001: 17, 18).

The task ahead is not just one of data collection but of finding optimal ways of handling data. By their use of the mobile phone and the Internet the Somali have shown that they can jump stages of development or 'leap frog poor communications infrastructure' (UNDP Somalia et al. 2001: 20). Recommended technologies should not be based on what has incrementally and gradually developed in Europe or America over long spans of time and is now existing practice. The Somali have thoroughly destroyed their entire infrastructure and now have a chance to have a completely new start. They do not need to worry about the best use of the things they have got. There is nothing. Whatever infrastructure they had has been sold as scrap metal by whoever got hold of it. Now they are in the unique position of starting from scratch. It might well be that the most modern information and telecommunication technology turns out not only to have the highest performance but also to be the cheapest.

Actions Recommended in Anticipation of the Success of the Mbagathi Process

Even if the Mbagathi process comes to a successful conclusion, i.e., if the remaining factions agree on a mode of power sharing and the Mbagathi parliament elects a transitional government, the failure of this government to establish itself in Somalia, or, if established, to remain in power for no more than a couple of weeks or months can be predicted, unless massive support is provided by the international community.

The highly political issue of a peacekeeping force with a mandate by some international organisations like the UN (United Nations) or the AU (African Union) is left aside here, since this chapter concentrates on the more modest issues of technical cooperation rather than international politics and diplomacy.

It is, however, in this field of technical cooperation that the way in which such a military intervention is carried out has important consequences. The legal economy in Somalia is small and regular forms of revenue collection hardly exist. The locally generated budget will therefore be extremely low for quite some time. Comparative studies of post-

---

52. On the peace process and the diaspora, remittances, problems of second-generation Somali in the diaspora, and informal banking, see Schlee (2004a).

war nations have shown that a high proportion of the mostly meagre budgets of these states is used for military expenditure.[53] If military expenditure can be kept low by the presence of foreign troops paid by foreign agencies, this will have a beneficial effect on the capacity of the government to allocate means to non-military ends.

Therefore, as long as they are financed from external sources, non-Somali soldiers might, apart from having a better chance of being considered neutral by rival factions, have the additional advantage of freeing Somali energies for other purposes than military activity. Demobilised Somali militiamen, whether or not organised in forms resembling a military organisation, can then direct their activities towards other community-oriented tasks and acquire skills which might be more useful for a peaceful future than handling a gun.

In general, post-war countries, especially those which had already belonged to the 'least developed' category before the war, have low rates of economic growth and do not have the capacity to absorb much economic aid immediately after the conflict. 'The earliest that economic recovery can realistically hope to take over the burden of maintaining the peace is by the middle of the first post-conflict decade. During this period growth rates are atypically high and, even more important, could be raised substantially more if aid were targeted to this phase'. (Collier 2003: 167)

While in the case of other post-war economies in the 'least developed' countries it is unrealistic to expect substantial growth in the first half of the first post-conflict decade, in the Somali case the economy can even be expected to shrink in this period. Large parts of the present Somali economy are illegal by standards applied elsewhere or infringe on import regulations of neighbouring countries. As these neighbouring countries are involved in the peace process, they will strive for a post-war order in which their custom regulations will be respected. If successful, such a policy may lead to the breakdown of large parts of the Somali economy.

Illegal trade is difficult to tax, because it is not transparent and because taxing it would involve problems of legitimacy. Such taxes may be construed as a way to legalise these forms of trade. In fact, states tend to have an interest in the continued existence of anything they can tax and may be accused of complicity if they attempted to derive revenues from activities which are regarded as illegal. The disappearance of illegal trade may therefore not affect state revenue directly and in a significant measure, but it may lead to livelihood crises and eventually to social and internal political problems.

Massive economic aid in a situation of weak institutional controls may also lead to the state itself becoming corrupt and aid-addicted. This is what characterised the late 1980s and led to the violent phase of the Somali crisis in the first place. At one stage, the Somali civil war was a war about aid money. Certainly no one wants to go down this path once more, knowing where it leads (Hancock 1989: 198; Schlee 2002b: 256).

---

53. There is a correlation between the level of military spending in post-war states and the risk of reversion to war. Apart from diverting means from civilian forms of development, high military spending generates mistrust and opposition, which in turn is answered by yet more military spending (see Collier 2003: 152).

If massive economic aid cannot be advised at an early post-war stage, what can be recommended? In addition to peacekeeping, a costly military engagement which will require a long effort by whoever provides it, functioning institutions need to be built up so that economic recovery can set in, before the remaining risk of reversion to conflict can be expected to be dealt with by the Somali themselves.

Apart from military intervention of the peacekeeping or peace-establishing type, many of the measures demanded by the various committees of the Eldoret/Mbagathi process and many of the ongoing activities of the aid community in Somalia should be intensified.

What are needed are knowledge and skill. There is a missing generation in Somalia in terms of education. Records and archives have got lost. The knowledge of how to run a country needs to be gathered and systematised again, and those who will apply and expand this knowledge have to be provided with the necessary skills. The focus of aid in the immediate post-war period should be on governance and capacity building, of the type for which examples have been given above, in the sections 'The Stated Needs: What Somali Expect from the International Community', 'Ongoing Activities in the Field of Technical Assistance', and 'Learning from Somaliland'.

Work in the fields of training administrative personnel, setting up libraries of policy-relevant documents (as started by the Somali Aid Coordination Body), and exploring the local conditions under which the measures decided in the Eldoret/Mbagathi resolutions are to be implemented, in fact should be taken up and, to the extent that it is already done, intensified immediately, even before a new transitional government is set up. Otherwise the government, once in place, might fall into a competence gap and lose its credibility very quickly.

Options in the Case of the Failure of the Mbagathi Peace Process

Given the intention of the international community (and within this community especially the 'West') not to tolerate statelessness in any territory of the post 9/11 world, there are basically two options in the case of the failure of the Mbagathi process.

The first is military intervention without a Somali transitional government as a partner. The country would be occupied, the militias disarmed, and a foreign military administration set up. Then, in a drawn-out process, civil society organisations, consultative bodies at various levels of government, and other elements of a democratic society would be encouraged to develop. Representative Somali institutions might be empowered step by step. At the end of such a process there would be 'independence', for the second time in Somali history.

Such an intervention without Somali consent and without a mandate by a Somali peace conference would have to overcome prolonged resistance. It would therefore have to be massive, and extended over time. The expenses for it would be high. In view of the difficulties the occupation forces have met in Iraq recently, it is unlikely that the international community or any part thereof will favour the option of non-consensual application of force in Somalia at the present moment, but it is not beyond imagination.

The other option is to give up the aim to abolish statelessness in Somalia in the short term. Intervention would then continue to be limited to technical assistance, and this technical assistance would continue to follow the 'peace dividend' approach. That means that cooperation would be limited to areas of relative peace where institutional life has developed and a degree of order been established. The reasons for this would be pragmatic (the security of aid workers) and programmatic (providing incentives for communities to be peaceful). If this form of intervention, which is basically what takes place already, were intensified, this would not lead to the abolition of statelessness in all parts of Somalia, but it might help in keeping violence at present levels or reducing it gradually and in making islands of relative peace multiply and grow. To combine conflict analysis and conflict mediation components with a local or district/regional focus to development projects might be advantageous in such a scenario.[54]

The importance of Somaliland as a separate unit, the degree to which it is de facto recognised by the international community, and its chances for ultimate official recognition, its capacity to attract technical assistance, and its role in a future political order in the Horn might all be enhanced by a failure of the Mbagathi process:

> Because of widespread insecurity in most of [Somalia] and because of an ongoing absence of a national government, the aid community has since 1995 had to relocate its country head offices to Nairobi, Kenya. Though security conditions are good in Somaliland, the fact that that administration's claim to sovereignty is not recognized makes it problematic for UN agencies and most NGOs to have a 'country' office in Hargeisa, so field operations in Somaliland are headquartered in Nairobi as well. (Menkhaus 2003: 44)

A failure of the Mbagathi process would substantially lower such hesitations to locate offices at Hargeisa. Future thinking about a more encompassing peace order might also take Hargeisa rather than Mogadishu as its starting point.[55]

Actions Recommended Irrespective of the Outcome of the Mbagathi Process

It is possible to define activities which will be required irrespective of the outcome of the Mbagathi process, and irrespective of the situation in Somalia getting better or worse. These comprise creating bodies of knowledge in the form of digitalised and conventional archives which collect studies done in connection with the many development projects of the 1980s, government records which might have been dispersed and need to be traced and preserved, scholarly writings, and anything else

---

54. An example is the EU-financed project on 'Improvement of Farming Systems in Bay and Bakool Regions, Somalia', which is administered by GTZ International Services; see below, the chapter 'On Methods: How to be a Conflict Analyst'.
55. This paragraph has considered the issue of recognition of Somaliland only from the perspective of the aid community and diplomacy. For other players, the advantages and disadvantages of recognition are discussed in Chapter 14.

which might become policy-relevant. The preservation of a public memory is essential for any future attempts to re-establish peace and justice and to build up functioning institutions at any level, be that locally, regionally, or nationally.

Much knowledge and many skills do not exist on paper or in electronic form but in human brains. As a whole generation of Somali in Somalia has not had a chance to get education, educated Somali in the diaspora[56] will have an important role to play. Wherever possible, even if this is only in certain regions, programmes should be set up to facilitate the return of skilled members of the diaspora for specific tasks (too vaguely defined remigration programmes might be counterproductive by favouring those who delay their return plans to wait for the facilitation funds).

There are, anyhow, other activities which the international community will carry out in one form or another, irrespective of the outcome of the Somali peace process and irrespective of any consideration of what is good for Somalia or not, because these activities are in the international community's own interest. These comprise monitoring environmental pollution (harmful substances, wherever they are dumped, have a way of getting into the food chain and travelling back to where they come from). Also the traffic in arms and drugs will have to be monitored in some form, whatever happens in Somalia.

---

56. There are strong tendencies in the Somali diaspora which work against repatriation. Because of the prolonged state of lawlessness in Somalia, the criteria for the choice of a country of residence in the West have changed from short-term to long-term benefits. While in the early 1990s welfare and health care were important considerations, later, as Somali migrants increasingly anticipated that their stay abroad might turn out to be permanent, security of status became more important. Somali often preferred countries where they could get secure residence status and preferably a prompt passport, to others where material benefits might be higher in the short term but long-term residence less secure (Alim 2002). The conditions in exile have often favoured women in the marital power balance. When confronted with the wish of their husbands to return to Somalia, women might fear to leave their enhanced status again in the process of remigration. Another dividing line runs between the generations. Diaspora children do not submit to parental control to the same degree as would be expected in Somalia (see Griffiths 2002: 108–118; Schlee 2004a). Middle-aged Somali have often taken an active interest in the Eldoret/Mbagathi process and have complained that their children did not bother about the future of Somalia at all. They described their children as 'Finnish' or 'Canadian' or whatever might be the case. Attempts to take diaspora children to Somalia, even just for a holiday, often fail miserably and end in generational conflict (Schlee 2004a).

Chapter 13

On Methods: How to be a
Conflict Analyst

Introduction

This chapter is drawn from a consultancy report. The consultancy was part of a Memorandum of Understanding between the Max Planck Institute for Social Anthropology and GTZ International Services concerning the conflict resolution and reconciliation component of the Improvement of Farming Systems Project (IFSP), Bay and Bakool Region.

The aim of the report was to carve out a role for a conflict analyst in an integrated multi-sector development project in a conflict-ridden area. As conflicts are not a separate sphere of life, conflict analysts do not work in isolation from people dealing with other aspects of life, like schooling, road building, water development, or food security. They will be attached to a branch of the administration, an NGO, or a national or international development agency and they have a role in facilitating other activities by working on security issues which might affect these. Conversely, the wider context of the project or institution in which they work provides them with transport, office facilities, and other amenities. The experience of establishing a conflict analysis component in this particular project might therefore provide hints and inspiration on how to organise similar activities elsewhere.

I stayed at Huddur from 3 March to 17 March 2004. Within this period of thirteen days, slightly shorter than planned because of an evacuation for 'security' reasons, I accompanied project staff on missions to the villages of El Lehele and El Garas and to the regional peace conference at Waajid.

The PICD Process and Conflict Analysis: Overlap and Complementarity of Methods

The work of the conflict analyst is an essential component of the Improvement of Farming Systems Project (IFSP), Bay and Bakool region. As the project takes place in an area without legitimate state authorities,[1] a constantly updated and competent

---

1. The local governor is a nominee of one of the power brokers in the Digil and Mirifle region, Sheikh Adan Madobe, a pretender to the chair of the RRA (Rahanweyn Resistance Army). There is still intermittent factional fighting within the RRA. Huddur is relatively calm, because the hot spot of these controversies is Baydhaabe (Baidoa). But also Huddur will be affected by the outcome of these power struggles. There have never been elections and the local authorities therefore have to be regarded as a faction which finds itself in power due to a (temporary) superiority in combat.

analysis of the local and regional social and political situation is essential to avoid disruption of development intervention in all technical fields and even for the security of the staff.

All parts of IFSP have a human factor, but the conflict analysis component is the only one which is exclusively concerned with the human environment of the project activities. It should be the eyes and the ears of the project. At an early stage it has therefore been suggested that, parallel to his or her other activities, the project analyst should learn the Somali language. This is a high priority. This can be done by lessons with bilingual Somali (project staff or hired from outside), and by spending as much time as possible with direct communication with Somali, gradually shifting away from the use of interpreters to speaking with them in Somali. Italian is also spoken by many local Somali of the older generation and can open another channel of direct communication. Participant observation in many daily activities of the local community should be carried out to the extent that having to live in a guarded camp permits.

The strength of the IFSP is its commitment to 'implement activities strictly under the premises of Participatory Integrated Community Development (PICD)'.[2] The PICD process starts with a 'cross walk of' a village and the mapping of resources by the local community and then proceeds, by village workshops, to identifying development priorities and implementing them with village input of all kinds, organisation, labour, and money. Lengthy as it may be, it leads to the stimulation of internal resources in terms of planning and ideas within the communities and – it is to be hoped – community ownership and community maintenance of any future material implementations of development measures. As resources are mapped, social structures depicted, and problems, as they are perceived by the community, listed in the PICD process, the PICD process is also an important source of information for the conflict analyst. It needs, however, to be complemented by other methods.

In addition to the organised group discussions of the PICD process, a mix of methods is required for conflict analysis. Individual conversations need to be held with people of all age and gender categories, and all clan and status groups, since it can be expected that statements in public meetings, especially if these public meetings go back to an outside intervention like a development project, are harmonised to some degree or are subject to group pressure, censorship, and self-censorship.

The types of information to be collected from individuals or small groups, if necessary with the guarantee of anonymity, include:

- The history of population movements in the area with a focus on recent changes in the composition of the population induced by the violence of the stateless period.[3]
- The life conditions, economic activities, and political status of minority groups (i.e., all but the clan of the present power-holders).

---

2.   Muchoki et al. (2003).
3.   The Hawiye and Darood with whom the local Rahanweyn have been engaged in fighting since 1991 have been expelled and territories restituted to earlier occupants. There are, however, people displaced from elsewhere residing in the area.

This information is essential for a wide range of project activities. A level of knowledge on these matters is required for deciding on the composition of the committees which prepare the community action plans (CAPs) and any form of agricultural improvement, because any such improvement which increases the value of land touches on the sensitive issue of land rights. Research on these matters by a mix of methods (group interviews, individual interviews, participating observation of everyday activities and economic activities accompanied by informal talks with subsequent note-taking) therefore needs to be carried out continuously and parallel to all other project activities so as to provide correctives and complements to these activities.

It is therefore suggested that open and explorative methods are used by the conflict analyst as soon as an area is accessible in terms of security, i.e., even before a formal PICD procedure is initiated. Such exploration may easily lead to the identification of groups which otherwise would not be represented or of problems which otherwise would not have been mentioned.

The mix of methods described in the preceding section is then to be applied to (in conjunction with) the PICD process in a complementary fashion. The conflict analyst will participate in the PICD process to an extent, but will also have to reserve time for other forms of data collection.

The mix of methods recommended is expected to lead to the following results:

- As conflict resolution and reconciliation are part of the PICD process, the communities will link conflict resolution to other aspects of development. In particular, they will recognise conflict resolution as an essential prerequisite for all other forms of development.
- As the conflict analyst is not limited to the PICD process as a source of knowledge, but will apply a whole range of methods of social science, especially open and semi-structured interviews, he or she will have an in-depth understanding of local conflicts and their wider ramifications.
- This in-depth understanding will enable him or her to assess in which localities and in which fields of activity the other members of the team will be safe, how their acceptance by the local communities can be enhanced, and how their role can be made more plausible, especially by helping to define and to promote their contribution to peace and development.

Material Support for the Activities of the Conflict Analyst

Travelling in the area is costly, due to the necessity of motor transport and armed guards. Such considerations of cost, however, need to be ignored, because mobility and familiarity with the region are essential for conflict analysis. The living situation inside a compound surrounded by walls and barbed wire in which each and every staff excursion needs transport and security provisions does not encourage spontaneous visits to the surroundings. The conflict analyst therefore needs to make a conscious effort to spend as much time as possible outside the compound, talking to Somali.

A part of the meetings, which require an informal character and a relaxed atmosphere, can, however, be held inside the project compound if the conflict analyst is provided with the facilities for Somali-type hospitality, which include:

- A hut or simple shade roof under which mats and cushions can be laid out.
- Food for invited elders, not more than one or two at a time, so that an element of confidentiality can be preserved.
- Tea. It may also be necessary to exempt this place from the general prohibition on chewing qat (*miraa*) in the compound.

As the project expands beyond Huddur and its immediate surroundings, clan affiliation, recent history, economic strategies, and other relevant data need to be gathered for a large number of settlements and the task will have to be shared with local researchers and consultants. It is, however, essential that the conflict analyst, in addition to coordinating the activities of others, first gets and then remains involved in the collection of first-hand data for the following reasons:

- In order to identify questions which might be relevant for his/her co-workers to ask in other localities.
- To cross-check the data collected by others.
- To get a feeling for the sensitivities and biases involved. What are the areas interlocutors tend to hide and disguise (the taboo subjects)? What are the investigator's effects (i.e., the influence of who is asking on how a question is answered) with regard to national/international staff and local researchers from different clan groups or political affiliation?

To summarise: the conflict analyst needs to be mobile and talk a great deal to people outside the compound. Transport and security (car, driver, guards) would be the wrong place to save money. He or she needs to be provided with the means to provide basic Somali-type hospitality.

As more areas become accessible to project activities with an improving security situation, and as dozens of additional villages are included in IFSP, the responsibilities of the conflict analyst need to be taken over by local staff and local and international consultants. The conflict analyst will then acquire coordinating and supervising functions. In part, however, he or she should remain involved in primary data collection for reasons already outlined in the preceding section.

The conflict analyst has to be provided with sound-recording equipment for interviews, which should then be selectively transcribed. To have the exact Somali wording of the conclusions of a peace negotiation, an often cited proverb, or a historical tradition which legitimises a land claim can be very important, both for the correct analysis of the situation, and for building the capacity of the conflict analyst in terms of language skills and general competence in local matters.

The material and personal equipment of the conflict analysis component must be designed with the following aims in mind:

- He or she is not tied down by repetitive activities, like organising similar workshops in dozens of villages, but is enabled to be the 'eyes and ears' of the project.

- He or she is mobile, flexible in his or her schedule (freedom in space and time), and free in the choice of methods.

Workshops on Conflict Resolution

During my two weeks with IFSP I had the opportunity to accompany project staff on a visit to El Lehele village to prepare a workshop on conflict resolution. I also spent several hours at that workshop on each day but one, when it was held in Huddur primary school from 10 March to 14 March 2004. The degree of openness, trust, and active community participation brought about by the PICD process was indeed impressive. All of the twenty representatives the community had selected to participate on the basis of the subclan divisions had come. As the community themselves had set the agenda, the items discussed captured everyone's interest and were hotly debated.

Meanwhile, the peace conference in Nairobi had been dragging on for a year and a half and its outcome had become more uncertain than ever. It was therefore felt that peace efforts in Somalia could not wait for the uncertain results of the peace process on the national level under the guidance and sponsorship of the international community, but had to focus on the local and the regional level. Instead of waiting for a new government to be set up or not to be set up in Nairobi, people had to organise their lives starting from the grass roots. What happened at this workshop, in fact, was that the community of El Lehele took over government functions.

They had put a re-examination of traditional law (*xeer*) on their agenda. They documented it on flip charts with the help of the facilitating staff members,[4] and they found fault with parts of it. So they engaged in a process of legislation. To cite just one example: traditionally the owner of a fenced field had the right to kill a trespasser whom he found on his land and who had left the fence behind him open, not caring about possible damage by stray livestock. It was now decided by majority vote that such a person should not be killed but fined a three-year-old camel bull. Any subsequent crop damage would not have to be paid for by that person but by the owner of the livestock. The alternatives that all or half of this damage should be paid by the primary offender were rejected. In the same spirit the law of adultery (*xeerka gogodhaafka*) was revised. The right of a husband to kill a lover caught with his wife was replaced by the right to demand compensation in the form of a camel bull of three years.

The reasoning employed in these debates was based on a rather elaborate case by case method. People constructed imaginary cases and discussed the positions of the various characters involved in these fictive case histories. Many of the participants in the discussion seemed to be natural lawyers.

There are large enclosures of many square kilometres of former communal grazing which rich people from among the Rahanweyn have fenced off for themselves. The participants of the workshop were hesitant to address that matter and said that it would have to be left to a future government. The objection was raised that the rich people in question were Hadama by clan, the governor of the

---

4.   Jery Sheikh Hussein and Abdullahi Sahal.

region is Hadama as well, and so are the District Commissioner and everyone at the workshop. So what were people waiting for to solve this matter? The return of the Marrehan (Siad Barre) government? This comment evoked laughter.

Another major issue at the workshop was livestock marketing. This touches on security issues, which extend much beyond El Lehele to the regional and the national level. I shall therefore come back to this theme in the following section on 'Geographical Scale and Levels of Organisation'.

The experience with the workshop on El Lehele was extremely encouraging and it can only be recommended to continue to use this format and to use it elsewhere wherever applicable. As the agenda for such workshops (in accordance with the PICD principles) is set by the communities themselves, future workshops cannot be planned to address the same themes, but it is very likely that security-related themes like livestock marketing (*suuq-geynta xoolaha*) will also come up in the workshops on other villages since the problems encountered in this field are ubiquitous in the entire region. This theme (with its wider national and international implications) deserves the special interest of the conflict analyst.

Local communities create institutions with governmental functions: they agree on rules (legislation), hold those who transgress these rules responsible (jurisdiction), and define and implement their own policies (executive). A future national government, if and when it comes into being, will have to accept these institutions as givens, and may very willingly accept them, because they are repositories of peace and development. An important proportion of the overall political power in Somalia will be located at the grass roots. Dictatorship and arbitrary rule will become very difficult to establish. Systems of extortion and intimidation, like that of the present warlords, will be difficult to maintain.

Geographical Scale and Levels of Organisation

The various levels of geographical inclusiveness (local, sub-national, regional, national, international) show multiple interconnections in the field of conflict analysis. The genesis of a violent conflict can take place at one level and it may then spread to another level. In the case of the Bay and Bakool region it can be shown that conflicts receive much of their dynamics from the sub-national level (conflict of leadership within the Rahanweyn Resistance Army/the projected south-western Somali regional state) but that this level is connected to other levels, namely:

- The international level (Libya or Ethiopia supporting one or the other faction).[5]
- The national level (regional forces struggling for recognition and for participation at the Eldoret/Mbagathi peace process).[6]
- The local level (the leadership struggle at the regional level causing clashes between localised clans).[7]

---

5.   Interview Sharif Yusuf Sharif Ahmad, Ashraaf, at Waajid, 8 March 2004.
6.   This volume, preceding chapter.
7.   Interview Sheikh Miris Mohammed Hussein Hadamo, Gaaljeel, at Waajid, 8 March 2004, and interview Marian Ruun Siraaji Ali, Eelay, at Waajid, 8 March 2004.

Apart from tracing these relationships of causation between different levels of conflict, conflict resolution and healing the consequences of a conflict may also require working from one level to the other.

It is to be hoped that in the not too distant future IFSP will have made substantial progress in helping to resolve local conflicts and in increasing the productivity in local farming systems. It is certainly on the right track to do so. It will then become even more obvious than now that the economic outlets of the districts where improvements have been achieved are blocked by violent conflicts or insecurity in the aftermath of violent conflict, or impaired by extortions by rival politico-military forces. The task ahead then will be to facilitate:

- Agreements on the free movement of goods, including livestock.
- Provision of security, possibly by combined forces representing different factions, for livestock treks and road transport.
- Establishment of conditions under which these security provisions can gradually be scaled down.

The regional dimensions of those aspects of livestock trade which need to be looked at from a conflict resolution perspective extend beyond the boundaries of Somalia. Livestock used to be taken from Bakool via the Somali region of Ethiopia to Somaliland (Berbera), but the Ethiopians block that route now. Livestock exports through Somaliland have declined, because in Somaliland Ogadeen youths have been arrested and expelled.[8] In retaliation for this, people in the Somali region of Ethiopia have started to seize animals destined for Somaliland.[9]

To resolve this matter, communication would have to be established with Ogadeen elders in the Ethiopian Somali region. The Somaliland administration should be made aware that their exclusivist clan and residence policies harm their own export trade. Everyday concerns of local livestock producers and traders are thus immediately linked to regional and even international issues.

As the district relies heavily on grain imports and therefore needs to export livestock, this matter has some urgency. Facilitating exports will have a positive effect on producer prices. At the moment, buyers buy cheap and the price difference to the cities is big, the security risks in taking the stock anywhere being also high. The connection between security and the flow of livestock to different markets is illustrated by Little (2003), who focuses on the Kenyan markets, which have grown in importance for Somali suppliers since the collapse of the Somali state and since the port of Kismayu and its hinterland are in the hands of rival militias.

Between 1988 and 1998 price differences in US dollar terms between Kenyan and Somali markets grew by about 20 percent, which implies a slight increase

---

8.   In addition to clannish and exclusivist policies of the Somaliland government, taxation might be a reason why much of the livestock trade has recently shifted from Berbera to Bosaso, (Christoph Langenkamp, oral communication, 18 March 2004).

9.   Information from Abdullahi Sahal at El Lehele, 6 March 2004.

in risks and transaction costs on the Somalia side. With few options, Somali traders are largely restricted to selling animals in the trans-border markets, which partially explains why their animals' prices have not grown as fast as their Kenyan counterparts who have several marketing opportunities. In terms of transaction costs, added expenses include new fees (4–6 percent fee) for currency transactions. (Little 2003: 99)

Somali traders convert their money into dollars in informal monetary markets and then have it transferred by telecommunication to Somalia, to avoid travelling with lots of cash. On difficulties implying currency transactions and travelling with money, see also the interview with Abdikarim Hajj Hassan in the appendix of Schlee (2004b). Little continues about transaction costs, which also include 'higher transport costs because of the need for additional security personnel to accompany transit animals. Security is a special problem between Mogadishu and Dinsoor and Baidoa and between those towns and the Kenya border' (Little 2003: 99).

In view of the problems of converting money into a currency which can be handled (the inflated Somali shilling being rather bulky for larger transactions)[10] and the difficulties of access to a banking system especially in rural areas, old proposals about the introduction of a form of banking suitable to marginal livestock producing areas might be reconsidered as a possible development intervention. Pastoralists are forced to sell animals at a time when they need grain and when animal prices are low and pastures depleted, namely in the dry season. Banking facilities might put them in a position to sell animals earlier and to keep the proceeds in a safe place, reducing also the pressure on dry season pastures (Schlee 1982; MoLD (Ministry of Livestock Development, Republic of Kenya) 1991).

It is therefore not surprising that the chairman at El Lehele insisted on putting livestock marketing on the agenda of the workshop on El Lehele, which was held at Huddur from 10 to 14 March 2004. He explained that people take animals to the local markets and often do not find buyers. When they want to return, sometimes buyers then collect animals at throwaway prices and take them to no one knows where.

The organisation of mutual agreements of free passage for livestock treks and security escorts of mixed clan/militia composition might be a solution to this problem. The participants of the village workshop of El Lehele even spoke of *xeer* agreements by which the community takes the responsibility for the safety of the herds of traders. 'Responsibility' is meant to entail that stolen animals or animals taken by raiders are to be paid for or to be replaced by the community. The community would then to seek to recover their losses by tracing the raiders or

---

10. The difficulties in handling the large amounts of Somali shillings (SoSh) necessary even for modest transaction, by the way, have little to do with the stateless period. Most of the inflation of the SoSh occurred in the 1980s, the decade preceding state collapse, when its value decreased by 98 per cent. As long as no fresh supply of banknotes came in the stateless period, the SoSh remained remarkably stable. Import of currency first by the warlord Hussein Aydiid, then by businessmen who supported the TNG, with the collusion of international money-printing firms, however, devalued the SoSh by another 25 per cent in 1999 to 2001 (see Little 2003: 139ff.).

thieves. When animals move out of an area, agreements with neighbouring communities should ensure that these neighbours then take over the responsibility, and so on, until the treks reach the final markets.

In the field of interconnections between various levels of conflict, it is therefore recommended that the conflict analyst of the project makes sure that the following activities are covered:

- Watching the media and following events at various levels (national, international) which influence politics and community relations in Bay and Bakool.
- Keeping in touch with experts on political and security-related issues in agencies and NGOs (UN security officers, UNDP, Somalia unit of the EU, and others).
- Semi-structured as well as open interviews with knowledgeable elders, clan leaders, and local law (xeer) specialists for the documentation of recent history and current events and their perception in local perspectives.
- Observing meetings and discussions at all levels of social/political organisations, initially with the help of an interpreter, later by the use of own Somali language skills, which need to be rapidly acquired.
- Facilitating contacts between peace promoters of different localities and regions to revive economic links and to open trade routes.[11]

To focus on these issues aims to help in the achievement of the following results. The project is enabled to situate its activities in wider contexts. It can assess influences and constraints on its own activities emerging from regional, national, and international configurations. It is also enabled to assess how players at these higher levels of geographical inclusiveness perceive its own activities at the village and district level and might be influenced by them.

The project facilitates regular forms of interaction (i.e., it facilitates institution building) beyond the local and the district level. This, in turn, will lead to the following results.

Livestock marketing becomes safer, thereby reducing the transaction costs of the livestock trade (balancing risks, paying for security, paying for extortion) and increasing producer prices and the profits of legitimate trade.

Livestock exports generate wealth, which can be used for imports. Food shortages resulting from a negative grain balance (especially in Bakool) may be redressed. The material standard of living will rise. Ways to measure this will be by monitoring all conventional development indicators such as nutrition, health, or education. Sectoral measures stimulating development in all these fields will fall on more fertile ground if more wealth has been generated locally.

---

11. The livestock export to Kenya, also from Bay and Bakool, already profits from such inter-clan cooperation. The Hagar District Council, dominated by Aulihan Ogadeen, and the Afmadow District Council (Mohammed Zubeyr Ogadeen) have cooperated in retrieving stolen trade goods, including livestock, and in providing safe passage for traders, in spite of their territorial conflict about pasture (see Little 2003: 156).

Peaceful inter-regional relations will generate wealth which is not derived from criminal activities. Increasingly stronger political interests will be attached to the preservation and the increase of these forms of wealth. The balance of wealth and the balance of power will gradually shift away from criminals,[12] and towards elements which are conducive to the common good or at least do not harm it.

A Regional Peace Conference in 2004

The peace talks held in the ruins of the hospital at Waajid between all Digil and Mirifle clans, including the Ashraaf of the area, have been going on for three months, after a similar period at Baidoa. So far, positive results include that many roadblocks in the area have disappeared and the general security situation has improved. The elders and traditional leaders (*malaqs*) have gained ground in holding militia leaders at various levels responsible for any incidents, and brought militias under clan control, although this aim is far from fully achieved.

In addition to being a peace conference, the gathering at Waajid has the character of being a mobile mediation unit. Delegations of elders have been sent from Waajid to wherever violence has newly erupted.

The principles of intervention in such a setting were clearly outlined last November by Magnus (2003) in her paper 'Support of the Bay and Bakool Peace and Reconciliation Initiative. Proposed Interventions by GTZ IS'. External agencies are not called upon to take sides in political disputes, but can greatly facilitate such peace initiatives with relatively modest means by relieving delegates from everyday worries like food and transport.

The measures proposed by Magnus to support this peace process include:

1. Training workshops.
2. Participation with an observer status.
3. Sharing experiences with Somaliland.
4. Study on local indigenous mechanisms of disarmament and reintegration.
5. Reconstruction and rehabilitation of local physical infrastructure.
6. Establishing and strengthening local and regional administrative and self-governing bodies.

On the whole it can be said that, while the Mbagathi process is still pending and its outcome more and more uncertain, such local and regional initiatives are the most rewarding targets for support. With a fraction of the expenses of a Nairobi-type conference, much faster and more tangible results can be achieved here. It is also beneficial that the initiative for this conference comes from elders, women, and traditional authorities and that the 'warlords' will be involved at a later stage or simply be excluded while new solutions are devised. A Somali peace process needs to

---

12. Examples of criminals who wield too much influence in Somalia at present are: extortionists, drug dealers, mercenaries of foreign powers, and environmental criminals (e.g., people who sell fishing rights which do not belong to them, sell the right to deposit poisonous waste, or commercially overexploit communal resources like wood).

'involve' the warlords (to this extent the organisers of the Eldoret/Mbagathi conference were right), but involving them should also mean to make them answerable, to expose them to scrutiny, to submit them to public pressure, to bring them under control, and not to court or pamper or privilege them, or give them a right to veto everything, including the power to block the whole peace process.

The 'peace constituency' is empowered by processes like the one taking place at Waajid. The constituency of peace consists of those who are tired of arbitrary violence and are interested in generating circumstances in which a living can be made by peaceful economic activities. Correspondingly, the constituency of war is weakened. This constituency is made up of people who gain from violence: those who create insecurity to be able to sell 'security', those who receive payments for continued fighting or profit from lawlessness by engaging in criminal activities.

People take over government functions. Democratic institutions growing from the grass roots to district and regional levels will provide checks and balances for a future national government, and, as long as there is no such national government in existence, they will be able to provide a measure of peace and stability by concluding inter-regional treaties with each other.

Chapter 14

An Update from 2007: Reconsidering the Peace Process

This chapter serves a dual purpose. One is that it brings events (more or less) up to date. The race with history as it unrolls is a race scholarly books can rarely win. Due to the nature of scholarly work, slowly overcoming one's own scepticism and then that of others in a peer-reviewing process, academic books are not put out fast. Therefore anyone who is really interested in the latest events should rather consult the daily press or the Internet. Ultimately, whatever I say about Somalia in this book will not be judged by its novelty on the level of facts but by whether or not it inspires a fresh perspective on conflict theory and conflict intervention, because that is what this book aims at. Still, since the last chapters were written, dramatic events have happened in Somalia which cannot simply be passed over in silence.

The second purpose is to reflect on my observations in 2002 and 2003 and to see where my bright spots and my blind spots were in retrospect. This certainly gives the reader a better insight into conflict analysis on the ground and its limitations than rewriting these chapters with the benefit of hindsight would have done.

Most of the text of Chapter 12, dates from 2002 and 2003, and that of Chapter 13, from 2004. The latest updates in the footnotes date from 2006. Here I resume the chronological account and take the events up at the point when the new government, appointed in late 2004 at Mbagathi, Nairobi, first ventured into Somalia.

By 2005, the Somali delegates to the Mbagathi peace process had long overstayed their welcome in Kenya. Public opinion had turned against them, suspecting them of just hanging on for the per diem payments and for private business. Press reports about brawls in their Parliament caused amusement. Expulsion of the Mbagathi-elected Transitional Federal Government (TFG) from Kenya was imminent, but the country this government was meant to rule was a dangerous place. The country (or whoever had spoken for it) had chosen a government, but now it seemed that the government wanted to choose another country. To put up a 'government in exile' in Cairo, Egypt, was one of the options explored. The new president, Abdullahi Yusuf, spent much time in the air between Egypt, Yemen, and other places. Apart from the Mogadishu warlords who had turned ministers, most other warlords/ministers considered Mogadishu to be a particularly dangerous place. Baidoa, as we have seen, was no place to go, since a warlord who had a grudge against the government for not receiving a ministerial post had brought that provincial town under his control. On 13 June, Abdullahi Yusuf was given a ceremonial goodbye in Kenya and boarded a plane 'to Jowhar'. He landed in Djibouti instead. But then Abdullahi Yusuf, a part of his government, and parts of the Parliament accepted Jowhar as their interim seat, although Abdullahi Yusuf felt uncomfortable there, because militarily the town was not under the control of his own militia but under that of another warlord, on whose goodwill he thus depended. One could almost speak of a government in exile in its own country.[1] The Mogadishu warlords/ministers and the other half of the Parliament ended up in Mogadishu. Their control of the capital was to be incomplete and transient.

'In September 2005, deteriorating relations between the Yusuf wing and the Mogadishu Group came dangerously close to precipitating a major conflict. For many observers, the fact that the TFG had not only failed to function after nearly a year but was on the verge of a war with itself was enough to conclude that it was beyond rescue' (ICG 2006: 6). Diplomatic recognition, however, came nevertheless and surprisingly fast. On 1 December 2005, Belgium opened an embassy at Jowhar.[2] Other EU member states and the EU opted for a more cautious course and wanted to postpone recognition to a time when the government would be firmly established. The government was also legal in the sense that it was or felt entitled to spend money allocated to it by international donors. Multimillion dollar contracts with Indian software companies and an American boat builder were signed without advertised tenders, biddings, or any system of monitoring and accountability.[3]

Finally a deal was struck with the warlord who was in power in Baidoa. The Jowhar part of the government and most of the parliamentarians from Mogadishu and Jowhar moved to Baidoa in February 2006. The Mogadishu warlords-cum-ministers had formed the Alliance for the Restoration of Peace and Counter-Terrorism (ARPCT), backed by the USA, and fought the United Islamic Courts (UIC) militias. The UIC militias defeated the 'armed ministers' and the TFG Prime Minister Ali Mohamed Gedi sacked them on 4 June 2006. Jowhar itself fell to the 'Islamists' on 12 June 2006. By then the TFG was in safety in Baidoa, enjoying the hospitality of the local warlord, who had earlier prevented the government from taking its seat in Baidoa but who now graciously provided security for the Parliament and UN offices. They also enjoyed the military protection of Ethiopia.[4]

The Islamic Courts were in no hurry to push on to Baidoa. They were in control of the coast and the major trade route to the north and left Baidoa as a Rahanweyn political enclave with a Darood president without a secure home base (the government of Puntland, which Abdullahi Yusuf had formerly ruled, had distanced itself from the TFG over rights to mineral exploitation[5]) to the side. However, the idea that the TFG was the government of Somalia still persisted in legal fiction and in the ambitions of the Ethiopians. In December 2006 it looked as if the Ethiopians

1.   See ICG (2006: 5); Jutta Bakonyi, personal communication.
2.   SomaliNet, http://www.somalinet.com, accessed 1 December 2005. The ambassador was Christina [Cristina] Funes-Noppen. The impression that Ms Funes-Noppen would take up residence at Jowhar, however, was corrected one day later (SomaliNet 2 December 2005, accessed 17 February 2007). Ms Funes-Noppen had just been appointed ambassador at Nairobi in October (http://www.communique-de-presse.com/content/view/3564/47). Apart from Kenya, the Seychelles, and Eritrea, Somalia had become her fourth simultaneous assignment.
3.   SomaliNet 30 November 2005: 'Somalia: National government or kids in a candy store?'
4.   ICG (2006: 8); Pelda (2006); Swiss Peace (2006: 9).
5.   ICG (2006: 9).

would make this ambition come true. At the side of TFG militias the Ethiopian army marched into Mogadishu. On 27 December 2006 the Council of Somali Islamic Courts dissolved itself. In view of the earlier successes of the Islamic Court militias it came as a surprise to some observers how little resistance the Ethiopians met. But one has to keep in mind that the earlier expansion of the Islamic Court militias was in a political, military, and moral vacuum. Their opponents were the generally hated warlords and their qat-chewing, marauding, rapist, and extortionist militias. The UIC and their militias distinguished themselves through discipline, political and religious visions and through effectively introducing basic law and order and some social services. Even those who did not share their views regarded them as the lesser evil in comparison with the warlords. Of course they were just an alliance of 'neighbourhood guards' or 'vigilante forces', as they might have been called elsewhere: a self-help organisation to provide a modicum of justice and security in the absence of a state. It would have been suicidal for them to face the regular army of a highly militarised neighbouring state with five times the population of Somalia and twenty times that of Mogadishu. So to abscond was the wisest thing to do.

To be in power in the capital for the TFG does not mean to be in control of the country. Nor does it mean to be accepted by the people. Mogadishu is now considered as occupied by an alliance of organised crime and a foreign power: an unpopular combination.

So far the bare chronology of events. I now go back to the topics discussed in Chapter 12 (and earlier in my report to IGAD from November 2003 (Schlee 2003b)) in order to identify a number of topics addressed there and to see what has become of them in the meantime.

Setting Up a Functioning State

One of the scenarios discussed above is entitled 'Actions Recommended in Anticipation of the Success of the Mbagathi Process'. Has the Mbagathi process, i.e., the fourteenth Somalia peace process started in October 2002 in Eldoret, now come to a successful conclusion? One needs to adopt a rather formalist view in order to answer this question in the affirmative. Such a formalist view would focus on the fact that none of the powers sponsoring or hosting the Mbagathi peace process has disclaimed the TFG as the outcome of their efforts and one of them, Ethiopia, even supports it militarily. Others support it less directly. Kenya has closed its boundaries to Somali refugees so that the 'Islamists' cannot escape, and the USA is flying air raids against these 'Islamists' inside Somalia.[6] So it cannot be denied that there is an amount of foreign support for the TFG and in addition we have seen that it enjoys a level of diplomatic recognition. Still, to call this outcome of the peace process a success is questionable. Already my observations from 2002/2003 show that there

---

6. According to an American intelligence report, the suspected terrorist Fazul Abdullah Mohamed was killed on 10 January 2007 when a CA-130 ('gunship') aeroplane fired at the village Hayo and the town Ras Kamboni in southern Somalia. One of the deputy leaders of the Islamic Courts Union was killed in another air raid 'against al-Qaida hide-outs'. The unconfirmed number of civilian casualties was thirty-one (*Daily Nation, Nairobi*, 11 January 2007: 1).

was a collusion of factors which led to the appropriation of the peace process by a group of warlords and Ethiopia. What became of the lofty principles like 'civil society representation', the 'rights-based approach', 'restitution of property or compensation' discussed at the conference is a question which sounds too naive to ask under the present circumstances. That the 'power sharing' discussed by the 'Leaders' Committee' (the warlords) had been strangely dissociated from the work of the committees which worked on the constitution and various aspects of policy has been noted in my reports at the time. Now we can say that the power struggle is still on and the other results of the peace process have been forgotten.

Ethiopia will not be able to face the costs we described as inevitable in Chapter 12, and no other power is going to provide the budget needed to run a state apparatus. Even if funds were forthcoming, whoever provides them would have to monitor how the money is spent. For this purpose a kind of parallel government would need to be set up to monitor the TFG, because given the criminal records of TFG members no one in his senses would expect them to spend such a budget in a lawful way. All this sounds so completely illusionary that we can safely say that it will not happen. A functional government which provides justice and security in Somalia will not come into existence in the foreseeable future. People in Somalia call for a kind of UN protectorate, similar to the one set up in Kosovo by NATO,[7] but I am not aware of the UN having such an intention and the means to realise it.

In another scenario we discussed how, in the case of the failure of the Mbagathi process, peace could be built up from below, region by region. We described a relatively promising peace conference at Waajid. What has become of it? The ruins of the Waajid hospital which housed the peace meeting in 2003 had turned by August 2005 into a camp for Ethiopian military advisers and trainers who built up a Somali peace force.[8] The elders may or may not continue their work elsewhere. They are as necessary as ever. The TFG does not set up a functioning judiciary even in the areas they control. One should not expect any government services from the TFG. Warlords do not render services. Their job is to take, not to give.[9]

Recognition

Another issue in Chapter 12, is recognition, de jure and de facto, and the 'peace dividend' approach to cooperate with those who organise peaceful interaction in a region so as to reward peace. We have discussed these issues mainly with regard to Somaliland. The recent intervention in Somalia was in direct contradiction to this policy: a warlike and politically isolated group (the remnants of TFG at Baidoa), in which even the individual members with good reason deeply mistrust each other (see also Terlinden and Hagmann 2005), was helped to power by a foreign intervention

---

7.   Markus Höhne, personal communication.
8.   The forces they train are those of two TFG-linked local warlords. Jutta Bakonyi, personal communication.
9.   'Warlord' here is a social type. In real persons, the characteristics of elders, businessmen, warlords, etc. might be mixed. Some warlords may at the same time be elders, rendering some services to and enjoying the respect of at least their own constituencies (subclans, followers, etc.).

and continues to enjoy the degree of official recognition just described. Recognition of this government, which, on the level of claims on paper and diplomatic fiction, represents all of pre-1991 Somalia, continues to prevent official recognition of Somaliland, which in 2005 held a peaceful parliamentary election[10] and progresses steadily in providing order and justice in a democratic framework.

Recognition, however, is a mixed blessing. Let us pause for a while to consider the advantages and disadvantages of recognition (of the country as a state and its government as legitimate) in the Somalia and the Somaliland case.

Somalia – Advantages of Recognition

Talking about advantages, one must ask for whom. The more recognition it receives, the better the TFG will be able to score moral points against their political adversaries. They are the 'government' and this makes the others 'insurgents'. Interfering foreign governments, who, for whatever reason, provide assistance for them, will be able to claim to be promoting peace and stabilising the country.

Somalia – Disadvantages of Recognition

The Somali people might have a quite different perspective on this, because they might have to pay one day for the consequences of diplomatic recognition extended to 'their' government. As Pogge (2005), talking about 'Sovereignty and Legitimacy' in general, explains:

> It is a basic principle of current international relations that respecting the sovereignty of another state presupposes accepting the legitimacy of its government—one need not believe it to be legitimate, but one must treat it as if it were. Relatedly, states must, in their international relations, treat their own previous governments as legitimate by paying off debts they had incurred, for example, and by honouring treaties they had signed. Insofar as we count as a state's government whatever person or group exercises effective power within its territory, these legitimacy principles serve to enhance the rewards of brute force. Such enhancement is morally problematic by increasing the staying power of domestically illegitimate regimes and by strengthening incentives to try to take power by force. It makes sense to seek plausible alternatives to the legitimacy principles. (Pogge 2005: 10)[11]

---

10. This refers to the House of Representatives. It is more difficult to find a mode of democratic elections for the other chamber, the House of Elders, which is meant to represent the traditional authorities.

11. One may ask to what extent these things have changed since 1989. During the cold war, the rival superpowers kept regimes which were allied to them in power, no matter what their human rights record was. Since then we have also seen interventions with the aim of changing regimes, especially in cases where human rights considerations combined with strategic or economic interests. Whatever the rhetoric, in practice, regimes are often tolerated for mere convenience. The status quo or support for the one who appears to be the strongest player is often the cheapest option.

This implies that the Somali as a nation might later be obliged to honour agreements concluded by their warlord government and to pay any debts it incurs. It also implies that the warlords, at least those who are part of the government, can continue to sell the resources of the nation (fishing rights, dumping rights for toxic waste). The difference will be that what they have so far done illegally will become legal. This includes printing money, the easiest way to devalue everyone else's accounts and to increase one's own wealth.

Advantages of Recognition for Somaliland

In the relatively peaceful environment of Somaliland, non-recognition in many cases is an obstacle to investment, which might otherwise grow faster. Foreign entrepreneurs in such a non-recognised political entity find it difficult to appeal to international bodies of arbitration or international courts of commercial law. Foreign insurance companies therefore hesitate to indemnify operations in such places. Legal claims based on Somaliland law are disadvantaged in the USA, because District Courts there have denied 'standing to litigants who base claims on laws of entities whose sovereignty is not recognised by the US Government' (Reno 2003: 30). Since Somaliland does not have the power to abrogate agreements by earlier Somali governments, companies cooperating with the Somaliland government in the field of mineral extraction might face litigation by these partners of earlier governments, who, although inactive at present, might still defend their contractual rights in courts outside Somaliland. Diplomatic recognition of Somaliland could therefore contribute in many ways to the safety of investment there. It would also enable Somaliland to join the postal union and to engage in dealings with the World Bank (Reno 2003: 30). Recognition and holding legally valid documents would also greatly improve the situation of many ordinary people. They would be able to travel legally.

Disadvantages of Recognition for Somaliland

Certain business networks in Somaliland have adapted to the consequences of the unclear diplomatic status of their country better then others and would forgo these competitive advantages if the situation changed. The contractors of earlier governments who might litigate against companies who take up the activities they themselves abandoned comprise powerful multinational oil companies. Chinese companies are willing to take the risk and thus make profits in the niche vacated by the multinationals. They and their local partners are beneficiaries of non-recognition.

Also, irrespective of such foreign partners, Somali networks have taken over commercial niches which in other places would be filled by economic actors who belong to a more formal and legalistic sphere. These might be among the losers if international recognition of Somaliland ever takes place (Reno 2003: 30).

The effect of diplomatic recognition of Somaliland on the boundary conflict with Puntland (see Höhne 2006: 411) would be difficult to predict. Creating harder legal facts may have escalating or de-escalating effects.

The 'Islamist Threat'

In 2002 it appeared that the terrorist attacks on the USA on 11 September 2001, apart from all the suffering they caused, had at least one positive effect. The fear that international terrorists might use regions beyond state control like Somalia as a basis for their operations, a justified fear or not, had motivated the international community to invest money in a renewed Somalia peace process after Somalia had already fallen into oblivion. Even people like myself, who were sceptical of the assumed dangers emanating from radicalised Muslims and of the terrorist threat issuing from Somalia,[12] thought that the fear of terrorism here might have a positive side effect: re-establishing statehood and human and civil rights in Somalia. I noticed that there were paradoxical effects like the peace process leading to conflict escalation by encouraging fights about participation but I would not have invested 100 days of my time if I had thought that there was not a chance for a just peace.

That the Somalia peace process on the international level was part of an anti-terrorist agenda had a number of effects which were embarrassing even to the observer: sheikhs outdoing each other in depicting themselves as 'traditional' and 'moderate', delegates doing the same and denouncing each other as 'radicals' and 'terrorists'. To assess what I mean by embarrassment I propose a mental experiment which mirrors the situation. Imagine an Arab-sponsored political campaign in the USA in which everyone plays down their religion: the Christians claim to be Christians only in name, the Jews not to be real Jews, everyone stresses how lax they are in the performance of their religion and that they are really only Christians and Jews by 'tradition', folklore so to say. This would invert the race for 'rigidification' and 'purification' (see above, Chapter 10) normally found in settings where religion and politics mix. In part, the Somali peace process reminded me of such an imaginary setting of a race for 'purity' in the opposite direction. For notorious mass murderers and extortionists it was, of course, easy to prove that they did not take the tenets of Islam too literally.

When discussing the categorical systems of identification (level A) right at the beginning of the exposition of our theoretical framework (Chapter 4), we found that some identifications might be more difficult than others. Identifications are part of systems of interconnected beliefs. They differ along variables like stability over time and resistance to change.

Much harm seems to have been done by the insistence on labels like 'Islamist' and the resistance of such constructs to critical analysis and modification. What is the reality behind fears of politicised or even violent 'Islamism'? Most observers agree, and this has already become clear in Chapter 12, that the organisations perceived as Islamists did not play a dominant role in Somali politics and belligerence before the recent 'peace process'. The Islamic Courts have always, since their beginnings in 1994, filled the vacuum caused by the absence of functioning state institutions. They only became a locally dominant political force after the government emerging from the latest peace process, the Mbagathi process, had failed

---

12. I was not alone in this scepticism: see Zitelmann (2003).

to reach peace even within itself and had failed to establish itself in Somalia as a credible authority.

Were the Islamic Courts and their militias terrorists linked to Al-Qaida? They were people who had had enough of extortion and chaos. They had popular support and just brushed away the 'armed warlords' of Mogadishu who were ministers appointed in Nairobi who subsequently had fallen out with Abdullahi Yusuf. They of course accepted money from local businessmen who for a long time had yearned to pay taxes (something quite unusual for businessmen!) to some force capable to establish a kind of order so as not to be blackmailed by warlords or alternatively to have to maintain their own militias.

Conspiracy theories about Islamists in Somalia often cite unidentified 'intelligence reports', and 'intelligence', as we have seen, has often been gathered from impecunious warlords for a fee. From the case of the 'weapons of mass destruction' which have served as a justification for the US intervention in Iraq we have learned that intelligence reports have a tendency to state what those who have ordered them want to hear. It is therefore difficult to incorporate that sort of information in scholarly writings, which describe their database and critically discuss their sources. I will therefore abstain from speculations as to how many or how few potential terrorists there actually are in Somalia. Those who are better placed than myself mostly come forward with very mixed assessments.

What I find remarkable in this context, however, is that Islamists, after a long history of ups and downs in Somalia without ever becoming the politically dominant force, had become much stronger by 2006 than they had been in 2002. This chronology suggests that the rise of political Islam in this case is a response to the 'war on terror' and therefore cannot be an element of its justification. If the 'international community' (in the shape of the powers actually engaged in the area)[13] had done just the opposite from what they have done, prospects for a sustainable peace in Somalia might now be better. They have supported a government composed of organised crime against the 'Islamists'. It might have been better to support the 'Islamists' against organised crime. The 'Islamists' might have softened in this process, being forced to cooperate with other Muslim and non-Muslim allies.

Fighting 'terrorism' or what we take for it, it is also worthwhile to pause from time to time to ask ourselves what values we want to defend and how these values are affected by the way in which we defend them. Are we fighting for freedom, peace, or justice? It is easy to show how physical violence undermines these values. Let us therefore take a non-violent example: As we have seen, in November 2001 the transfer bank Al-Barakaat was closed all over the world, wherever the USA had enough influence to have this done. Somali families suffered because they could not

---

13. Here I speak of Ethiopia, Kenya, the USA, and all the other states and international organisations who assisted in the Mbagathi process and still stand by its results. Some powers like Eritrea (a country dominated by Christian highlanders in which internally Islamists are in a difficult position) have supported the Islamic Courts against the Ethiopian-sponsored forces (*Daily Nation*, Nairobi, 10 January 2007: 14), just like the USA supported the *mujaahidiin* against the Russians in Afghanistan earlier.

receive the remittances from their relatives in Europe and America. Al-Barakaat wanted to take legal action against this, but they did not find even a proper lawyer.[14] What if the rumours that Al-Barakaat supported Al-Qaida prove unfounded? Maybe Usama bin Laden has never even made a transfer through Al-Barakaat. What if instead there had been rumours of Usama bin Laden making transfers through Dresdner Bank and Barclay's Bank? (Maybe he has.) Would these banks have been dealt with in the same way as Al-Barakaat? If it is legality we want to defend, this might not be the way to do it.

---

14. Two made no progress and a third dropped the case, because people probably told him: "do you know what you're doing? Barakaat? These people are terrorists"' (ICG 2005: 24).

References

Abbink, Jon 2003. 'Dervishes, *moryaan* and Freedom Fighters: Cycles of Rebellion and the Fragmentation of Somali Society, 1900-2000', in Jon Abbink, Mirjam de Bruijn, and Klaas van Walraven (eds), *Rethinking Resistance: Revolt and Violence in African History.* Leiden, Boston: Brill, 328–356.

Abdel Ghaffar Mohamed Ahmed 2006. 'The Darfur Crisis: Mapping the Root Causes', in Abdel Ghaffar Mohamed Ahmed and Leif Manger (eds), *Understanding the Crisis in Darfur. Listening to Sudanese Voices.* Bergen: BRIC, 10–19.

Abun-Nasr, Jamil M. 1965. *The Tijaniyya: A Sufi Order in the Modern World.* London: Oxford University Press.

Ahlzweig, Claus 1994. *Muttersprache-Vaterland: die deutsche Nation und ihre Sprache.* Opladen: Westdeutscher Verlag.

Alim, Abdulkadir M. 2002. 'The Changing Nature of the Global Refugee and Immigration Movement: The Case of Somali People'. Ph.D. thesis, Bielefeld, University of Bielefeld: Faculty of Sociology.

Allen, Tim 1994. 'Ethnicity and Tribalism on the Sudan–Uganda Border', in Katsuyoshi Fukui and John Markakis (eds), *Ethnicity and Conflict in the Horn of Africa.* London: James Currey, 112–139.

Anderson, Terry Lee and Randy T. Simmons (eds) 1993. *The Political Economy of Customs and Culture.* Lanham, Maryland: Rowman & Littlefield.

Andrzejewski, Bogumil Witalis 1972. 'Allusive Diction in Galla Hymns in Praise of Sheikh Hussein of Bale'. *African Language Studies* vol. 13: 1–31.

———. 1974. 'Sheikh Hussein of Bale in Galla Oral Traditions'. *IV Congresso Internazionale di Studi Etiopici (Roma, 10–15 aprile 1972).* Rome: Accademia Nazionale dei Lincei, 463–480.

Asad, Talal 1972. 'Market Model, Class Structure and Consent: A Reconsideration of Swat Political Organisation'. *MAN* vol. 7, no. 1: 74–94.

Atkinson, Adrain and Pierre Couté 2003. 'Feasibility and Design Study for an Urban Development Programme in Somalia – An Urban Development Strategy for Somalia'. (Report drawn up on behalf of the European Commission, September 2003.)

Bakonyi, Jutta and Kirsti Stuvoy 2005. 'Violence and Social Order beyond the State'. *Review of African Political Economy* vol. 32, no. 104: 359–382.

Bartels, Lambert 1983. *Oromo Religion: Myths and Rites of the Western Oromo of Ethiopia, an Attempt to Understand.* Berlin: Dietrich Reimer Verlag.

Barth, Fredrik 1959. *Political Leadership among the Swat Pathans.* London: Athlone Press.

———. (ed.) 1969. *Ethnic Groups and Boundaries.* London: Allen & Unwin.

———. 1981. *Features of Person and Society in Swat: Collected Essays on Pathans.* London: Routledge & Kegan Paul.

Baxter, Paul Trevor William 1965. 'Repetition in Certain Boran Ceremonies', in Meyer Fortes and Germaine Dieterlen (eds), *African Systems of Thought.* London: Oxford University Press, 64–78.

———. 1970. 'Stock Management and the Diffusion of Property Rights among the Boran'. *Proceedings of the Third International Conference of Ethiopian Studies (1966),* 3. Addis Ababa: Haile Sellassi I University, Institute of Ethiopian Studies, 116–127.

——. 1979. 'Boran Age-Sets and Warfare', in David Turton and Katsuyoshi Fukui (eds), *Warfare among East African Herders*. Senri Ethnological Studies. Osaka: National Museum of Ethnology, 69–94.

——. 1987. 'Some Observations on the Short Hymns Sung in Praise of Shaikh Nur Hussein of Bale', in Ahmed Al-Shahi (ed.), *The Diversity of the Muslim Community: Anthropological Essays in Memory of Peter Lienhardt*. London: Ithaca Press, 139–152.

Baxter, Paul Trevor William and Hector Blackhurst 1978. 'Vercingetorix in Ethiopia: Some Problems Arising from Levine's Inclusion of the Oromo in his Delineation of Ethiopia as a Culture-Area'. *Abbay* no. 9: 159–166.

Becker, Gary S. 1998 [1993]. *A Treatise on the Family*. Cambridge, Massachusetts: Harvard University Press.

Behrends, Andrea 2007a. 'Neither Nomads versus Settlers nor Ethnic Conflicts – The Long History of Changing Alliances and Politicized Group on the Chad/Sudan Border'. *Orientwissenschaftliche Hefte* no. 23. Halle/Saale: Orientwissenschaftliches Zentrum der Martin-Luther-Universität Halle-Wittenberg.

——. 2007b. 'The Dafur Conflict and the Chad/Sudan Border – Regional Context and Local Re-Configurations', in Andrea Behrends and Jan Patrick Heiß (eds), *Sociologus*, vol. 57, Special Issue (Crisis in Chad. Approaching the Anthropological Gap), no. 1: 99–131.

Besteman, Catherine L. 1999. *Unraveling Somalia: Race, Violence, and the Legacy of Slavery. The Ethnography of Political Violence*. Philadelphia: University of Pennsylvania Press.

Besteman, Catherine L. and Lee V. Cassanelli 1996. *The Struggle for Land in Southern Somalia: The War behind the War*. Boulder: Westview Press.

Boddy, Janice 1989. *Wombs and Alien Spirit: Women, Men, and the Zar Cult in Northern Sudan*. Madison: University of Wisconsin Press.

Braukämper, Ulrich 1984. 'On Food Avoidances in Southern Ethiopia: Religious Manifestation and Socio-Economic Relevance', in Sven Rubenson (ed.), *Proceedings of the Seventh International Conference of Ethiopian Studies 1982, Lund*. Addis Ababa: Institute of Ethiopian Studies, 429–445.

——. 1989. 'The Sanctuary of Shaykh Husayn and the Oromo-Somali Connections in Bale (Ethiopia)'. *Frankfurter Afrikanistische Blätter* vol. 1: 108–134.

Campbell, John Kennedy 1964. *Honour, Family and Patronage: A Study of Institutions and Moral Values in a Greek Mountain Community*. Oxford: Oxford University Press.

Casanova, José 1994. *Public Religions in the Modern World*. Chicago and London: University of Chicago Press.

Cashman, Greg 1993. *What Causes War? An Introduction to Theories of International Conflict*. Lanham, Massachusetts: Lexington Books.

Cerulli, Enrico 1933. *Ethiopia Occidentale II*. Rome: Sindicato Italiano Arti Grafiche.

Collier, Paul 2003. *Breaking the Conflict Trap: Civil War and Development Policy*. Washington D.C.: World Bank Publications.

Dahl, Gudrun 1989. 'Possession as Cure. The *Ayaana* Cult of Waso Borana', in Anita Jacobson-Widding and David Westerlund (eds), *Culture, Experience and Pluralism: Essays on African Ideas of Illness and Healing*. Uppsala: Almquist and Wiksell, 151–165.

Dench, Geoff 1986. *Minorities in the Open Society: Prisoners of Ambivalence*. London: Routledge & Kegan Paul.

De Saussure, Ferdinand 1969 [1915]. *Cours de linguistique générale*. Paris: Payot.

De Silva, Purnaka L. 2002. 'Combat Modes, Mimesis and the Cultivation of Hatred: Revenge/Counter Revenge Killings in Sri Lanka', in Günther Schlee (ed.), *Imagined Differences: Hatred and the Construction of Identity*. Münster: Lit-Verlag, 215–239.

De Waal, Alex 1996. 'Class and Power in a Stateless Somalia' (a discussion paper). http://www.justiceafrica.org/wp-content/uploads/2006/07/DeWaal_ClassandPowerin Somalia.pdf (accessed 26 July 2006).

———. 2004. 'Counter-Insurgency on the Cheap. The Road to Darfur'. *London Review of Books* vol. 26, no. 15, www.lrb.co.uk/v26/n15/waal01_.html.

Dizdarevic, Svebor 1993. 'In der Geiselhaft der Milizen. Eine bosnische Kritik des Vance-Owens-Plans'. *Blätter für deutsche und internationale Politik*, vol. 38, no. 5: 553–557.

Donahoe, Brian 2004. 'A Line in the Sayans: History and Divergent Perceptions of Property among the Tozhu and Tofa of South Siberia'. Ph.D. thesis, Indiana University: Department of Anthropology.

———. 2005. 'Southern Siberia'. *The Indigenous World 2005.* Copenhagen: International Work Group for Indigenous Affairs, 56–63.

Donahoe, Brian, Dereje Feyissa, Veronika Fuest, Markus Höhne, Boris Nieswand, Günther Schlee, and Olaf Zenker 2009. 'The Formation and Mobilization of Collective Identities'. *Max Planck Institute for Social Anthropology Working Paper.* Halle/Saale: Max Planck Institute for Social Anthropology.

Donahoe, Brian, Otto Habeck, Agnieszka Halemba, and Istvan Santha 2008. 'Size and Place in the Construction of Indigeneity in the Russian Federation' *Current Anthropolgy* vol. 49, no. 6: 993-1020.

Donham, Donald L. 1999. *Marxist Modern: An Ethnographic History of the Ethiopian Revolution.* Berkeley and Los Angeles: University of California Press.

Douglas, Mary 1966. *Purity and Danger: An Analysis of Concepts of Pollution and Taboo.* London: Routledge & Kegan Paul.

Dow, James R. (ed.) 1991. *Language and Ethnicity.* Amsterdam: Benjamins.

Duesenberry, James Stemble 1960. 'Comment on "An Economic Analysis of Fertility"', in Universities National Bureau Committee for Economic Research (ed.), *Demographic and Economic Change in Developed Countries.* Princeton: Princeton University Press, 231–240.

Durkheim, Emile 1984 [1893]. *The Division of Labor in Society.* New York: The Free Press.

EC (European Commission) 2002. 'European Commission Strategy for the Implementation of Special Aid to Somalia 2002–2007'. http://ec.europa.eu/comm/development/body/csp_rsp/print/so_csp_en.pdf (accessed July 2006).

Edwards, David B. 1996. *Heroes of the Age: Moral Fault Lines on the Afghan Frontier.* Berkeley, Los Angeles: University of California Press.

El-Battahani, Atta 2005. 'Ideologische, expansionistische Bewegungen und historische indigene Rechte in der Region Darfur, Sudan'. *Zeitschrift für Genozidforschung* vol. 5, no. 2: 8–51.

Elias, Norbert 1997 [1939]. *Über den Prozeß der Zivilisation.* Frankfurt/Main: Suhrkamp. (*The Civilizing Process.* Oxford: Blackwell, 2000.)

Elwert, Georg 1989. 'Nationalismus und Ethnizität. Über die Bildung von Wir-Gruppen'. *Kölner Zeitschrift für Soziologie und Sozialpsychologie* no. 3: 440–464.

———. 1995. 'Gewalt und Märkte', in Wolf R. Dombrowsky and Ursula Pasero (eds), *Wissenschaft, Literatur, Katastrophe. Festschrift für Lars Claussen.* Opladen: Westdeutscher Verlag, 120–138.

———. 1997. 'Gewaltmärkte. Beobachtungen zur Zweckrationalität der Gewalt', in Trutz von Trotha (ed.), *Soziologie der Gewalt, Kölner Zeitschrift für Soziologie und Sozialpsychologie,* Special Issue 37: 86–101.

———. 2002. 'Switching Identity Discourses: Primordial Emotions and the Social Construction of We-Groups', in Günther Schlee (ed.), *Imagined Differences: Hatred and the Construction of Identity.* Münster: Lit-Verlag, 33–54.

Esser, Hartmut 1999. 'Inklusion und Exklusion'. Lecture at Bielefeld University, 11 February 1999.

Evans-Pritchard, Edward E. 1954. *The Sanusi of Cyrenaica*. Oxford: Clarendon Press.

Everitt, Alan 1973. *Perspectives in English Urban History*. London: MacMillan.

Evers, Hans-Dieter and Heiko Schrader (eds) 1994. *The Moral Economy of Trade: Ethnicity and Developing Markets*. London: Routledge.

Evers, Hans-Dieter and Günther Schlee 1995. 'Die Strukturierung sozialer Welten: Zur Konstruktion von Differenz in den Handlungsfeldern Markt und Staat'. *Sociology of Development Research Centre Working Paper No. 234*. Bielefeld: University of Bielefeld, Faculty of Sociology.

Falge, Christiane 2006. 'The Global Nuer. Modes of Transnational Livelihoods'. Ph.D. thesis, Martin-Luther-Universität Halle-Wittenberg: Institute for Social Anthropology, Halle/Saale, and Max Planck Institute for Social Anthropology, Halle/Saale.

Feaver, George 1969. *From Status to Contract: A Biography of Sir Henry Maine 1822–1888*. London: Longmans.

Feyissa, Dereje 2003. 'Ethnic Groups and Conflict: The Case of Anywaa-Nuer Relations in the Gambela Region, Ethiopia'. Ph.D. thesis, Martin-Luther-Universität Halle-Wittenberg: Institute for Social Anthropology, Halle/Saale, and Max Planck Institute for Social Anthropology, Halle/Saale.

Firth, Raymond 1973. *Symbols Public and Private*. London: Allen & Unwin.

Fishman, Joshua A. 1989. *Language and Ethnicity in Minority Socio-Linguistic Perspective*. Clevedon, Avon: Multilingual Matters.

Flint, Julie and Alex de Waal 2005. *Darfur. A Short History of a Long War*. London: Zed Books.

Fox, Robin 1993. *Reproduction and Succession: Studies in Anthrolopogy, Law, and Society*. New Brunswick: Transaction Publishers.

Freeman, Deena and Alula Pankhurst (eds) 2001. *Living on the Edge: Marginalised Minorities of Craftworkers and Hunters in Southern Ethiopia*. Addis Ababa: Addis Ababa University, Department of Sociology and Social Administration.

Gellner, Ernest 1981. *Muslim Society*. Cambridge: Cambridge University Press.

Giddens, Anthony 1976. *New Rules of Sociological Method: a Positive Critique of Interpretative Sociologies*. New York: Basic Books.

———. 1979. *Central Problems in Social Theory*. London: Macmillan Press.

Gluckman, Max 1955. *Custom and Conflict in Africa*. Oxford: Blackwell.

Graebner, Fritz 1911. *Methode der Ethnologie*. Heidelberg: Carl Winter's Universitätsbuchhandlung.

Gräfrath, Bernd 1997. *Evolutionäre Ethik? Philosophische Programme, Probleme und Perspektiven der Soziobiologie*. Berlin, New York: Mouton de Gruyter.

Grätz, Tilo 2004. 'Friendship Ties among Young Artisanal Gold Miners in Northern Benin'. *africa spectrum* no. 39: 95–117.

Grätz, Tilo, Barbara Meier, and Michaela Pelican 2004. 'Freundschaftsprozesse in Afrika aus sozialanthropologischer Perspektive'. *africa spectrum* no. 39: 9–39.

Griffiths, David J. 2002. *Somali and Kurdish Refugees in London: New Identities in the Diaspora*. Aldershot: Ashgate.

Guichard, Martine 2007. 'Hoch bewertet und oft unterschätzt: Theoretische und empirische Einblicke in Freundschaftsbeziehungen aus sozialanthropologischer Perspektive', in Johannes Schmidt, Martine Guichard, Fritz Trillmich, and Peter Schuster (eds), *Freundschaft und Verwandtschaft: Zur Unterscheidung und Verflechtung zweier Beziehungssysteme*. Constance: Universitätsverlag Konstanz, 313–342.

Guidi, Ignazio 1973 [1907]. 'Historia gentis galla', in Carlo Conti-Rossini (ed.), *Historia Regis Sarsa Dengel Vol. 3*. Louvain: Peeters, 195–208.

Haaland, Gunnar 1969. 'Economic Determinants in Ethnic Processes', in Fredrik Barth (ed.), *Ethnic Groups and Boundaries. The Social Organization of Culture Difference*. Bergen, Oslo: Universitetsforlaget, 58–73.

Haarmann, Harald 1986. *Language in Ethnicity. A View of Basic Ecological Relations*. Berlin: Mouton de Gruyter.

Haberland, Eike 1963. *Galla Südäthiopiens*. Vol. 2. Stuttgart: Kohlhammer.

Habermas, Jürgen 1968. *Erkenntnis und Interesse*. Frankfurt am Main: Suhrkamp.

Hallpike, Christopher Robert 1977. *Bloodshed and Vengeance in the Papuan Mountains. The Generation of Conflict in Tauade Society*. London: Oxford University Press.

Hancock, Graham 1989. *Lords of Poverty*. London: Mandarin.

Hardin, Garrett 1968. 'The Tragedy of the Commons'. *Science*, vol. 162, no. 3859: 1243–1248.

Harrison, Simon 1993. *The Mask of War: Violence, Ritual and the Self in Melanesia*. Manchester: Manchester University Press.

Hechter, Michael 1988. *Principles of Group Solidarity*. Berkeley, Los Angeles: University of California Press.

Helbling, Jürg 2006. *Tribale Kriege: Konflikte in Gesellschaften ohne Zentralgewalt*. Frankfurt am Main: Campus Verlag.

Hobbes, Thomas 1994 [1651]. *Leviathan*. (Ed. with introduction by Edwin Curley.) Indianapolis: Hackett Publishing Company.

Hobsbawm, Eric J. and Terence Ranger (eds) 1983. *The Invention of Tradition*. Cambridge: Cambridge University Press.

Höhne, Markus V. 2006: 'Political Identity and the State. Reflections on Emerging State Structures and Conflict in Northern Somalia'. *Journal of Modern African Studies* vol. 44, no. 3: 397–414.

Holt, Peter M. 1961. *A Modern History of the Sudan. From the Funj Sultanate to the Present Day*. London: Weidenfeld & Nicolson.

ICG (International Crisis Group) 2003. 'Negotiating a Blueprint for Peace in Somalia'. *International Crisis Group Africa Report* no. 59, 6 March. Mogadishu/Brussels: International Crisis Group.

———. 2005. 'Somalia's Islamists'. *International Crisis Group Africa Report* no. 100, 12 December. Nairobi/Brussels: International Crisis Group.

———. 2006. 'Can the Somali Crisis Be Contained?'. *International Crisis Group Africa Report* no. 116, 10 August. Nairobi/Brussels: International Crisis Group.

Jakobson, Roman 1971. *Selected Writings II: Word and Language*. The Hague, Paris: Mouton.

Jakobson, Roman and Morris Halle 1956. *Fundamentals of Language*. The Hague: Mouton.

Janzen, Jörg 1991. 'Somalias Küstenfischerei: Gegenwärtige Situation und zukünftige Entwicklungsmöglichkeiten'. *Die Erde* vol. 122: 131–143.

Jensen, Adolf E. 1936. *Im Lande des Gada*. Stuttgart: Strecker und Schröder.

Kaiser, Birgit Mara 2002. 'Exclusivist Rhetorics: The Constitution of Political Identities in Present-Day Algeria', in Günther Schlee (ed.), *Imagined Differences: Hatred and the Construction of Identity*. Münster: Lit-Verlag, 183–214.

Kenney, Mary C. 2002. 'Targeting the Victims of Violence: The Role of Folk Histories and Voluntary Associations in Northern Ireland', in Günther Schlee (ed.), *Imagined Differences: Hatred and the Construction of Identity*. Münster: Lit-Verlag, 241–249.

Khazanov, Anatoly and Günther Schlee (eds) (forthcoming). *Who Owns the Stock? Collective and Multiple Forms of Property in Animals*.

Klare, Michael T. 2001. *Resource Wars: The Landscape of Local Conflict*. New York: Metropolitan Books.

Knighton, Ben 2003. 'The State as Raider among the Karamojong: "Here there are no guns, they use the threat of guns"'. *Africa: Journal of the International African Institute* vol. 73, no. 3: 427–455.

Lang, Hartmut 1977. *Exogamie und interner Krieg in Gesellschaften ohne Zentralgewalt.* Hohenschäftlarn: Kommissionsverlag Klaus Renner.

Leach, Edmund 1954. *Political Systems of Highland Burma.* London: Athlone Press.

Le Page, Robert B. and Andrée Tabouret-Keller 1985. *Acts of Identity: Creole Based Approaches to Language and Ethnicity.* Cambridge: Cambridge University Press.

Le Sage, André 2001. 'Prospects for *Al Itihad* and Islamic Radicalism in Somalia'. *Review of Afrian Political Ecomomy* no. 28: 472–477.

Levine, Donald N. 1974. *Greater Ethiopia: the Evolution of a Multiethnic Society.* Chicago: University of Chicago Press.

Lewis, Bernard 1998. *The Multiple Identities of the Middle East.* London: Weidenfeld and Nicolson.

Lewis, Ioan M. 1961a. *A Pastoral Democracy: A Study of Pastoralism and Politics among the Northern Somali of the Horn of Africa.* London: Oxford University Press.

———. 1961b. 'Force and Fission in Northern Somali Lineage Structure'. *American Anthropologist* vol. 63, no. 1: 94–112.

———. (ed.) 1977. *Symbols and Sentiments: Cross-Cultural Studies in Symbolism.* London, New York: Academic Press.

———. 1978. *Ecstatic Religion: an Anthropological Study of Spirit Possession and Shamanism.* Harmondsworth: Penguin.

———. 1982. *The Somali Lineage System and the Total Genealogy.* Ann Arbor: University Microprints (reproduction of a typescript from 1957).

———. 2002. 'Mohamad Siyad Barre's Ghost in Somalia'. Paper presented at Walta Information Center, Rome. http://www.waltainfo.com/conflict/articles/2002/april/article8.htm (accessed July 2006).

Little, Peter D. 2003. *Somalia: Economy without State.* Oxford: James Currey. Bloomington and Indianapolis: Indiana University Press. Hargeisa: Btec Books for the International African Institute.

Lockwood, William G. 1975. *European Moslems: Economy and Ethnicity in Western Bosnia.* New York: Academic Press.

Longley, Catherine, Richard Jones, Mohamed Hussein Ahmad, and Patrick Andi 2001 (July). 'Supporting Local Seed Systems in Southern Somalia: A Developmental Approach to Agricultural Rehabilitation in Emergency Situations'. *Network Paper* No. 115. London: The Overseas Development Institute, Agricultural Research and Extension Network.

Luling, Virginia 2002. *Somali Sultanate: The Geledi City-State over 150 Years.* London: HAAN.

Machiavelli, Niccolò 1975 [1531]. *The Discourses of Niccolò Machiavelli,* trans. Leslie J. Walker, Volume 2. London and Boston: Routledge & Kegan Paul.

Magnus, Hege T. (GTZ IS, IFSP Bay and Bakool) 2003 (November). 'Support of the Bay and Bakool Peace and Reconciliation Initiative. Proposed Interventions by GTZ IS'. (Unpublished manuscript.)

Maine, Henry 1986 [1861]. *Ancient Law.* Tucson: University of Arizona Press.

Marchal, Roland 2004. 'Islamic Political Dynamics in the Somali Civil War', in Alex De Waal (ed.), *Islamism and its Enemies in the Horn of Africa.* London: Hurst & Company, 114–146.

Max Planck Institute for Social Anthropology 2005. *Report 2004–2005.* Halle/Saale: Max Planck Institute for Social Anthropology.

McLellan, David 2000 [1977]. *Karl Marx Selected Writings.* Oxford: Oxford Universtiy Press.

Meggit, Mervyn 1977. *Blood is their Argument: Warfare among the Mae Enga Tribesmen of the New Guinea Highlands.* Palo Alto: Mayfield Publishing Company.

Meillassoux, Claude 1986. *Anthropologie de l'esclavage: le ventre de fer et d'argent.* Paris: Presses Universitaires de France.

Meinertzhagen, Richard 1984 [1957]. *Kenya Diary (1902–1906).* London: Eland Books.

Menkhaus, Kenneth 2003 (August). 'Somalia: a Situation Analysis and Trend Assessment'. UNHCR (United Nations High Commissioner for Refugees) Protection Information Section: Department of International Protection. WRITENET paper. http://www.somali-civilsociety.org/downloads/Menkhaus%20unhcrsomstudyrevised.03.pdf (accessed July 2006).

———. n.d. 'Bantu Ethnic Identity in Somalia'. http//www.jimonet.com/news_bantu_identity-somalia.htm (accessed July 2006).

Mohamed, Ahmed Farah and Jasmin Touati 1991. *Sedentarisierung von Nomaden – Chancen und Gefahren einer Entwicklungsstrategie am Beispiel Somalias.* Saarbrücken: Verlag Breitenbach (later: Verlag für Entwicklungspolitik).

MoLD (Ministry of Livestock Development, Republic of Kenya) 1991, 1992. *Kenya Range Management Handbook,* Volume 2, 1: Marsabit District (1991). Volume 2, 3: Wajir District (1992). Volume 2, 4: Mandera District (1992). Nairobi.

Muchoki, Jackson, Julius Muchemi, and Günter Wessel (GTZ, IFSP) 2003. 'Participatory Integrated Community Development Process'. Paper presented at an experience-sharing meeting, Nairobi, with GAA, DRC, and CEFA (Somalia EC-funded projects).

Mutie, Pius Mutuku 2003. '"In Spite of Difference": Making Sense of the Co-Existence between the Kamba and the Maasai Peoples in Kenya'. Ph.D. thesis, University of Bielefeld, Faculty of Sociology: Sociology of Development Research Centre.

Nadel, Siegfried F. 1951. *Foundations of Social Anthropology.* London: Cohen & West.

Nageeb, Salma 2004. *New Spaces and Old Frontiers: Women, Social Space, and Islamization in Sudan.* Lexington: Lexington Books.

Newbury, David S. 1980. 'The Clans of Rwanda: An Historical Hypothesis'. *Africa* vol. 50, no. 4: 389–403.

Odenwald, Michael, Margarete Schauer, Birke Lingenfelder, and Thomas Elbert, in cooperation with Harald Hinkel 2002. 'War-Trauma, Khat Abuse and Psychosis: Mental Health in the Demobilization and Reintegration Program Somaliland'. Final Report of the vivo mission 2 within the EC/GTZ Demobilization and Reintegration Program in Somaliland. http://www.delken.cec.eu.int/en/publications/war%20trauma%20khat%20and%20psychosis%20vivo%20report.pdf. (accessed July 2006).

Owens, Jonathan 1995. 'Language in the Graphics Mode: Arabic among the Kanuri of Nigeria'. *Language Science* vol. 17, no. 2: 181–199.

Pelda, Kurt 2006. 'Somalias Regierung im Dauerprovisorium'. *Neue Zürcher Zeitung,* 30 May. http://www.fcaea.org/content/view/178/64/ (accessed February 2007).

Pogge, Thomas 2005. 'Sovereignty and Legitimacy'. Presentation at the biennial meeting of the German Anthropological Associaton (GAA, DGV), 6 October 2005. (Abstract in *Mitteilungen der Deutschen Gesellschaft für Völkerkunde e. V.* no. 35: 10.)

Polanyi, Karl 1957 [1944]. *The Great Transformation.* Boston: Beacon Press.

Portes, Alejandro 1994. 'The Informal Economy and its Paradoxes', in Neil J. Smelser and Richard Swedberg (eds), *The Handbook of Economic Sociology.* Princeton: Princeton University Press, 426–449.

Prunier, Gérard 2005. *Darfur – The Ambiguous Genocide.* London: Hurst.

Ra'anan, Uri 1989. 'The Nation-State Fallacy', in Joseph V. Montville (ed.), *Conflict and Peacemaking in Multiethnic Societies.* Lexington: Lexington Books, 5–20.

Radcliffe-Brown, Alfred Reginald 1952. *Structure and Function in Primitive Society.* London: Cohen & West.

Rahman, Afzalur 1980. *Islam: Ideology and the Way of Life.* London: The Muslim Schools Trust.

———. 1982. *Islam and Modernity: Transformation of an Intellectual Tradition.* Chicago: University of Chicago Press.

Reno, William 2003. 'Somalia and Survival in the Shadow of the Global Economy'. *QEH Working Paper Series – QEHWPS 100.* Oxford: University of Oxford.

Riker, William H. 1962. *The Theory of Political Coalitions.* New Haven and London: Yale University Press.

Roth, Eric A. 1993. 'A Re-Examination of Rendille Population Regulation'. *American Anthropologist* vol. 95, no. 3: 597–611.

Rousseau, Jean-Jacques 1999 [1762]. *Discourse on Political Economy and the Social Contract,* trans. Christopher Betts. Oxford: Oxford University Press.

Samatar, Abdi Ismail and Ahmed I. Samatar 2003. 'Somali Reconciliation: Editorial Note'. *Bildhaan: an International Journal of Somali Studies* vol. 3: 1–15.

Schimmel, Annemarie 1995 (1985). *Al-Halladsch- "O Leute, rettet mich vor Gott". Texte islamischer Mystik.* Freiburg: Herder.

Schlee, Günther 1979. *Das Glaubens- und Sozialsystem der Rendille. Kamelnomaden Nordkenias.* Berlin: Dietrich Reimer Verlag.

———. 1982. 'Zielkonflikte und Zielvereinheitlichung zwischen Entwicklungsplanung und Wanderhirten in Ostafrika', in Fred Scholz and Jörg Janzen (eds), *Nomadismus – ein Entwicklungsproblem?* Berlin: Dietrich Reimer Verlag, 96–109.

———. 1987a. 'L'Islamisation du passé: à propos de l'effet réactif de la conversion de groupes somalis et somaloides à l'islam sur la représentation de l'histoire dans leurs traditions orales', in Wilhelm Möhlig, Hermann Jungraithmayr, and Josef F. Thiel (eds), *La Littérature orale en Afrique comme source pour la découverte des cultures traditionelles. Collectanea Instituti Anthropos, No. 36.* Berlin: Dietrich Reimer Verlag, 269–299.

———. 1987b. 'Rendille Ornaments as Identity Markers'. *Kenya Past and Present* 20: 31–37.

———. 1988. 'Camel Management Strategies and Attitudes towards Camels in the Horn', in Jeffrey C. Stone (ed.), *The Exploitation of Animals in Africa.* Aberdeen: Aberdeen University African Studies Group, 143–154.

———. 1989a. *Identities on the Move: Clanship and Pastoralism in Northern Kenya.* Manchester: University Press. New York: St Martin's Press. (Reprinted 1994 Nairobi: Gideon S. Were. Hamburg, Münster: Lit-Verlag.)

———. 1989b. 'Zum Ursprung des Gada-Systems'. *Paideuma* vol. 35: 231–246.

———. 1994a. 'Loanwords in Oromo and Rendille as a Mirror of Past Interethnic Relations', in Richard Fardon and Graham Furniss (eds), *African Languages, Development, and the State.* London: Routledge, 191–212.

———. 1994b. 'Ethnicity Emblems, Diacritical Features, Identity Markers: Some East African Examples', in David Brokensha (ed.), *River of Blessings: Essays in Honor of Paul Baxter.* Syracuse, New York: Maxwell School of Citizenship and Public Affairs, 129–143.

———. 1995. 'Ethnizität und interethnische Beziehungen in Kenia: Vorbemerkungen zu den Fallstudien von Falkenstein und Odak'. *Zeitschrift für Ethnologie* vol. 120, no. 2: 191–200.

———. 1996. 'Regelmässigkeiten im Chaos: die Suche nach wiederkehrenden Mustern in der jüngsten Geschichte Somalias', in Günther Schlee and Karin Werner (eds), *Inklusion und Exklusion: die Dynamik von Grenzziehungen im Spannungsfeld von Markt, Staat und Ethnizität.* Cologne: Rüdiger Köppe Verlag, 133–159.

———. 1997. 'Cross-Cutting Ties and Interethnic Conflict: The Example of Gabbra, Oromo and Rendille', in Katsuyoshi Fukui, Kurimoto Eisei, and Shigeta Masayoshi (eds),

Ethiopia in Broader Perspective. Papers of the XIIIth International Conference of Ethiopian Studies, vol. 2. Kyoto: Shokado Book Sellers, 577–596.

——. 2000. 'Identitätskonstruktionen und Parteinahme'. *Sociologus* vol. 10, no. 1: 64–89.

——. 2001. 'Language and Ethnicity', in Neil Smelser and Paul B. Baltes (eds), *International Encyclopedia of the Social and Behavioral Sciences*, 1st edn, vol. 12. Amsterdam, Paris, New York, Oxford, Shannon, Singapore, Tokyo: Elsevier Science, 8285–8288.

——. (ed.) 2002a. *Imagined Differences: Hatred and the Construction of Identity*. Münster: Lit-Verlag.

——. 2002b. 'Regularity in Chaos: the Politics of Difference in the Recent History of Somali', in Günther Schlee (ed.), *Imagined Differences: Hatred and the Construction of Identity*. Münster: Lit-Verlag, 251–280.

——. 2003a. 'Redrawing the Map of the Horn: The Politics of Difference'. *Africa: Journal of the International African Institute* vol. 73, no. 3: 343–368.

——. 2003b. 'Support for the Somali Peace Process' (in Eldoret/Mbagaathi). Report to IGAD, 20 November.

——. 2003c. 'Interethnische Beziehungen', in Hans Fischer and Bettina Beer (eds), *Ethnologie – Einführung und Überblick*. Berlin: Dietrich Reimer Verlag, 375–390.

——. 2003d. 'Competition and Exclusion in Islamic and Non-Islamic Societies: Essay on Purity and Power'. *Max Planck Institute for Social Anthropology Working Paper No 52*. Halle/Saale: Max Planck Institute for Social Anthropology.

——. 'Identitätspolitik und Gruppengröße', Inaugural Lecture, Martin Luther University Halle-Wittenberg, Halle (Saale), 30 June 2004.

——. 2004a. 'Somalia und die Somali-Diaspora vor und nach dem 11. September 2001', in Hartmut Lehmann (ed.), *Koexistenz und Konflikt von Religionen im vereinten Europa*. Göttingen: Wallstein Verlag, 140–156.

——. 2004b. 'Conflict Analysis in Bay and Bakool'. Report on a two-week consultancy in the framework of the conflict resolution and reconciliation component of the Improvement of Farming Systems Project (IFSP), Bay and Bakool Region, 3 to 17 March 2004. Halle/Saale: Max Planck Institute for Social Anthropology. http://www.eth.mpg.de/people/schlee/pdf/consultancy_report_mar_2004.pdf.

——. 2004c. 'Taking Sides and Constructing Identities: Reflections on Conflict Theory'. *Journal of the Royal Anthropological Institute* vol. 10, no. 1: 135–156.

——. 2005. 'Conflict Resolution and Reconciliation as a Component of the Improvement of "Farming Systems Project (IFSP)"'. Report on a consultancy at Dinsoor, Somalia, 6–20 April 2005. http://www.eth.mpg.de/people/schlee/pdf/consultancy_report_abr_2005.pdf.

——. 2006a. 'The Somali Peace Process and the Search for a Legal Order', in Hans-Jörg Albrecht, Jan-Michael Simon, Hassan Rezaei, Holger-C. Rohne, and Ernesto Kiza (eds), *Conflicts and Conflict Resolution in Middle Eastern Societies – Between Tradition and Modernity*. Berlin: Duncker & Humblot, 117–167.

——. 2006b. *Wie Feindbilder entstehen. Eine Theorie religiöser und ethnischer Konflikte*. Munich: C.H. Beck Verlag.

——. 2007. '"Diebe haben keine Kinder": Väter, Gevattern, Erzeuger und die soziale Konstruktion des Biologischen', in Johannes Schmidt, Martine Guichard, Fritz Trillmich, and Peter Schuster (eds), *Freundschaft und Verwandtschaft: Zur Unterscheidung und Verflechtung zweier Beziehungssysteme*. Constance: Universitätsverlag Konstanz, 261–290.

Schlee, Günther and Alexander Horstmann (eds) 2001. *Integration durch Verschiedenheit: Lokale und globale Formen interkultureller Kommunikation*. Bielefeld: transcript.

Schlee, Günther and Abdullahi Shongolo (forthcoming). *Islam and Ethnicity in Northern Kenya.*

Schlee, Günther and Fritz Trillmich 2007. 'Verwandtschaft und Freundschaft im Verhältnis von biologischer, sozialer und handlungstheoretischer Rationalität', in Johannes Schmidt, Martine Guichard, Fritz Trillmich, and Peter Schuster (eds), *Freundschaft und Verwandtschaft: Zur Unterscheidung und Verflechtung zweier Beziehungssysteme.* Constance: Universitätsverlag Konstanz, 369–394.

Schlesinger, Izchak M. 1991. 'The Wax and Wane of Whorfian Views', in Robert L. Cooper and Bernard Spolsky (eds), *The Influence of Language on Culture and Thought.* Berlin: Mouton de Gruyter, 7–44.

Schuster, Peter; Rudolf Stichweh, Johannes Schmidt, Fritz Trillmich, Martine Guichard, and Günther Schlee 2003. 'Freundschaft und Verwandtschaft als Gegenstand interdisziplinärer Forschung'. *Sozialersinn* no. 1: 3–20.

Simons, Anna 2000. 'Mobilizable Male Youths, Indigenous Institutions and War'. *VAD – German African Studies Association, 17th Biennial Conference.* Leipzig (CD).

Smith, Adam 1998 [1776]. *An Inquiry into the Nature and Causes of the Wealth of Nations.* Oxford: Oxford University Press.

Sokolovski, Sergei V. 2005. 'Identity Politics and Indigeneity Construction in the Russian Census 2002'. *Max Planck Institute for Social Anthropology Working Paper No. 77.* Halle/Saale: Max Planck Institute for Social Anthropology.

Spencer, Paul 1973. *Nomads in Alliance: Symbiosis and Growth among the Rendille and Samburu of Kenya.* London: Oxford University Press.

Swiss Peace 2006. *FAST Update: Somalia. Semi-Annual Risk Assessment February to July 2006.* http:/www.swisspeace.org/uploads/FAST/updates/Somalia%20FAST%20Update%201_2006.pdf (accessed February 2007).

Tadesse, Wolde Gossa 1999. 'Warfare and Fertility: A Study of the Hor (Arbore) of Southern Ethiopia'. Ph.D. thesis, London School of Economics and Political Sciences: Department of Anthropology.

Terlinden, Ulf and Tobias Hagmann 2005. 'Faking a Government for Somalia'. *Sub-Saharan Informer* 29 July: 9.

Thomason, Sarah Grey and Terrence Kaufman 1988. *Language Contact, Creolization, and Genetic Linguistics.* Berkeley: University of California Press.

Tönnies, Ferdinand 1991 [1935]. *Gemeinschaft und Gesellschaft: Grundbegriffe der reinen Soziologie.* Darmstadt: Wissenschaftliche Buchgesellschaft. (In English: 2001. *Community and Civil Society,* trans. Margaret Hollis. Cambridge: Cambridge University Press.)

Turton, David 1994. 'Mursi Political Identity and Warfare: the Survival of an Idea', in Katsuyoshi Fukui and John Markakis (eds), *Ethnicity and Conflict in the Horn of Africa.* London: James Currey, 15–31.

UNDP (United Nations Development Programme) 1998. 'Human Development Report, Somalia 1998'. Compiled by Kenneth Menkhaus and Roland Marchal. Nairobi: United Nations Development Programme.

———. 2001. 'Human Development Report, Somalia 2001'. Compiled by Mark Bradbury, Kenneth Menkhaus, and Roland Marchal. Nairobi: United Nations Development Programme, Somalia Country Office.

UNDP Somalia. Somali Aid Coordination Body/Governance Working Group 2001. 'Talking Peace in Somalia'. Somali Civil Protection Programme Workshop 'Demobilisation and Reintegration in Somalia', Nairobi, January 2001.

UNDP Somalia, Government of Italy, Government of Norway 2001 (June). 'Capacity Building for Governance (CBG)'. Project Document: SOM/01/003/A/01/34.

UNHCR Somalia: Update to end August 1996. http://www.unhcr.org/cgi-bin/texis/vtx/publ/opendoc (accessed 26 July 2006).

United Nations Security Council 2003. *Report of the Panel of Experts on Somalia Pursuant to Security Council Resolution 1425 (2002)*. Compiled by Ernst Jan Hogendoorn, Mohamed Abdulaye M'Backe, and Brynjulf Mugaas. S/2003/223. http://daccessdds.un.org/doc/UNDOC/GEN/N03/259/25/IMG/N0325925.pdf?OpenElement.

University of Pennsylvania – African Studies Centre 1995. 'WFP in Somalia, February 1995', from Ben Parker. http://www.africa.upenn.edu/Hornet/WFP_smlia.html (accessed July 2006).

US Department of State 1996 (March). 'Somalia Human Rights Practice, 1995'. http://dosfan.lib.uic.edu/ERC/democracy/1995_hrp_report/95hrp_report_africa/Somalia.html (accessed July 2006).

Van Nahl, Andreas 1999. 'Market Expansion, Globalized Discourses and Changing Identity Politics in Kenya', in Richard Fardon, Wim van Bimsbergen, and Rijk van Dijk (eds), *Modernity on a Shoestring: Dimensions of Globalization, Consumption and Development, in Africa and Beyond*. Leiden et al.: EIDOS (European Inter-University Development Opportunities Study-Group), 303–313.

Von Humboldt, Wilhelm 1988 [1836]. *On Language: The Diversity of Human Language Structure and its Influence on the Mental Development of Mankind*. Cambridge: Cambridge University Press.

Watson, Elizabeth E. 1998. 'Ground Truths: Land and Power in Konso, Ethiopia'. Ph.D. thesis, University of Cambridge.

Weber, Max 1990 [1922]. *Wirtschaft und Gesellschaft*. Tübingen: Mohr. (*Economy and Society*. Berkeley: University of California Press, 1978.)

Werner, Karin 1997. *Between Westernization and the Veil: Contemporary Lifestyles of Women in Cairo*. Bielefeld: transcript.

Whorf, Benjamin L. 1962. *Language, Thought, and Reality: Selected Writings*. Wiley: New York.

Wimmer, Andreas 1995. 'Interethnische Konflikte: ein Beitrag zur Integration aktueller Forschungsansätze'. *Kölner Zeitschrift für Soziologie und Sozialpsychologie* vol. 47: 464–493.

Zenker, Olaf 2006. 'De Facto Exclusion through Discursive Inclusion: Autochthony in Discourses on Irishness and Politics in Catholic West Belfast'. *Paideuma* vol. 52: 183–195.

Zitelmann, Thomas 1999. 'Des Teufels Lustgarten: Themen und Tabus der politischen Anthropologie Nordostafrikas'. Habilitation thesis, Freie Universität Berlin: Institut für Ethnologie.

———. 2003. 'Somalia, das Horn von Afrika und die Gerüchte vom Einfluss Usama Bin Ladens', in Günter Meyer, Robert Pütz, and Andreas Thimm (eds), *Terrorismus und Dritte Welt*. Mainz: Johannes-Gutenberg-Universität, 59–95.

Index

www.ingramcontent.com/pod-product-compliance
Lightning Source LLC
Chambersburg PA
CBHW072129020426
42334CB00018B/1723